Transform Your Life

Also by Geshe Kelsang Gyatso

Meaningful to Behold
Clear Light of Bliss
Heart of Wisdom
Universal Compassion
Joyful Path of Good Fortune
Guide to Dakini Land
The Bodhisattva Vow
Heart Jewel
Great Treasury of Merit
Introduction to Buddhism
Understanding the Mind
Tantric Grounds and Paths
Ocean of Nectar
Essence of Vajrayana
Living Meaningfully, Dying Joyfully
Eight Steps to Happiness
The New Meditation Handbook
How to Solve Our Human Problems
Mahamudra Tantra

Profits received by Tharpa Publications from
the sale of this book will be donated to the
NKT-International Temples Project
Part of the New Kadampa Tradition
*A Nonprofit Buddhist Organization,
Building for World Peace*
www.kadampa.org/temples.htm

GESHE KELSANG GYATSO

Transform Your Life

A BLISSFUL JOURNEY

THARPA PUBLICATIONS
Glen Spey, New York
Ulverston, England

Published 2007
First UK edition published in 2001

Tharpa Publications USA
47 Sweeney Rd
Glen Spey, NY 12737
USA

Tharpa Publications
Conishead Priory
Ulverston
Cumbria, LA12 9QQ, England

Photos on pages 21 and 95 by Kathia Rabelo.
Photos on pages 13 and 115 ©2001 www.arttoday.com.
Photo on page 313 by René Knopfel.

Library of Congress Control Number: 2007901723

ISBN-13 978-0-9789067-4-0 paperback
ISBN-10 0-9789067-4-8 paperback

ISBN-13 978-0-9789067-3-3 hardcover
ISBN-10 0-9789067-3-X hardcover

Set in Adobe Garamond Pro by Tharpa Publications USA.
Printed on acid-free longlife paper.

Contents

Preface

*W*e should consider how our human life is precious, rare, and meaningful. Due to the limitations of their body and mind, those who have taken rebirth as animals, for example, have no opportunity to understand or practice the spiritual path. Only humans are free from such hindrances and have all the necessary conditions for engaging in spiritual paths, which alone lead to everlasting happiness. This freedom and possession of necessary conditions are the special characteristics that make our human life so precious.

Although there are many humans in this world, each one of us has only one life. One person may own many cars and houses, but even the richest person in the world cannot possess more than one life. When that life is coming to an end he or she cannot buy, borrow, or manufacture another. When we lose this life, it will be very difficult to find another similarly qualified human life in the future. Our human life is therefore very rare.

If we use our human life to accomplish spiritual realizations, it becomes immensely meaningful. By using it in this way, we actualize our full potential and progress from the state of an ordinary, ignorant being to that of a fully enlightened being, the highest of all beings. When we have done this we will have the power to benefit all living beings without exception. Thus, by using our human life for gaining spiritual realizations we can solve all our human problems and fulfill all our own and others' wishes. What could be more meaningful than this?

Through contemplating these points, we will arrive at the determination to engage in spiritual practice. This book, which I have prepared for daily spiritual practice, is a collection of many important instructions from my other books. Its subject matter is profound, but because its presentation is simple, even if you are a beginner you will not find it difficult to understand. If you put the instructions into practice, you can solve your daily problems and find true happiness. In particular, I believe that for those who are already familiar with my other books, the instructions presented here will provide a powerful method for gaining the deepest experience of both the stages of the path to enlightenment and training the mind. If you read this book with a positive mind, free from negative views, you will definitely receive great benefits.

I pray that everyone who reads this book experiences inner peace and accomplishes the real meaning of human life.

Geshe Kelsang Gyatso
USA, March 2001

PART ONE

Foundation

Inner Peace

Inner Peace

All living beings have the same basic wish to be happy and avoid suffering, but very few people understand the real causes of happiness and suffering. We generally believe that external conditions such as food, friends, cars, and money are the real causes of happiness, and as a result we devote nearly all our time and energy to acquiring these. Superficially it seems that these things can make us happy, but if we look more deeply we will see that they also bring us a lot of suffering and problems.

Happiness and suffering are opposites, so if something is a real cause of happiness it cannot give rise to suffering. If food, money, and so forth are really causes of happiness, they can never be causes of suffering; but we know from our own experience that they often do cause suffering. For example, one of our main interests is food, but the food we eat is also the principal cause of most of our ill health and sickness. In the process of producing the things we feel will make us happy, we have polluted our environment to such an extent that the very air we breathe and the water we drink now threaten our health and well-being. We love the freedom and independence a car can give us, but the cost in accidents and environmental destruction is enormous. We feel that money is essential for us to enjoy life, but the pursuit of money also causes immense problems and anxiety. Even our family and friends, with whom we enjoy so many happy moments, can also bring us a lot of worry and heartache.

In recent years our understanding and control of the external world have increased considerably, and as a result we have witnessed remarkable material progress, but there has not been a corresponding increase in human happiness. There is no less suffering in the world today and there are no fewer problems. It could even be said that there are now more problems and greater unhappiness than ever before. This shows that the solution to our problems, and to those of society as a whole, does not lie in knowledge or control of the external world.

Why is this? Happiness and suffering are states of mind, and so their main causes cannot be found outside the mind. The real source of happiness is inner peace. If our mind is peaceful, we will be happy all the time, regardless of external conditions, but if it is disturbed or troubled in any way, we will never be happy, no matter how good our external conditions may be. External conditions can only make us happy if our mind is peaceful. We can understand this through our own experience. For instance, even if we are in the most beautiful surroundings and have everything we need, the moment we get angry any happiness we may have disappears. This is because anger has destroyed our inner peace.

We can see from this that if we want true, lasting happiness we need to develop and maintain a special experience of inner peace. The only way to do this is by training our mind through spiritual practice—gradually reducing and eliminating our negative, disturbed states of mind and replacing them with positive, peaceful states. Eventually, through continuing to improve our inner peace we will experience permanent inner peace, or *nirvana*. Once we have attained nirvana we will be happy throughout our life, and in life after life. We will have solved all our problems and accomplished the true meaning of our human life.

Since we all have within us our own source of peace and happiness, we may wonder why it is so hard to maintain a continually peaceful and joyful mind. This is because of the delusions that so often crowd our mind. Delusions are distorted ways of looking at ourself, other people, and the world around us—like a distorted mirror they reflect a distorted world. The deluded mind of hatred, for example, views other people as intrinsically bad, but there is no such thing as an intrinsically bad person. Desirous attachment, on the other hand, sees its object of desire as intrinsically good and as a true source of happiness. If we have a strong craving to eat chocolate, chocolate appears to be intrinsically desirable. However, once we have eaten too much of it and start to feel sick, it no longer seems so desirable and may even appear repulsive. This shows that in itself chocolate is neither desirable nor repulsive. It is the deluded mind of attachment that projects all kinds of pleasurable qualities onto its objects of desire and then relates to them as if they really did possess those qualities.

All delusions function like this, projecting onto the world their own distorted version of reality and then relating to this projection as if it were true. When our mind is under the influence of delusions, we are out of touch with reality and are not seeing things as they really are. Since our mind is under the control of at least subtle forms of delusion all the time, it is not surprising that our lives are so often filled with frustration. It is as if we are continually chasing mirages, only to be disappointed when they do not give us the satisfaction we had hoped for.

When things go wrong in our life and we encounter difficult situations, we tend to regard the situation itself as the problem, but in reality whatever problems we experience come from the mind. If we responded to difficulties with a positive or peaceful mind, they would not be problems for us. Eventually we might even regard them as challenges or opportunities for growth and development. Problems arise only if we respond to situations with a negative state of mind. Therefore if we want to transform our life and be free from problems, we must learn to transform our mind. Sufferings, problems, worries, unhappiness, and pain all exist within our mind—they are all unpleasant feelings, which are part of the mind. Through controlling and purifying our mind we can stop them once and for all.

To understand this fully, we need to understand the relationship between the mind and external objects. All objects, whether pleasant, unpleasant, or neutral, are mere appearances to the mind, just like things experienced in a dream. This is not easy to understand at first, but we can gain some understanding by thinking about the following. When we are awake many different things exist, but when we fall asleep they cease. This is because the mind to which they appear ceases. When we dream, the only things that appear are dream objects. Later, when we wake up, these dream objects cease. This is because the dreaming mind to which they appear ceases. If we think deeply about this, we will understand how we can cause all the unpleasant things that we dislike to cease simply by abandoning impure, deluded states of mind, and we can cause all the pleasant things that we desire to arise simply by developing a pure mind. Purifying our mind of delusions through spiritual practice fulfills our deepest longing for true, lasting happiness.

We should understand that although delusions are deeply ingrained, they are not an intrinsic part of our mind and so they can definitely be removed. Delusions are just bad mental habits, and like all habits they can be broken. At the moment our mind is like muddy water, murky and polluted by delusions. However, just as it is possible to separate mud from water, so it is possible to purify the mind of all delusions. With no delusions remaining in our mind, there is nothing that can disturb our inner peace and joy.

Since time without beginning we have been under the control of our mind, like a puppet on a string. We are like a servant working for our mind—whenever our mind wants to do something, we have to do it without any choice. Sometimes our mind is like a crazy elephant, creating so many problems and dangers for ourself and others. By sincerely engaging in spiritual practice we can reverse this situation and gain mastery over our mind. Transforming our mind in this way, we will finally enjoy real freedom.

For our spiritual practice to be successful, we need the blessings and inspiration of those who have already gained deep inner realizations, but we also need to give ourself constant encouragement. If we cannot encourage ourself, how can we expect anyone else to? When we understand clearly that inner peace is the real source of happiness, and how through spiritual practice we can experience progressively deeper levels of inner peace, we will develop tremendous enthusiasm to practice. This is very important because to attain the permanent inner peace of nirvana we need to engage in spiritual practice sincerely and diligently.

This does not mean that we ignore external conditions. We need inner peace, but we also need good physical health, and for this we need certain external conditions such as food and a comfortable environment to live in. There are many people who concentrate exclusively on developing the material side of their life, while completely ignoring spiritual practice. This is one extreme. However, there are other people who concentrate exclusively on spiritual practice, while ignoring the material conditions that are necessary for supporting a healthy human life. This is another extreme. We need to maintain a middle way that avoids both extremes of materialism and spirituality.

Some people believe that those who strive to attain nirvana are being selfish because they seem to be concentrating only on their own inner peace, but this belief is incorrect. Our real purpose in attaining the permanent inner peace of nirvana is to help others do the same. Just as the only way to solve our own problems is to find inner peace, so the only way to help others to solve theirs is to encourage them to engage in spiritual practice and discover their own inner peace. This way of benefiting others is by far the best. Yet we can do this effectively only if we first work on our own mind. There is little benefit in telling people how important it is to overcome their delusions if we are unable to control our own. However, if through training our mind we succeed in pacifying—or even completely eliminating—our own anger, for example, we can certainly help others control theirs. Then our advice will not be mere words, but will have behind it the power of personal experience.

We can sometimes help others by providing them with money or better material conditions, but we should remember that the greatest benefit we can give is to help them overcome their delusions and find true, lasting happiness within. Through technological progress and by organizing society in fairer, more humane ways, we can certainly help improve people's lives in some respects. But whatever we do will inevitably have some unwanted side effects. The best we can hope for is to provide people with conditions that bring some temporary relief from problems and difficulties, but we cannot give them true, lasting happiness. This is because the real cause of happiness is inner peace, which can be found only within the mind, not in external conditions.

Without inner peace, outer peace is impossible.

Without inner peace, outer peace is impossible. We all wish for world peace, but world peace will never be achieved unless we first establish peace within our own minds. We can send so-called "peacekeeping forces" into areas of conflict, but peace cannot be imposed from the outside with guns. Only by creating peace within our own mind and helping others do the same can we hope to achieve peace in this world.

This book presents many profound methods of spiritual training, all of which are practical ways to purify and control our mind. If we put these methods into practice we will definitely gain a special experience of mental peace. By continuing to improve this experience, deluded states of mind will gradually diminish and our inner peace will grow. Eventually, by abandoning delusions altogether, we will attain the permanent inner peace of nirvana. Having overcome our own delusions, such as anger, attachment, and ignorance, and developed profound spiritual realizations of universal love, compassion, concentration, and wisdom, our ability to help others will be far greater. In this way we can help others solve their problems not just for a few days or a few years, but forever. We can help them find an inner peace and joy that nothing, not even death, can destroy. How wonderful!

What is the Mind?

What is the Mind?

Since happiness and suffering depend on the mind, if we want to avoid suffering and find true happiness we need to understand the nature and functions of the mind. At first, this might seem straightforward since we all have minds, and we all know what state our mind is in—whether it is happy or sad, clear or confused, and so forth. However, if someone asked us what the nature of our mind is and how it functions, we would probably not be able to give a precise answer. This indicates that we do not have a clear understanding of the mind.

Some people think the mind is the brain or some other part or function of the body, but this is incorrect. The brain is a physical object that can be seen with the eyes and that can be photographed or operated on in surgery. The mind, on the other hand, is not a physical object. It cannot be seen with the eyes, photographed or repaired by surgery. The brain, therefore, is not the mind but simply part of the body.

There is nothing within the body that can be identified as being our mind because our body and mind are different entities. For example, sometimes when our body is relaxed and immobile, our mind can be very busy, darting from one object to another.

This indicates that our body and mind are not the same entity. In Buddhist scriptures, our body is compared to a guest house and our mind to a guest residing within it. When we die, our mind leaves our body and goes to the next life, just like a guest leaving a guest house and going somewhere else.

If the mind is not the brain or any other part of the body, what is it? It is a formless continuum that functions to perceive and understand objects. Because the mind is formless, or non-physical by nature, it is not obstructed by physical objects. Thus, it is impossible for our body to go to the moon without traveling in a spaceship, but our mind can reach the moon in an instant just by thinking about it. Knowing and perceiving objects is a function that is unique to the mind. Although we say, "I know such and such," in reality it is our mind that knows. We know things only by using our mind.

It is very important to be able to distinguish between disturbed states of mind and peaceful states. As explained in the previous chapter, states of mind that disturb our inner peace, such as anger, jealousy, and desirous attachment, are called *delusions*. These are the principal causes of all our suffering. We may think that our suffering is caused by other people, by poor material conditions, or by society, but in reality it all comes from our own deluded states of mind. The essence of spiritual practice is to reduce and eventually to eradicate altogether our delusions, and to replace them with permanent inner peace. This is the real meaning of our human life.

Normally we seek happiness outside ourself. We try to obtain better material conditions, a better job, higher social status, and so forth. But no matter how successful we are in improving our external situation, we still experience many problems and much dissatisfaction. We never experience pure, lasting happiness. This shows us that we should not seek happiness outside ourself but instead establish it within by purifying and controlling our mind through sincere spiritual practice. If we train in this way we can ensure that our mind remains calm and happy all the time. Then, no matter how difficult our external circumstances may be, we will always be happy and peaceful.

In our ordinary life, even though we work very hard to find happiness it remains elusive for us, while suffering and problems seem to come naturally, without any effort. Why is this? It is because the cause of happiness within our mind—inner peace—is very weak and can give rise to its effect only if we apply great effort, while the internal causes of suffering and problems— delusions—are very strong and can give rise to their effects with no effort on our part. This is the real reason why problems come naturally while happiness is so difficult to find.

From this we can see that the principal causes of both happiness and problems are in the mind, not in the external world. If we were able to maintain a calm and peaceful mind all day long we would never experience any problems or mental suffering. For example, if our mind remains peaceful all the time, then even if we are insulted, criticized, or blamed, or if we lose our job or our friends, we will not become unhappy. No matter how difficult our external circumstances may become, as long as we maintain a calm and peaceful mind they will not be a problem for us. Therefore, if we wish to be free from problems there is only one thing to do—learn to maintain a peaceful state of mind by following the spiritual path.

The essential point of understanding the mind is that liberation from suffering cannot be found outside the mind. Permanent liberation can be found only by purifying the mind. Therefore, if we want to become free from problems and attain lasting peace and happiness we need to increase our knowledge and understanding of the mind.

There are three levels of mind: gross, subtle, and very subtle. Gross minds include sense awarenesses such as eye awareness and ear awareness, and all our normal waking minds, including delusions such as anger, jealousy, attachment, and strong self-grasping ignorance. These gross minds are related to gross inner winds and are relatively easy to recognize. Inner winds are subtle energy winds that flow through the channels of our body and function to move our mind to its object. When we fall asleep or die, our gross minds dissolve inward and our subtle minds become manifest. Subtle minds are related to subtle inner winds and are more difficult to recognize than gross minds. During deep sleep, and at the end of the death process, the inner winds dissolve into the center of the heart channel wheel inside the central channel, and then the very subtle mind, the mind of clear light, becomes manifest. The very subtle mind is related to the very subtle inner wind and is extremely difficult to recognize. The continuum of the very subtle mind has no beginning and no end. It is this mind that goes from one life to the next, and if it is completely purified by training in meditation, it is this mind that will eventually transform into the omniscient mind of an enlightened being.

Liberation from suffering cannot be found outside the mind.

Living beings experience countless thoughts or minds, all of which are included within two: primary minds and mental factors. A detailed explanation of this can be found in *Understanding the Mind*.

If we understand clearly the nature of our mind, we will definitely realize that the continuum of our mind does not cease when we die, and there will be no basis for doubting the existence of our future lives. If we realize the existence of our future lives, we will naturally be concerned for our welfare and happiness in those lives, and we will use this present life to make the appropriate preparations. This will prevent us from wasting our precious human life on the preoccupations of this life alone. Therefore, a correct understanding of the mind is absolutely essential.

Reincarnation

Reincarnation

Many people believe that when the body disintegrates at death, the continuum of the mind ceases and the mind becomes non-existent, like a candle flame that goes out when all the wax has burned. There are even some people who contemplate committing suicide in the hope that if they die their problems and sufferings will end. These ideas, however, are completely wrong. As already explained, our body and mind are separate entities, so even though the body disintegrates at death, the continuum of the mind remains unbroken. Instead of ceasing, the mind simply leaves the present body and goes to the next life. For ordinary beings, therefore, instead of releasing us from suffering, death only brings new sufferings. Because they do not understand this, many people destroy their precious human life by committing suicide.

There is a special spiritual practice called *transference of consciousness into another body*, which was quite widespread in ancient times. There are many examples of past practitioners who could transfer their consciousness from their normal body into another body. If mind and body were the same entity, how would it be possible for these practitioners to transfer their consciousness in this way? Even now, it is not that unusual for the mind temporarily to leave the physical body before death. For example, many people who are not spiritual practitioners have had so-called "out of body" experiences.

We can also gain an understanding of past and future lives by examining the process of sleeping, dreaming, and waking, because this closely resembles the process of death, intermediate state, and rebirth. When we fall asleep our gross inner winds gather and dissolve inward, and our mind becomes progressively more and more subtle until it transforms into the very subtle mind of the clear light of sleep. While the clear light of sleep is manifest we experience deep sleep, and to others we resemble a dead person. When it ends, our mind becomes gradually more and more gross, and we pass through the various levels of the dream state. Finally our normal powers of memory and mental control are restored and we wake up. When this happens our dream world disappears and we perceive the world of the waking state.

A very similar process occurs when we die. As we die our inner winds dissolve inward and our mind becomes progressively more and more subtle until the very subtle mind of the clear light of death becomes manifest. The experience of the clear light of death is very similar to the experience of deep sleep. After the clear light of death has ceased, we experience the stages of the intermediate state, or *bardo* in Tibetan, which is a dream-like state that occurs between death and rebirth. After a few days or weeks, the intermediate state ends and we take rebirth. Just as when we awaken from sleep, the dream world disappears and we perceive the world of the waking state, similarly when we take rebirth, the appearances of the intermediate state cease and we perceive the world of our next life.

The only significant difference between the process of sleeping, dreaming, and waking and the process of death, intermediate state, and rebirth is that after the clear light of sleep has ceased, the relationship between our mind and our present body remains intact, while after the clear light of death this relationship is broken. By contemplating this, we can gain conviction in the existence of past and future lives.

We generally believe that the things we perceive in dreams are unreal while the things we perceive when we are awake are true. But in reality everything we perceive is like a dream in that it is mere appearance to mind. For those who can interpret them correctly, dreams have great significance. For example, if we dream that we visit a particular country that we have never been to in this life, our dream will indicate one of four things: that we have been to that country in a previous life, that we will visit it later in this life, that we will visit it in a future life, or that it has some personal significance for us—for example, if we had recently received a letter from that country or had seen a television program about it. Similarly, if we dream we are flying, it may mean that in a previous life we were a being who could fly, such as a bird or a meditator with miracle powers, or it may predict that we will become such a being in the future. A flying dream may also have a less literal meaning, symbolizing an improvement in our health or state of mind.

It was with the help of dreams that I was able to discover where my mother was reborn after she had died. Just before she died, my mother dozed off for a few minutes and when she woke she told my sister, who was caring for her, that she had dreamed of me and that in her dream I had offered her a traditional white scarf. I interpreted this dream to mean that I would be able to help my mother in her next life, and so after she died, I prayed every day for her to be reborn in England, where I was living, so that I would have the opportunity to meet and recognize her reincarnation. I made strong prayers to see clear signs of where my mother's reincarnation could be found.

Later I had three dreams that seemed to be significant. In the first I dreamed that I met my mother in a place that appeared to be England. I asked her how she had traveled from India to England, but she replied that she had not come from India, but from Switzerland. In the second dream I dreamed that I saw my mother talking to a group of people. I approached her and spoke to her in Tibetan, but she did not seem to understand what I was saying. While she was alive my mother spoke only Tibetan, but in this dream she spoke English fluently. I asked her why she had forgotten Tibetan, but she did not reply. Later in the same dream, I dreamed of a Western couple who were helping me with the development of my spiritual activities in England.

Both dreams seemed to give clues about where my mother had been reborn. Two days after the second dream, the husband of the couple I had dreamed of visited me and told me that his wife was pregnant. I immediately remembered my dream and thought that her baby might be my mother's reincarnation. The fact that in the dream my mother had forgotten Tibetan and spoke only English suggested that she would be reborn in an English-speaking country, and the presence of this couple in the dream might have been an indication that they were her parents. I then performed a traditional divination together with ritual prayers, and this indicated that their child was my mother's reincarnation. I was very happy but did not say anything to anyone.

One night I dreamed about my mother again and again. The next morning I considered the matter carefully and reached a decision. If the baby had been born that night then it was definitely my mother's reincarnation, but if it had not, I would need to check further. Having made this decision I phoned the husband, who gave me the good news that his wife had given birth to a baby girl the previous night. I was delighted and performed a special offering ceremony.

A few days later, the father phoned and told me that if he recited the mantra of Buddha Avalokiteshvara, OM MANI PÄME HUM, when the baby cried, she would immediately stop crying and appear to be listening to the mantra. He asked me why this was, and I replied that it was because of her tendencies from her previous life. I knew that my mother had recited this mantra with strong faith throughout her life.

The child was named Amaravajra. Later when my mother's brother, Kuten Lama, visited England and saw Amaravajra for the first time he was astonished by how affectionate she was toward him. He said that it was as if she recognized him. I also had the same experience. Although I was able to visit the young child only occasionally, she was always extremely happy to see me.

When Amaravajra started to talk, one day she pointed to a dog and said, "kyi, kyi." After this she used to say "kyi" many times whenever she saw a dog. Her father asked me if "kyi" meant anything, and I told him that in the dialect of western Tibet, where my mother used to live, "kyi" means "dog." This was not the only Tibetan word the little girl uttered spontaneously.

I later heard through my sister's husband that after my mother's death a Tibetan astrologer had predicted that my mother would be born as a female in a country with a language other than Tibetan. This story comes from my own personal experience, but if we investigate we can find many other true stories about how people have been able to recognize the reincarnations of their husband, wife, teachers, parents, friends, and others.

In western Tibet, near my first monastery, there lived a man who had a reputation for being very bad tempered. He collected many silver coins and put them into a teapot, which he kept secret even from his wife. Later as he lay dying, out of attachment for the coins he became obsessed with the thought that they might be stolen. He tried to tell his wife about the coins, but because he was very weak he could only repeat the one word "tib," which means "teapot." Hearing this, his wife assumed that he wanted some tea, but when she offered him some he had no interest in it. Shortly afterwards he died.

The happiness of future lives is more important than the happiness of this life.

Sometime later, the wife found the hidden teapot. Wondering why it was so heavy, she opened the lid and discovered the coins. Coiled around these was a small snake. Terrified of the snake, she called for her family, who together tried to remove it from the teapot. But however hard they tried they could not separate the snake from the coins. They were surprised and confused about this, and wondered where the snake had come from.

The wife then remembered her husband's last words, and realized that at the time of his death he had been trying to tell her about the coins. But what about the snake? Why was it so attached to the coins? She decided to visit a clairvoyant Yogi living nearby, who told her that the snake was the reincarnation of her husband. Due to the actions he had created out of anger, and due to his attachment to the coins when he was about to die, he had taken rebirth as a snake and had gone inside the teapot to be close to the coins. With tears falling from her eyes, she beseeched the Yogi, "Please tell me what I can do to help my husband." He suggested that she offer the coins to the nearby community of ordained Sangha, requesting them to pray for her husband to be released from his animal rebirth.

By contemplating such stories with a positive mind, and reflecting on the nature of the mind and the analogy of sleeping, dreaming, and waking, we will definitely gain a deep understanding of the existence of our future lives. This knowledge is very precious and helps us gain great wisdom. We will understand that the happiness of future lives is more important than the happiness of this life for the simple reason that countless future lives are far longer than this one short human life. This will motivate us to prepare for the happiness of our future lives, or to try to attain permanent liberation from suffering by abandoning our delusions.

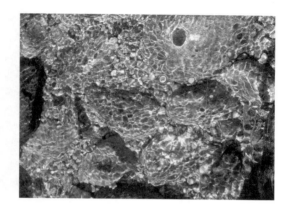

Death

Death

No one wants to suffer. Day and night, even in our dreams, we instinctively try to avoid even the slightest suffering. This indicates that, although we are not fully aware of it, deep down what we are really seeking is permanent liberation from suffering.

There are times when we are free from physical suffering and mental pain, but these times never last. It does not take long before our body again becomes uncomfortable or sick, and our mind is disturbed by worries and unhappiness. Whatever problem we overcome, it is only a matter of time before another arises to take its place. This shows that despite our wish for permanent liberation from suffering we have never managed to attain it. As long as delusions remain in our mind, we will never be completely free from suffering. We may enjoy moments of relief, but before long our problems will return. The only way to finally end our suffering is by following the spiritual path. Since in the depths of their hearts everyone wants complete liberation from suffering, we can see that in reality everyone needs to follow the spiritual path.

However, because our desire for worldly enjoyment is so strong, we have little or no interest in spiritual practice. From a spiritual point of view, this lack of interest in spiritual practice is a type of laziness called the *laziness of attachment*. As long as we have this laziness the door to liberation will be closed to us, and consequently we will continue to experience misery in this life and endless suffering in life after life. The way to overcome this laziness is to meditate on death.

We need to contemplate and meditate on our death again and again until we gain a deep realization of death. Although on an intellectual level we all know that eventually we are going to die, our awareness of death remains superficial. Since our intellectual knowledge of death does not touch our hearts, each and every day we continue to think, "I will not die today, I will not die today." Even on the day of our death we are still thinking about what we will do tomorrow or next week. This mind that thinks every day "I will not die today" is deceptive—it leads us in the wrong direction and causes our human life to become empty. On the other hand, through meditating on death we will gradually replace the deceptive thought "I will not die today" with the non-deceptive thought "I may die today." The mind that spontaneously thinks each and every day "I may die today" is the realization of death. It is this realization that directly eliminates our laziness of attachment and opens the door to the spiritual path.

In general, we may die today or we may not die today—we do not know. However, if we think each day, "I may not die today," this thought will deceive us because it comes from our ignorance. If instead we think each day, "I may die today," this thought will not deceive us because it comes from our wisdom. This beneficial thought will prevent our laziness of attachment, and will encourage us to prepare for the welfare of our countless future lives or to put great effort into entering the path to liberation. In this way, we will make our human life meaningful.

To meditate on death, we contemplate that our death is certain and that the time of our death is uncertain. We then need to understand that at the time of death and after death only spiritual practice can help us.

DEATH IS CERTAIN

Death will definitely come and there is nothing that can prevent it. We contemplate:

> *No matter where I am born, whether in fortunate or unfortunate states of existence, I will definitely have to die. Whether I am born in the happiest condition of higher rebirth or in the deepest hell, I will have to experience death. However far and wide I travel, I will never find a place where I can hide from death, even if I voyage far into space or tunnel deeply underground.*
>
> *No one alive at the time of the first century remains alive today, and no one alive at the time of the second century and so forth remains alive today. Only their names survive. All those who were alive two hundred years ago have passed away, and everyone alive today will be gone within two hundred years.*

Contemplating these points we should ask ourself, "Could I alone outlive death?"

When our karma to experience this life comes to an end, no one and nothing can prevent our death. When the time of our death arrives, there is no escape. If it were possible to prevent death by using clairvoyance or miracle powers, those who had such powers would have become immortal—but even clairvoyants die. The most powerful leaders who have ruled in this world have been helpless before the power of death. The king of beasts, the lion, who can kill an elephant, is immediately destroyed when he encounters the Lord of Death. Even billionaires have no way of avoiding death. They cannot distract death with a bribe or buy time, saying, "If you postpone my death, I will give you wealth beyond your wildest dreams."

Death is relentless and will not be compromised. It is like the collapse of an immense mountain in all four directions—there is no way to hold back its devastation. This is also true of aging and sickness. Aging progresses surreptitiously and undermines our youth, our strength, and our beauty. Although we are hardly aware of the process, it is already underway and cannot be reversed. Sickness destroys the comfort, power, and strength of our body. If doctors help us overcome our first illness, others take its place until eventually our sickness cannot be cured and we die. We cannot escape from sickness and death by running away from them. We cannot appease them with money or use miracle powers to make them vanish. Every single being in this world must suffer aging, sickness, and death.

We live in the very embrace of death.

Our lifespan cannot be increased, and in fact it is decreasing continuously. From the moment of our conception we head inexorably toward death, just like a racehorse galloping toward the finish line. Even racehorses occasionally relax their pace, but in our race toward death we never stop, not even for a second. While we are sleeping and while we are awake, our life slips away. Every vehicle stops and breaks its journey from time to time, but our lifespan never stops running out. One moment after our birth, part of our lifespan has perished. We live in the very embrace of death. After our birth we have no freedom to remain even for a minute. We head toward the embrace of the Lord of Death like an athlete running. We may think that we are among the living, but our life is the very highway of death.

Imagine if our doctor were to break the news to us that we are suffering from an incurable disease and that we have only one week left to live. If our friend were then to offer us a fantastic gift such as a diamond, a new car, or a free vacation, we would not get very excited about it. Yet in reality, this is our predicament, because we are all suffering from a mortal disease. It's foolish to become overly interested in the passing pleasures of this brief life!

If we find it difficult to meditate on death, we can just listen to a clock ticking and be aware that every tick marks the end of a moment of our life and brings us closer to death. We can imagine that the Lord of Death lives a few miles up the road from our home, and as we listen to the clock ticking we can imagine ourself taking steps in death's direction. In this way we will become real travelers.

Our world is as impermanent as autumn clouds, with our birth and death being like the entrance and exit of an actor on the stage. Actors frequently change their costumes and their roles, making their entrance in many different disguises. In the same way, living beings take different forms continually and enter new worlds. Sometimes they are human beings, sometimes they are animals, and sometimes they enter hell. We should understand that the lifespan of a living being passes like lightning in the sky, and perishes quickly like water falling from a high mountain.

Death will come regardless of whether or not we have made time for spiritual practice. Although life is short, it would not be so bad if we had plenty of time for spiritual practice, but most of our time is taken up with sleeping, working, eating, shopping, talking, and so on, leaving very little time for pure spiritual practice. Our time is easily consumed by other pursuits until suddenly we die.

We keep thinking that we have plenty of time for spiritual practice, but if we closely examine our way of life we will see that the days slip by without our getting down to serious practice. If we do not make time to engage in spiritual practice purely, we will look back on our life at the time of death and see that it has been of very little benefit. However, if we meditate on death, we will develop such a sincere wish to practice purely that we will naturally begin to modify our daily routine so that it includes at least a little time for practice. Eventually we will find more time for practice than for other things.

If we meditate on death again and again we may feel afraid, but it is not enough just to feel fear. Once we have generated an appropriate fear of dying unprepared, we should search for something that will offer real protection. The paths of future lives are very long and unfamiliar. We have to experience one life after another and we cannot be sure where we will take rebirth—whether we will have to follow the paths to unhappy states of existence or the paths to happier realms. We have no freedom or independence but must go wherever our karma takes us. Therefore, we need to find something that will show us a safe way to future lives, something that will direct us along correct paths and away from wrong paths. The possessions and enjoyments of this life cannot protect us. Since only spiritual teachings reveal a flawless path that will help and protect us in the future, we must apply effort with our body, speech, and mind to put spiritual teachings such as those presented in this book into practice. The Yogi Milarepa said:

> There are more fears in future lives than in this one. Have you prepared anything that will help you? If you have not prepared for your future lives, do so now. The only protection against those fears is the practice of holy spiritual teachings.

If we think about our own life, we will see that we have spent many years with no interest in spiritual practice, and that even now that we have the wish to practice, still, due to laziness, we do not practice purely. A scholar called Gungtang said:

> I spent twenty years not wanting to practice spiritual teachings. I spent the next twenty years thinking that I could practice later on. I spent another twenty years engrossed in other activities and regretting that I had not engaged in spiritual practice. This is the story of my empty human life.

This could be our own life story, but if we meditate on death we will avoid wasting our precious human life and we will strive to make it meaningful.

Through contemplating these points, we should deeply think, "I will definitely die." Considering that at the time of death only our spiritual practice will be of any real assistance to us, we make a firm resolution, "I must put spiritual teachings into practice." When this new thought arises strongly and clearly in our mind, we do placement meditation to become more and more familiar with it, until we never lose it.

THE TIME OF OUR DEATH IS UNCERTAIN

Sometimes we fool ourself by thinking, "I'm young and so I will not die soon," but we can see how misguided this thought is just by observing how many young people die before their parents. Sometimes we think, "I'm healthy and so I will not die soon," but we can see that people who are healthy and looking after the sick sometimes die before their patients. People who go to visit their friends in the hospital may die sooner in a car crash, because death does not confine itself to those who are old and sick. Someone who is alive and well in the morning could be dead by the afternoon, and someone who is well when he falls asleep may die before he wakes up. Some people die while they are eating, and some people die in the middle of a conversation. Some people die as soon as they are born.

Death may not give any warning. This enemy can come at any time and often he strikes quickly, when we least expect it. He may come as we are driving to a party, or switching on our television, or as we are thinking to ourself "I will not die today" and making plans for our summer vacation or our retirement. The Lord of Death can creep up on us as dark clouds creep across the sky. Sometimes when we go indoors the sky is bright and clear, but when we step outside again the sky is overcast. In the same way, death can quickly cast its shadow over our life.

There are many more conditions conducive to death than to survival. Although our death is certain and our lifespan is indefinite, it would not be so bad if the conditions that lead to death were rare; but there are innumerable external and internal conditions that can bring about our death. The external environment causes deaths by famine, floods, fires, earthquakes, pollution, and so on. In a similar way, the four internal bodily elements of earth, water, fire, and wind cause death when their harmony is lost and one of them develops in excess. When these internal elements are in harmony they are said to be like four snakes of the same species and strength abiding together peacefully; but when they lose their harmony it is like one snake becoming stronger than the others and consuming them, until finally it dies of hunger itself.

Besides these inanimate causes of death, other living beings such as thieves, hostile soldiers, and wild animals can also cause our death. Even things that we do not consider to be threatening—things that we think of as supporting and protecting our life, such as our house, our car, or our best friend—can turn out to be causes of our death. People are sometimes crushed to death by their own house or they fall to their death from their own staircase, and each day many people are killed in their cars. Some people die on vacation, and some are killed by their hobbies and entertainments, such as horseback riders who are thrown to their death. The very food we eat to nourish and sustain our life can be a cause of death. Even our friends and lovers can become causes of our death, by mistake or intentionally. We read in the newspapers how lovers sometimes kill one another, and how parents sometimes kill their own children. If we investigate carefully, we will not be able to find any worldly enjoyment that is not a potential cause of death and that is solely a cause of remaining alive. The great scholar Nagarjuna said:

We maintain our life in the midst of thousands of conditions that threaten death. Our life force abides like a candle flame in the breeze. The candle flame of our life is easily extinguished by the winds of death that blow from all directions.

Each person has created the karma to remain in this life for a certain period, but since we cannot remember what karma we have created we cannot know the exact duration of our present life. It is possible for us to die an untimely death before completing our lifespan because we can exhaust our merit, the cause of good fortune, sooner than we exhaust the karma that determines our lifespan. If this happens we become so sick that doctors cannot help us, or we find that we are unable to obtain food and other necessities to support our life. However, even when we become seriously ill, if our lifespan has not ended and we still have merit we can find all the conditions necessary for recovery.

The human body is very fragile. Although there are many causes of death it would not be so bad if our body were strong like steel, but it is delicate. It does not take guns and bombs to destroy our body; it can be destroyed by a small needle. As Nagarjuna said:

There are many destroyers of our life force.
Our human body is like a water bubble.

Just as a water bubble bursts as soon as it is touched, so a single drop of water in the heart or the slightest scratch from a poisonous thorn can cause our death. Nagarjuna said that at the end of this eon the entire world system will be consumed by fire and not even its ashes will remain. Since the entire universe will become empty, there is no need to say that this delicate human body will decay very swiftly.

We can contemplate the process of our breathing and how it continues without interruption between inhalation and exhalation. If it were to stop, we would die. But even when we are asleep and our mindfulness is no longer functioning, our breathing continues, although in many other respects we resemble a corpse. Nagarjuna said, "This is a most wonderful thing!" When we wake up in the morning we should rejoice, thinking, "How amazing it is that my breathing has kept me alive throughout sleep. If it had stopped during the night I would now be dead!"

Contemplating that the time of our death is completely uncertain, and understanding that there is no guarantee that we will not die today, we should think deeply, day and night, "I may die today, I may die today." Meditating on this feeling, we will then come to a strong determination:

Since I will soon have to leave this world, there is no point in my becoming attached to the things of this life. Instead I will take to heart the real essence of my human life by sincerely engaging in spiritual practice.

What does "engaging in spiritual practice" mean? Essentially it means transforming the mind—overcoming delusions and negative actions and cultivating constructive thoughts and actions. This is something we can be doing all the time, not just while seated in meditation. An explanation of the different levels of the practice of *training the mind* will be given in Part Two. Whenever we put these teachings into practice we are engaging in spiritual practice. The practice of training the mind is especially appropriate in these times, when people experience so many difficulties.

The foundation of an authentic spiritual life is moral discipline. This means avoiding negative actions such as killing, stealing, sexual misconduct, lying, divisive speech, hurtful speech, idle chatter, covetousness, malice, and holding wrong views—recognizing them as harmful to both ourself and others.

It is also important to practice giving. Not only can we give material help to those who need it, but we can also give our time, goodwill, and love to everyone we meet; we can give protection to those who are afraid or in danger, especially animals; and we can give spiritual teachings or good advice whenever it is appropriate.

Another essential practice is patience. Patience is a mind that accepts harm or hardship with a virtuous intention, and is the opponent to anger. We are practicing patience whenever we prevent ourself from getting angry even if we are harmed or insulted, or when we calmly accept difficult situations such as illness, poverty, loneliness, losing our job or partner, or not fulfilling our wishes. By accepting harm and hardship as an opportunity to train or purify our mind, we can maintain a happy mind all the time.

We should also put great effort into the study and practice of spiritual teachings so that we can fulfill our spiritual goals. We should train in meditative concentration, which is the source of inner peace. The deeper our concentration, the more profound and stable our mental peace will be, and the clearer and more powerful our mind will become. Most importantly, we should train in the wisdom that understands how things really exist. By gaining deep knowledge of ultimate truth, or emptiness, we can remove the ignorance of self-grasping from our mind and thereby fulfill our deepest wish for permanent liberation from suffering.

Karma

Karma

The law of karma is a special instance of the law of cause and effect, according to which all our actions of body, speech, and mind are causes and all our experiences are their effects. The law of karma explains why each individual has a unique mental disposition, a unique physical appearance, and unique experiences. These are the various effects of the countless actions that each individual has performed in the past. We cannot find any two people who have created exactly the same history of actions throughout their past lives, and so we cannot find two people with identical states of mind, identical experiences, and identical physical appearances. Each person has a different individual karma. Some people enjoy good health while others are constantly sick. Some people are very beautiful while others are very ugly. Some people have a happy disposition that is easily pleased while others have a sour disposition and are rarely delighted by anything. Some people easily understand the meaning of spiritual teachings while others find them difficult and obscure.

Karma means "action," and refers to the actions of our body, speech, and mind. Every action we perform leaves an imprint, or potentiality, on our very subtle mind, and each imprint eventually gives rise to its own effect. Our mind is like a field, and performing actions is like sowing seeds in that field. Virtuous actions sow seeds of future happiness, and non-virtuous actions sow seeds of future suffering. The seeds we have sown in the past remain dormant until the conditions necessary for their germination come together. In some cases this can be many lifetimes after the original action was performed.

It is because of our karma or actions that we are born in this impure, contaminated world and experience so many difficulties and problems. Our actions are impure because our mind is contaminated by the inner poison of self-grasping. This is the fundamental reason why we experience suffering. Suffering is created by our own actions or karma—it is not given to us as a punishment. We suffer because we have accumulated many non-virtuous actions in our previous lives. The source of these non-virtuous actions is our own delusions such as anger, attachment, and self-grasping ignorance.

Once we have purified our mind of self-grasping and all other delusions, all our actions will naturally be pure. As a result of our pure actions or pure karma, everything we experience will be pure. We will abide in a pure world, with a pure body, enjoying pure enjoyments and surrounded by pure beings. There will no longer be the slightest trace of suffering, impurity, or problems. This is how to find true happiness from within our mind.

THE GENERAL CHARACTERISTICS OF KARMA

For every action we perform, we experience a similar result. If a gardener sows a seed of a medicinal plant, a medicinal plant and not a poisonous one will grow. And if he or she does not sow any seeds, then nothing will grow. In a similar way, if we perform positive actions we will experience happy results and not unhappiness, if we perform negative actions we will experience only unhappy results, and if we perform neutral actions we will experience neutral results.

For example, if we now experience any mental disturbance it is because at some time in the past we disturbed the minds of others. If we experience a painful physical illness it is because in the past we caused pain to others, such as by beating or shooting them, intentionally administering wrong medicines, or serving them poisonous food. If we have not created the karmic cause to become sick it is impossible for us to experience the suffering of physical illness, even if we find ourself in the midst of an epidemic where everyone else around us is dying. Those who have attained nirvana, for example, never experience any physical or mental pain, because they have stopped engaging in harmful actions and purified all the non-virtuous potentialities that are the main causes of pain.

The main cause of the sufferings of poverty is an action of stealing. The main causes of being oppressed are looking down on, beating, or demanding work from people of inferior position, or despising others instead of showing them loving kindness. The main causes of the sufferings of being separated from friends and family are actions such as seducing other people's partners or purposefully alienating their friends and the people who work for them.

Usually we assume that bad experiences arise only in dependence upon the conditions of this present life. Since we cannot account for many of them in these terms, we often feel that they are inexplicable and undeserved, and that there is no justice in the world. In reality, however, most of our experiences in this life are caused by actions we committed in past lives.

Through the following example given in Buddhist scriptures, we can begin to understand how our experiences in this life arise from actions in previous lives, as well as how the results of actions increase over time, just as a small seed can grow into a large tree.

Most of our experiences in this life are caused by actions we committed in past lives.

There was once a nun called Upala, who before her ordination experienced many horrible sufferings. Married three times, each time her husband and her children met a tragic end; and her parents also perished in a fire. Having experienced one terrible misery after another, Upala developed a very strong wish to find freedom from every kind of suffering existence, and so she sought Buddha and told him her story. Buddha explained that in a previous life she had been one of the wives of a king, and that, being very jealous of the other wives, she had continually plotted to destroy their relationships. Her jealous actions alone were enough to cause the extravagant sufferings of her present life. Buddha then explained how she could purify her mind, and by sincerely practicing these teachings she attained nirvana in that life.

By contemplating how the results of our actions are definite and how they increase, we will develop a strong determination to avoid even the slightest non-virtue and to nurture even the smallest positive thoughts and constructive deeds. We then meditate on this determination to make it constant and stable. If we can keep our determination all the time and put it into practice, our actions of body, speech, and mind will become increasingly more pure, until there is no longer any basis for suffering.

If we do not perform an action, we cannot experience its effect. In a battle, some soldiers are killed while others survive. The survivors are not saved because they are braver than the others, but because they did not create any action that would cause them to die at that time. We can find many similar examples in the daily newspapers. When a terrorist plants a bomb in a large building, some people are killed while others escape despite being at the center of the blast. When there is an airplane crash or a volcanic eruption, some people are killed while others, as if by a miracle, escape. In many accidents the survivors themselves are astonished to be alive when others right next to them were killed.

The actions of living beings are never wasted, even though a long time may pass before their effects are experienced. Actions cannot simply vanish, and we cannot give them away to someone else and thus avoid our responsibility. Although the momentary mental intentions that initiated our past actions have ceased, the potentialities they have created in our mind do not cease until their results have ripened. The only way to destroy negative potentialities before they ripen as suffering is to purify them.

Unfortunately, it is easier to destroy our positive potentialities, because if we fail to dedicate our virtuous actions they can be made completely powerless by just one moment of anger. Our mind is like a treasure chest and our virtuous actions are like the jewels. If we do not safeguard these through dedication, whenever we become angry it is as if we have allowed a thief access to our treasures.

THE SIX REALMS OF REBIRTH

The seeds that ripen when we die are very important because they determine what kind of rebirth we will take. Which particular seed ripens at death depends on the state of mind in which we die. If we die with a peaceful mind, this will stimulate a virtuous seed and we will experience a fortunate rebirth. But if we die with a disturbed mind, in a state of anger, for example, this will stimulate a non-virtuous seed and we will experience an unfortunate rebirth. This is similar to the way in which nightmares are triggered by our being in an agitated state of mind just before falling asleep.

The analogy of falling asleep is not accidental. As explained in the chapter on reincarnation, the process of sleeping, dreaming, and waking closely resembles the process of death, intermediate state, and rebirth. While we are in the intermediate state, we experience different visions that arise from the karmic seeds that were activated immediately before death. If negative seeds were activated, these visions will be nightmarish, but if positive seeds were activated they will be predominantly pleasant. In either case, when the karmic seeds have matured sufficiently, they impel us to take rebirth in one or another of the six realms of samsara.

The six realms are actual places where we can be reborn. They are brought into existence through the power of our actions, or karma. There are three types of action: bodily actions, verbal actions, and mental actions. Since our bodily and verbal actions are always initiated by our mental actions, or intentions, ultimately the six realms are created by our mind. For example, a hell realm is a place that arises as a result of the worst actions, such as murder or extreme mental or physical cruelty, which depend on the most deluded states of mind.

To form a mental image of the six realms, we can compare them to the floors of a large, old house. In this analogy the house represents samsara, the cycle of contaminated rebirth. The house has three floors above ground and three below. Deluded living beings are like the inhabitants of this house. They are continually moving up and down the house, sometimes living above ground, sometimes below.

The ground floor corresponds to the human realm. Above this, on the next floor, is the realm of the demi-gods—non-human beings who are continually at war with the gods. In terms of power and prosperity they are superior to humans, but they are so obsessed with jealousy and violence that their lives have little spiritual value.

On the top floor live the gods. The lower classes of gods, the desire realm gods, live a life of ease and luxury, devoting their time to enjoyment and the satisfaction of their desires. Though their world is a paradise and their lifespan is very long, they are not immortal and they eventually fall to lower states. Since their lives are filled with distractions, it is difficult for them to find the motivation to engage in spiritual practice. From a spiritual point of view, a human life is much more meaningful than a god's life.

Higher than the desire realm gods are the gods of the form and formless realms. Having passed beyond sensual desire, the form realm gods experience the refined bliss of meditative absorption and possess bodies made of light. Transcending even these subtle forms, the gods of the formless realm abide without form in a subtle consciousness that resembles infinite space. Though their minds are the purest and most exalted within samsara, they have not overcome the ignorance of self-grasping, which is the root of samsara, and so after experiencing bliss for many eons, eventually their lives end and they are once again reborn in the lower states of samsara. Like the other gods, they consume the merit they have created in the past and make little or no spiritual progress.

The three floors above ground are called the *fortunate realms* because the beings who inhabit them have relatively pleasant experiences, which are caused by the practice of virtue. Below ground are the three lower realms, which are the result of negative bodily, verbal, and mental actions. The least painful of these is the animal realm, which in the analogy is the first floor beneath the ground. Included in this realm are all mammals apart from humans, as well as birds, fish, insects, worms—the whole animal kingdom. Their minds are characterized by great stupidity, without any spiritual awareness, and their lives by fear and brutality.

On the next floor down live the hungry spirits. The principal causes of rebirth here are greed and negative actions motivated by miserliness. The consequence of these actions is extreme poverty. Hungry spirits suffer continuous hunger and thirst, which they are unable to bear. Their world is a vast desert. If by chance they come across a drop of water or a scrap of food it disappears like a mirage, or transforms into something repulsive such as pus or urine. These appearances are due to their negative karma and lack of merit.

The lowest floor is hell. The beings here experience unrelenting torment. Some hells are a mass of fire; others are desolate regions of ice and darkness. Monsters conjured up by the minds of the hell beings inflict terrible tortures on them. The suffering continues unremittingly for what seems like an eternity, but eventually the karma that caused the beings to be born in hell is exhausted and the hell beings die and are reborn elsewhere in samsara. Hell is simply what appears to the most negative and distorted type of mind. It is not an external place, but is like a nightmare from which we do not wake up for a long, long time. For those living in hell, the sufferings of the hell realm are as real as our present experience of the human realm.

This is a general picture of samsara. We have been trapped in samsara since beginningless time, wandering meaninglessly without any freedom or control from the highest heaven to the deepest hell. Sometimes we reside on the upper floors with the gods, sometimes we find ourself on the ground floor with a human rebirth, but most of the time we are trapped on the underground floors experiencing terrible physical and mental suffering.

Although samsara resembles a prison, there is however one door through which we can escape. That door is emptiness, the ultimate nature of phenomena. By training in the spiritual paths described in this book, we will eventually find our way to this door and, stepping through, discover that the house was simply an illusion, the creation of our impure mind. Samsara is not an external prison—it is a prison made by our own mind. It will never end by itself, but by diligently practicing the true spiritual path, and thereby eliminating our self-grasping and other delusions, we can bring our samsara to an end. Once we attain liberation ourself, we will then be in a position to show others how to destroy their mental prison by eradicating their delusions.

TYPES OF ACTION

Although there are countless different actions of body, speech, and mind, they are all included within three types: virtuous actions, non-virtuous actions, and neutral actions. The practices of giving, moral discipline, patience, effort in spiritual training, meditative concentration, and wisdom are examples of virtuous actions. Killing, stealing, and sexual misconduct are bodily non-virtuous actions; lying, divisive speech, hurtful speech, and idle chatter are verbal non-virtuous actions; and covetousness, malice, and holding wrong views are mental non-virtuous actions. In addition to these ten non-virtuous actions, there are many other kinds of non-virtuous action, such as beating or torturing others, or otherwise deliberately causing them to suffer. Every day we also perform many neutral actions. Whenever we engage in daily actions such as shopping, cooking, eating, sleeping, or relaxing without a specific good or bad motivation, we are performing neutral actions.

All non-virtuous actions are contaminated because they are motivated by delusions, particularly the delusion of self-grasping ignorance. Most of our virtuous and neutral actions are also based on self-grasping and are thus also contaminated. At the moment, even when we are observing moral discipline, for example, we still grasp at an inherently existent I or self who is acting in a moral way, and so our practice of moral discipline is contaminated virtue.

We grasp at an inherently existent I and mine all the time, day and night. This mind is the delusion of self-grasping ignorance. Whenever we are embarrassed, afraid, angry, indignant, or puffed up with pride, we have a very strong sense of self or I. The I that we are grasping on these occasions is the inherently existent I. Even when we are relaxed and relatively peaceful we still grasp our I as inherently existent, though in a less pronounced way. This mind of self-grasping is the basis of all our delusions and the source of all our problems. To free ourself from delusions and the problems they cause, we need to understand that the inherently existent I we grasp so firmly and continuously does not exist at all. It never has existed and never will. It is merely the fabrication of our self-grasping ignorance.

To fulfill the wishes of this I—the inherently existent I that we believe actually exists—we normally perform innumerable positive and negative actions. These actions are known as *throwing actions*, which means actions that are motivated by strong self-grasping and that are the main cause of samsaric rebirth. Contaminated virtuous actions throw us into higher samsaric rebirths as a human, demi-god, or god, while non-virtuous actions throw us into lower rebirths in the animal, hungry spirit, or hell realms. When we are about to die, if we develop a negative state of mind such as anger, this causes the potential of a non-virtuous throwing action to ripen so that after death we will take a lower rebirth. Alternatively, if at the time of death we develop a virtuous state of mind—for example by remembering our daily spiritual practice—this causes the potential of a virtuous throwing action to ripen, so that after death we will be reborn as a human being or one of the other two types of higher samsaric being, and will have to experience the sufferings of these beings.

There is another type of contaminated action, which is called a *completing action*. This is a contaminated action that is the main cause of the happiness or suffering we experience once we have taken a particular rebirth. All human beings are thrown into the human world by virtuous throwing actions, but the experiences they have as human beings vary considerably depending on their different completing actions. Some experience a life of suffering, while others experience a life of comfort. Similarly, animals have all been thrown into the animal world by non-virtuous throwing actions, but their experiences as animals vary considerably depending on their different completing actions. Some animals, such as some domestic pets, can experience a life of luxury, receiving more care and attention than many human beings. Hell beings and hungry spirits experience only the results of non-virtuous throwing actions and non-virtuous completing actions. From the day they are born to the day they die, they experience nothing but suffering.

One throwing action may throw us into many future lives. In Buddhist scriptures an example is given of a man who became very angry with an ordained monk and told him he looked like a frog. As a result, this unfortunate man was reborn many times as a frog. However, just one rebirth is sometimes sufficient to exhaust the power of our throwing action.

Some of our actions ripen in the same life in which they are performed, some ripen in the next life, and some ripen in lives after that.

In conclusion, we can see that first we develop strong self-grasping, from which all the other delusions arise. These delusions impel us to create throwing karma, which causes us to take another samsaric rebirth in which we experience fear, suffering, and problems. Throughout this rebirth we continuously develop self-grasping and other delusions, impelling us to create more throwing actions, and leading to further contaminated rebirths. This process of samsara is an endless cycle—unless we attain nirvana.

Our Human Life

Our Human Life

 O ur human life is precious and of real value only when we use it to train in spiritual paths. In itself it is a true suffering. We experience various types of suffering because we have taken a rebirth that is contaminated by the inner poison of delusions. This experience has no beginning, because we have taken contaminated rebirths since beginningless time, and it will have no end unless we attain the supreme inner peace of nirvana. If we contemplate and meditate on how we experience sufferings and difficulties throughout our life, and in life after life, we will come to the strong conclusion that every single one of our sufferings and problems arises because we took contaminated rebirth. We will then develop a strong wish to abandon the cycle of contaminated rebirth, samsara. This is the first step toward the happiness of nirvana, or liberation. From this point of view, contemplating and meditating on suffering has great meaning. The main purpose of this meditation is to avoid having to go through all of these experiences again in the future.

While we remain in this cycle of contaminated rebirth, sufferings and problems will never end—we will have to experience them over and over again every time we take rebirth. Although we cannot remember our experience while we were in our mother's womb or during our very early childhood, the sufferings of human life began from the time of our conception. Everyone can see that a newborn baby experiences anguish and pain. The first thing a baby does when it is born is scream. Rarely has a baby ever been born in complete serenity, with a peaceful, smiling expression on its face.

BIRTH

When our consciousness first enters the union of our father's sperm and our mother's ovum, our body is a very hot, watery substance like white yogurt tinted red. In the first moments after conception, we have no gross feelings, but as soon as these develop, we begin to experience pain. Our body gradually becomes harder and harder, and as our limbs grow, it feels as if our body is being stretched out on a rack. Inside our mother's womb it is hot and dark. Our home for nine months is this small, tightly compressed space full of unclean substances. It is like being squashed inside a small water tank full of filthy liquid with the lid tightly shut so that no air or light can come through.

While we are in our mother's womb, we experience much pain and fear all on our own. We are extremely sensitive to everything our mother does. When she walks quickly, it feels as if we are falling from a high mountain and we are terrified. If she has sexual intercourse, it feels as if we are being crushed and suffocated between two huge weights and we panic. If our mother makes just a small jump, it feels as if we are being thrown against the ground from a great height. If she drinks anything hot, it feels like boiling water scalding our skin, and if she drinks anything cold, it feels like an ice-cold shower in midwinter.

When we are emerging from our mother's womb, it feels as if we are being forced through a narrow crevice between two hard rocks, and when we are newly born our body is so delicate that any kind of contact is painful. Even if someone holds us very tenderly, his or her hands feel like thorn bushes piercing our flesh, and the most delicate fabrics feel rough and abrasive. By comparison with the softness and smoothness of our mother's womb, every tactile sensation is harsh and painful. If someone picks us up, it feels as if we are being swung over a huge cliff and we feel frightened and insecure. We have forgotten everything we knew in our past life—we bring only pain and confusion from our mother's womb. Whatever we hear is as meaningless as the sound of wind and we cannot comprehend anything we perceive. In the first few weeks, we are like someone who is blind, deaf, and dumb, and suffering from profound amnesia. When we are hungry we cannot say, "I need food," and when we are in pain we cannot say, "This is hurting me." The only signs we can make are hot tears and furious gestures. Our mother often has no idea what kinds of pain and discomfort we are experiencing. We are completely helpless and have to be taught everything—how to eat, how to sit, how to walk, how to talk.

Although we are most vulnerable in the first few weeks of our life, our pains do not cease as we grow up. We continue to experience various kinds of suffering throughout our life. Just as when we light a fire in a large house, the heat from the fire pervades the whole house and all the heat in the house comes from the fire, so when we are born in samsara, suffering pervades our whole life, and all the miseries we experience arise because we took a contaminated rebirth.

Since we have been born as a human, we cherish our human body and mind and cling to them as our own. In dependence upon observing our body and mind, we develop self-grasping, which is the root of all delusions. Our human rebirth is the basis of our human suffering; without this basis, there are no human problems. The pains of birth gradually turn into the pains of aging, sickness, and death—they are one continuum.

AGING

Our birth gives rise to the pains of aging. Aging steals our beauty, our health, our figure, our fine complexion, our vitality, and our comfort. Aging turns us into objects of contempt. It brings many unwanted pains and takes us swiftly to our death.

As we grow old, we lose all the beauty of our youth and our strong, healthy body becomes weak and burdened with illness. Our figure, once firm and well-proportioned, becomes bent and disfigured, and our muscles and flesh shrink so that our limbs become like thin sticks and our bones poke out. Our hair loses its color and shine, and our complexion loses its luster. Our face becomes wrinkled and our features grow distorted. Milarepa said:

> How do old people get up? They get up as if they were heaving a stake out of the ground. How do old people walk around? Once they are on their feet, they have to walk gingerly, like bird-catchers. How do old people sit down? They crash down like heavy luggage whose harness has snapped.

We can contemplate the following poem on the sufferings of growing old:

When we are old, our hair becomes white,
But not because we have washed it clean;
It is a sign we will soon encounter the Lord of Death.

We have wrinkles on our forehead,
But not because we have too much flesh;
It is a warning from the Lord of Death:
  "You are about to die."

Our teeth fall out,
But not to make room for new ones;
It is a sign we will soon lose the ability to eat human food.

Our faces are ugly and unpleasant,
But not because we are wearing masks;
It is a sign we have lost the mask of youth.

Our heads shake back and forth,
But not because we are in disagreement;
It is the Lord of Death striking our head with the stick he
  holds in his right hand.

We walk bent and gazing at the ground,
But not because we are searching for lost needles;
It is a sign we are searching for our lost beauty and
  memories.

We get up from the ground using all four limbs,
But not because we are imitating animals;
It is a sign our legs are too weak to support our bodies.

We sit down as if we had suddenly fallen,
But not because we are angry;
It is a sign our body has lost its strength.

Our body sways as we walk,
But not because we think we are important;
It is a sign our legs cannot carry our body.

Our hands shake,
But not because they are itching to steal;
It is a sign the Lord of Death's itchy fingers are stealing
    our possessions.

We eat very little,
But not because we are miserly;
It is a sign we cannot digest our food.

We wheeze frequently,
But not because we are whispering mantras to the sick;
It is a sign our breathing will soon disappear.

When we are young we can travel around the whole world, but when we are old we can hardly make it to our own front yard. We become too weak to engage in many worldly activities, and our spiritual activities are often reduced. For example, we do not have much physical strength to perform virtuous actions, and we have less mental energy to memorize, contemplate, and meditate. We cannot attend teachings that are given in places that are hard to reach or uncomfortable to inhabit. We cannot help others in ways that require physical strength and good health. Deprivations such as these often make old people very sad.

When we grow old, we become like someone who is blind and deaf. We cannot see clearly, and we need stronger and stronger glasses until we can no longer read. We cannot hear clearly, and so it becomes more and more difficult to listen to music or to the television, or to hear what other people are saying. Our memory fades. All activities, worldly and spiritual, become more difficult. If we practice meditation, it becomes harder for us to gain realizations, because our memory and concentration are too weak. We cannot apply ourself to study. Thus, if we have not learned and trained in spiritual practices when we were younger, the only thing to do when we grow old is to develop regret and wait for the Lord of Death to come.

When we are old, we cannot derive the same pleasure from the things we used to enjoy, such as food, drink, and sex. We are too weak to play games and we are often too exhausted even for entertainment. As our lifespan runs out, we cannot join young people in their activities. When they travel, we have to stay behind. No one wants to take us with them when we are old and no one wants to visit us. Even our own grandchildren do not want to stay with us for very long. Old people often think to themselves, "How wonderful it would be if young people would stay with me. We could go out for walks and I could show them things." But young people do not want to be included in their plans. As their life comes to an end, old people experience the sorrow of abandonment and loneliness. They have many special sorrows.

SICKNESS

Our birth also gives rise to the sufferings of sickness. Just as the wind and snow of winter take away the glory of green fields, trees, forests, and flowers, so sickness takes away the youthful splendor of our body, destroying its strength and the power of our senses. If we are usually fit and well, when we become sick we are suddenly unable to engage in all our normal physical activities. Even a champion boxer who is usually able to knock out all his opponents becomes completely helpless when sickness strikes.

When we get sick, we are like a bird that has been soaring in the sky and is suddenly shot down. When a bird is shot, it falls straight to the ground like a lump of lead, and all its glory and power are immediately destroyed. In a similar way, when we become sick we are suddenly incapacitated. If we are seriously ill, we may become completely dependent upon others and even lose the ability to control our bodily functions. This transformation is hard to bear, especially for those who pride themselves on their independence and physical well-being.

When we are sick, we feel frustrated at not being able to do our usual work or complete everything we have to do. We easily become impatient with our illness and depressed about all the things we cannot do. We cannot enjoy the things that usually give us pleasure, such as sports, dancing, drinking, eating rich foods, or the company of our friends. All these limitations make us feel even more miserable. And to add to our unhappiness, we have to endure all the physical pain the illness brings.

When we are sick, not only do we have to experience all the unwanted pains of the illness itself, but we also have to experience all kinds of other undesirable things. For example, we have to accept whatever our doctor prescribes, whether it is a bad-tasting medicine, a series of injections, a major operation, or abstinence from something we like very much. If we need to have an operation, we have to go to the hospital and accept all the conditions there. We may have to eat food we do not like and stay in bed all day long with nothing to do, and we may feel anxious about the operation. Our doctor may not explain to us exactly what the problem is and whether or not he or she expects us to survive.

If we learn that our sickness is incurable, and we have no spiritual experience, we will suffer anxiety, fear, and regret. We may become depressed and give up hope, or we may become angry with our illness, feeling that it is an enemy that has maliciously deprived us of all our joy.

DEATH

Our birth also gives rise to the sufferings of death. If during our life we have worked hard to acquire possessions, and if we have become very attached to them, we will experience great suffering at the time of death, thinking, "Now I have to leave all my precious possessions behind." Even now we find it difficult to lend one of our most treasured possessions to someone else, let alone to give it away. No wonder we become so miserable when we realize that, in the hands of death, we have to abandon everything.

When we die, we are separated from even our closest friends. We have to leave our partner, even though we may have been together for years and never spent a day apart. If we are very attached, we will experience great misery at the time of death, but all we will be able to do is hold their hands. We will not be able to stop the process of death, even if they plead with us not to die. Usually when we are very attached to someone, we feel jealous if they leave us on our own and spend time with someone else, but when we die we will have to leave our friends with others forever.

We will have to leave everyone, including our family and all the people who have helped us in this life.

When we die, this body that we have cherished and cared for in so many ways will have to be left behind. It will become mindless like a stone, and will be buried in the ground or cremated. If we do not have the inner protection of spiritual experience, at the time of death we will experience fear and distress, as well as physical pain.

When our consciousness departs from our body at death, all the potentialities we have accumulated in our mind by performing virtuous and non-virtuous actions will go with it. Other than these, we cannot take anything else out of this world. All other things deceive us. Death ends all our activities—our conversation, our eating, our meeting with friends, our sleep. Everything comes to an end on the day of our death and we have to leave all things behind, even the rings on our fingers. In Tibet, beggars carry a stick to defend themselves against dogs. To understand the complete deprivation of death, we should remember that at the time of death beggars have to leave even this old stick, the most meager of human possessions. All over the world, we can see that names carved on stone are the only possessions of the dead.

OTHER TYPES OF SUFFERING

Living beings also have to experience the sufferings of separation, having to encounter what we do not like, and failing to satisfy our desires. Before the final separation at the time of death, we often have to experience temporary separation from the people and things we like, which causes us mental pain. We may have to leave our country where all our friends and relatives live, or we may have to leave the job we like. We may lose our reputation. Many times in this life we have to experience the misery of departing from the people we like, or abandoning and losing the things we find pleasant and attractive. But when we die we have to part from all the companions and enjoyments of this life forever.

We often have to meet and live with people that we do not like, or encounter situations that we find unpleasant. Sometimes we may find ourself in a very dangerous situation such as in a fire or a flood, or where there is violence such as in a riot or a battle. Our lives are full of less extreme situations that we find annoying. Sometimes we are prevented from doing the things we want to do. On a sunny day we may set out for the beach, but find ourself stuck in a traffic jam. Sometimes we experience interference from spirits who disturb our mind and our spiritual practices. There are countless conditions that frustrate our plans and prevent us from doing what we want. It is as if we are living in a thorn bush—whenever we try to move, we are wounded by circumstances. People and things are like thorns piercing our flesh and no situation ever feels entirely comfortable. The more desires and plans we have, the more frustrations we experience. The more we want certain situations, the more we find ourself stuck in situations we do not want. Every desire seems to invite its own obstacle. Undesired situations happen to us without our looking for them. In fact, the only things that come effortlessly are the things we do not want. No one wants to die, but death comes effortlessly. No one wants to be sick, but sickness comes effortlessly. If we take rebirth without freedom or control, we have an impure body and we inhabit an impure environment, and so undesirable things pour down on us. In samsara, this kind of experience is entirely natural.

We have countless desires but no matter how much effort we make, we never feel that we have satisfied them. Even when we get what we want, we do not get it in the way we want. We possess the object but we get no satisfaction from possessing it. For example, we may dream of becoming wealthy, but if we actually become wealthy our life is not the way we imagined it would be, and we do not feel that we have fulfilled our desire. This is because our desires do not decrease as our wealth increases. The more wealth we have, the more we desire. The wealth we seek cannot be found because we seek an amount that will satisfy our desires, and no amount of wealth can do that. To make things worse, in obtaining the object of our desire we create new occasions for dissatisfaction. With every object we desire come other objects we do not want. For example, with wealth come taxes, insecurity, and complicated financial affairs. These unwished for side effects prevent us from ever feeling fully satisfied. Similarly, we may dream of a tropical vacation, and we may actually go on vacation, but the experience is never quite what we expect, and with our vacation come other things such as sunburn and great expense.

With every object we desire come other objects we do not want.

If we examine our desires, we will see that they are inordinate. We want all the best things in samsara—the best job, the best partner, the best reputation, the best house, the best car, the best vacation. Anything that is not the best leaves us with a feeling of disappointment—still searching for but not finding what we want. No worldly enjoyment, however, can give us the complete and perfect satisfaction we desire. Better things are always being produced. Everywhere new advertisements announce that the very best thing has just arrived on the market, but a few days later another best thing arrives that is better than the best thing of a few days ago. There is no end of new things to captivate our desires.

Children in school can never satisfy their own or their parents' ambitions. Even if they become first in their class, they feel they cannot be content unless they do so again the following year. If they go on to be successful in their jobs, their ambitions will be as strong as ever. There is no point at which they can rest with the feeling that they are completely satisfied with what they have done.

We may think that at least people who lead a simple life in the country must be content, but if we look at their situation, we will find that even farmers search for but do not find what they want. Their lives are full of problems and anxieties, and they do not enjoy real peace and satisfaction. Their livelihoods depend on many uncertain factors beyond their control, such as the weather. Farmers have no more freedom from discontent than businesspeople who live and work in the city. Business people look well-dressed and efficient as they go to work each morning carrying their briefcases, but although they look so smooth on the outside, in their hearts they carry a lot of dissatisfaction. They are still searching for but not finding what they want.

If we reflect on this situation, we may decide that we can find what we are searching for by abandoning all our possessions. We can see, however, that even poor people are looking for but not finding what they seek, and many poor people have difficulty in finding the most basic necessities of life.

We cannot avoid the suffering of dissatisfaction by frequently changing our situation. We may think that if we keep getting a new partner or a new job, or keep traveling around, we will eventually find what we want. But even if we traveled to every place on the globe, and had a new lover in every place, we would still be seeking another place and another lover. In samsara, there is no real fulfillment of our desires.

Whenever we see anyone in a high or low position, male or female, they differ only in appearance, dress, behavior, and status. In essence they are all equal—they all experience problems in their lives. Whenever we have a problem, it is easy to think that it is caused by our particular circumstances, and that if we changed our circumstances our problem would disappear. We blame other people, our friends, our food, our government, our times, the weather, society, history, and so forth. However, external circumstances such as these are not the main causes of our problems. We need to recognize that these painful experiences are the consequences of our taking a rebirth that is contaminated by the inner poison of delusions. Human beings have to experience human sufferings because they took a contaminated human rebirth. Animals have to experience animal suffering, and similarly hungry spirits and hell beings have to experience their own particular sufferings because they took a contaminated rebirth. Even gods are not free from suffering, because they too have taken a contaminated rebirth. By contemplating all the miseries of contaminated rebirth, we make the strong determination:

As long as I remain in the cycle of contaminated rebirth—samsara—I will have to experience all these sufferings endlessly, life after life. Therefore I must abandon samsara and attain the supreme inner peace of nirvana.

We meditate on this determination for as long as possible. We need to continually repeat the cycle of contemplations on the sufferings of contaminated rebirth, and then meditate deeply on the determination to abandon samsara. The mind that holds this determination is renunciation. Once we have attained nirvana, we will never again experience contaminated environments, enjoyments, bodies, or minds. We will experience everything as pure because our mind will have become pure, free from the inner poison of delusions.

In conclusion, the first step toward the attainment of nirvana is gaining the realization of renunciation, the spontaneous wish to abandon samsara, or contaminated rebirth. We then abandon samsara and attain nirvana by gaining a direct realization of emptiness, the ultimate nature of phenomena, which will be explained in detail in the chapter on ultimate truth.

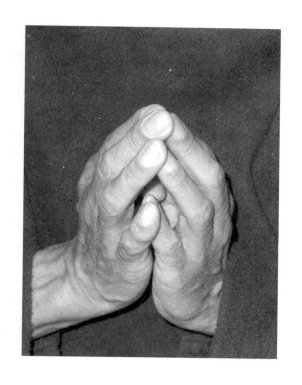

A Daily Practice

A Daily Practice

We need to create virtuous or positive actions because these are the root of our future happiness; we need to abandon non-virtuous or negative actions because these are the root of our future sufferings; and we need to control our delusions because these are the root of our contaminated rebirths. We can do all of this by sincerely engaging in the following practices of faith, sense of shame, consideration for others, non-attachment, non-hatred, and effort.

FAITH

Faith is the root of all virtuous qualities and spiritual realizations. In particular, our ability to enter the spiritual path depends on our having the faith that believes that spiritual realizations directly protect us from suffering and fear.

The great Yogi Ensapa said that all spiritual experiences, great and small, depend on faith. Since faith is the root of all attainments, it should be our main practice. While the famous Buddhist Master Atisha was in Tibet, a man once approached him asking for spiritual instructions. Atisha remained silent and so the man, thinking that he had not been heard, repeated his request very loudly. Atisha then replied, "I have good hearing, but you need to have faith."

What exactly is faith? Faith is a naturally virtuous mind that functions mainly to oppose the perception of faults in the object it is focused on. The object of faith is any object that is regarded as holy or pure, such as enlightened beings, spiritual teachings, spiritual realizations, and spiritual Teachers and friends.

Faith is more than just belief. For example, we might believe that human beings have been to the moon, but this belief is not faith, because faith views its object as pure and holy. Without faith everything is mundane. We are blind to anything beyond the ordinary and imperfect world we normally inhabit, and we cannot even imagine that pure, faultless beings, worlds, or states of mind exist. Faith is like pure eyes that enable us to see a pure and perfect world beyond the suffering world of samsara.

According to Buddhism, enlightened beings are called *Buddhas*, their teachings are called *Dharma*, and the practitioners who have gained realizations of these teachings are called *Sangha*. These are known as the *Three Jewels*—Buddha Jewel, Dharma Jewel, and Sangha Jewel—and are the objects of faith and refuge. They are called "Jewels" because they are very precious. In dependence upon seeing the fears and sufferings of samsara, and developing strong faith and conviction in the power of Buddha, Dharma, and Sangha to protect us, we make the determination to rely on the Three Jewels. This is the simple way of going for refuge to Buddha, Dharma, and Sangha.

There are three types of faith: believing faith, admiring faith, and wishing faith. If we believe that our spiritual practice is the very heart of our life, this is an example of believing faith. An example of admiring faith is the faith we have when, by recognizing the good qualities of our Spiritual Teacher or the good qualities of his or her teachings, we develop admiration for these and our mind becomes very clear and free from disturbing, negative conceptions. This faith is pure-hearted, and it comes when we develop sincere respect and deep admiration for someone or something that we recognize as being worthy

Faith is like pure eyes that enable us to see a pure and perfect world beyond the suffering world of samsara.

or beneficial. On the basis of believing faith and admiring faith, when we develop the sincere wish to put spiritual teachings into practice, this is wishing faith.

Without faith our mind is like a burnt seed, because just as a burnt seed cannot germinate, so knowledge without faith can never produce spiritual realizations. Faith in spiritual teachings or Dharma induces a strong intention to practice them, which in turn induces effort. With effort we can accomplish anything.

Faith is essential. If we have no faith, even if we master profound teachings and become capable of skillful analysis our mind will remain untamed because we will not be putting these teachings into practice. No matter how well we understand spiritual teachings on an intellectual level, if we have no faith this will never help us reduce our problems of anger and other delusions. We may even become proud of our knowledge, thereby actually increasing our delusions. Spiritual knowledge without faith will not help us purify our negativity. We may even create heavy negative karma by using our spiritual position for money, reputation, power, or political authority. Faith should therefore be cherished as extremely precious. Just as all places are pervaded by space, so all virtuous states of mind are pervaded by faith.

If a practitioner has strong faith, then even if they make some mistake they will still receive benefits. Once in India there was a famine in which many people died. One old woman went to see her Spiritual Guide and said, "Please show me a way of saving my life." Her Spiritual Guide advised her to eat stones. The woman asked, "But how can I make stones edible?" and he replied, "If you recite the mantra of the Goddess Tsunda, you will be able to cook the stones." He taught her the mantra, but he made a slight mistake. He taught OM BALE BULE BUNDE SÖHA, instead of OM TZALE TZULE TZUNDE SÖHA. However, the old woman placed great faith in this mantra, and reciting it with concentration, she cooked stones and ate them.

This old woman's son was a monk and he began to worry about his mother, and so he went home to see her. He was astonished to find her plump and well. He said, "Mother, how are you so healthy when even young people are dying of starvation?" His mother explained that she had been eating stones. Her son asked, "How have you been able to cook stones?" and she told him the mantra that she had been given to recite. Her son quickly spotted the mistake and declared, "Your mantra is wrong! The mantra of the Goddess Tsunda is OM TZALE TZULE TZUNDE SÖHA." When she heard this, the old woman was plunged into doubt. She tried reciting both the mantras, but now neither of them would work because her faith was destroyed.

To develop and increase our faith in spiritual teachings, we need a special way of listening and reading. For example, when we are reading a book that reveals the spiritual path, we should think:

This book is like a mirror that reflects all the faults of my bodily, verbal, and mental actions. By exposing all my shortcomings, it provides me with a great opportunity to overcome them and thereby remove all faults from my mental continuum.

This book is supreme medicine. Through practicing the instructions contained within it, I can cure myself of the diseases of the delusions, which are the real source of all my problems and suffering.

This book is the light that dispels the darkness of my ignorance, the eyes with which I can see the actual path to liberation and enlightenment, and the supreme Spiritual Guide from whom I can receive the most profound and liberating advice.

It does not matter whether the author is famous or not—if a book contains pure spiritual teachings it is like a mirror, like medicine, like light, and like eyes; and it is a supreme Spiritual Guide. If we always read Dharma books and listen to teachings with this special recognition, our faith and wisdom will definitely increase. Contemplating in this way, we can develop and maintain faith in spiritual teachings, in Teachers who show us spiritual paths, and in our spiritual friends. This will make it easier for us to make progress in our spiritual practice.

SENSE OF SHAME AND CONSIDERATION FOR OTHERS

The difference between sense of shame and consideration for others is that with the former we avoid inappropriate actions for reasons that concern ourself, while with the latter we avoid inappropriate actions for reasons that concern others. In this way, sense of shame restrains us from committing such actions by reminding us that it is not appropriate to engage in these actions because, for example, we are a spiritual practitioner, an ordained person, a spiritual Teacher, an adult, and so on; or because we do not want to experience negative results from our actions. If we think, "It's not right for me to kill insects because this will cause me to experience suffering in the future," and then make a firm decision not to kill them, we are motivated by sense of shame. Our sense of shame guards us against committing negative actions by appealing to our conscience and to the standards of behavior that we feel are appropriate. If we are unable to generate sense of shame, we will find it extremely difficult to practice moral discipline.

Examples of consideration for others are holding back from saying something unpleasant because it will upset another person, or giving up fishing because of the suffering it causes the fish. We need to practice consideration whenever we are with other people by being mindful of how our behavior might disturb or harm them. Our desires are endless, and some of them would cause other people great distress if we acted on them. Therefore, before we act on a wish, we should consider whether it will disturb or harm others, and if we think that it will, we should not do it. If we are concerned for the welfare of others, we will naturally show them consideration.

Consideration for others is important for everyone. If we are considerate, others will like and respect us, and our relationships with our family and friends will be harmonious and long lasting. Without consideration for others, however, relationships quickly deteriorate. Consideration prevents others from losing faith in us and is the basis for developing a mind of rejoicing.

Whether we are a good person or a bad person depends on whether or not we have sense of shame and consideration for others. Without these two minds, our daily behavior will soon become negative and cause others to turn away from us. Sense of shame and consideration are like beautiful clothes that cause others to be attracted to us. Without them we are like a naked person whom everyone tries to avoid.

Both sense of shame and consideration for others are characterized by a determination to refrain from engaging in negative and inappropriate actions and from breaking vows and commitments. This determination is the very essence of moral discipline. We generate and sustain this determination by contemplating the benefits of practicing moral discipline and the dangers of breaking it. In particular, we need to remember that without moral discipline we have no chance of taking any higher rebirth, let alone of attaining nirvana.

Sense of shame and consideration for others are the foundations of moral discipline, which is the basis for gaining spiritual realizations and the main cause of higher rebirth. The great Spiritual Teacher Nagarjuna said that while enjoyments come from giving, the happiness of higher rebirth comes from moral discipline. The results of practicing giving can be experienced in a higher realm or a lower realm, depending on whether or not we practice it in conjunction with moral discipline. If we do not practice moral discipline, our action of giving will ripen in a lower realm. For example, as the result of actions of giving they accumulated in previous lives, some pet dogs have far better conditions than many humans—pampered by their owners, given special food and soft cushions, and treated like a favorite child. Despite these comforts, these poor creatures have nevertheless taken rebirth in a lower life form with the body and mind of an animal. They have neither the bodily nor the mental basis to continue with their practice of giving or any other virtuous action. They cannot understand the meaning of the spiritual path or transform their minds. Once their previous karma of giving is exhausted through enjoying these good conditions, since they have had no opportunity to create more virtuous actions, their enjoyments will come to an end, and in a future life, they will experience poverty and starvation. This is because they did not practice giving in conjunction with moral discipline and so did not create the cause for a higher rebirth. Through practicing sense of shame and consideration for others, we can abandon non-virtuous or inappropriate actions, the root of our future sufferings.

NON-ATTACHMENT

Non-attachment in this context is the mind of renunciation, which is the opponent to attachment. Renunciation is not a wish to abandon our family, friends, home, job, and so forth and become like a beggar. Instead it is a mind that functions to stop attachment to worldly pleasures and that seeks liberation from contaminated rebirth.

We must learn to stop our attachment through the practice of renunciation or it will be a serious obstacle to our pure spiritual practice. Just as a bird cannot fly if it has stones tied to its legs, so we cannot make progress on the spiritual path if we are tightly tied down by the chains of attachment.

The time to practice renunciation is now, before our death. We need to reduce our attachment to worldly pleasures by realizing that they are deceptive and cannot give real satisfaction. In reality, they cause us only suffering. This human life with all its suffering and problems is a great opportunity for us to improve both our renunciation and our compassion. We should not waste this precious opportunity. The realization of renunciation is the gateway through which we enter the spiritual path to liberation, or nirvana. Without renunciation, it is impossible even to enter the path to the supreme happiness of nirvana, let alone to progress along it.

To develop and increase our renunciation, we can repeatedly contemplate the following:

Because my consciousness is beginningless, I have taken countless rebirths in samsara. I have already had countless bodies; if they were all gathered together, they would fill the entire world, and all the blood and other bodily fluids that have flowed through them would form an ocean. My suffering in all these previous lives has been so great that I have shed enough tears of sorrow to form another ocean.

In every single life, I have experienced the sufferings of sickness, aging, death, being separated from those I love, and being unable to fulfill my wishes. If I do not attain permanent liberation from suffering now, I will have to experience these sufferings again and again in countless future lives.

Contemplating this, from the depths of our heart we make a strong determination to abandon attachment to worldly pleasures and attain permanent liberation from contaminated rebirth. By putting this determination into practice, we can control our attachment and thereby solve many of our daily problems.

NON-HATRED

Non-hatred in this context is love, which is the opponent to hatred. Many people experience problems because their love is mixed with attachment; for such people, the more their "love" increases, the more their desirous attachment grows. If their desires are not fulfilled, they become upset and angry. If the object of their attachment, such as their lover, even talks to another person, they may become jealous or aggressive. This clearly indicates that their "love" is not real love but attachment. Real love can never be a cause of anger; it is the opposite of anger and can never cause problems. If we love everyone as a mother loves her dearest child, there will be no basis for any problems to arise because our mind will always be at peace. Love is the real inner protection against suffering.

Love is a virtuous mind motivated by equanimity to which its object appears as beautiful or pleasant. Equanimity is a balanced mind that prevents us from developing anger and attachment by applying specific opponents. Recognizing anger and attachment to be harmful, like poison, equanimity prevents them from developing and keeps our mind peaceful. When the mind of equanimity is manifest, we are very balanced and calm because we are free from the disturbing minds of attachment, anger, and other delusions.

Developing equanimity is like plowing a field—clearing our mind of the rocks and weeds of anger and attachment, thereby making it possible for true love to grow. We need to learn to love all living beings. Whenever we meet anyone, we should be happy to see them and try to generate a warm feeling toward them. On the basis of this feeling of affection, we should develop cherishing love so that we genuinely come to feel that they are precious and important. If we cherish others in this way, it will not be difficult to develop wishing love, wanting to give them happiness. Through learning to love everyone, we can solve all our daily problems of anger and jealousy and our life will become happy and meaningful. A more detailed explanation of how to develop and increase our love will be given in later chapters.

EFFORT

If we do not apply ourself to our spiritual practice, no one can grant us liberation from suffering. We are often unrealistic in our expectations. We wish we could accomplish high attainments swiftly without having to apply any effort, and we want to be happy without having to create the cause of happiness. Unwilling to endure even the slightest discomfort we want all our suffering to cease, and while living in the jaws of the Lord of Death we wish to remain like a long-life god. No matter how much we long for these wishes to be fulfilled, they never will be. If we do not apply energy and effort to our spiritual practices, all our hopes for happiness will be in vain.

Effort in this context is a mind that delights in virtue. Its function is to make our mind happy to engage in virtuous actions. With effort we delight in actions such as listening to, reading, contemplating, and meditating on spiritual teachings, and engaging in the path to liberation. Through effort we will eventually attain the ultimate supreme goal of human life.

By applying effort in our meditation, we develop mental suppleness. Even though we may experience problems such as heaviness, tiredness, or other forms of mental or physical discomfort when we first begin to meditate, we should neverthe-

Laziness makes our human life meaningless.

less patiently persevere and try to become familiar with our practice. Gradually, as our meditation improves, it will induce mental suppleness—our mind and body will feel light, healthy, and tireless, and be free from obstacles to concentration. All our meditations will become easy and effective, and we will have no difficulty making progress.

However difficult meditation may be at the beginning, we should never give up hope. Instead, we should engage in the practice of moral discipline, which protects us from gross distractions and acts as the basis for developing pure concentration. Moral discipline also strengthens mindfulness, which is the life of concentration.

We need to abandon laziness—laziness arising from attachment to worldly pleasures, laziness arising from attachment to distracting activities, and laziness arising from discouragement. With laziness, we will accomplish nothing. As long as we remain with laziness, the door to spiritual attainments is closed to us. Laziness makes our human life meaningless. It deceives us and causes us to wander aimlessly in samsara. If we can break free from the influence of laziness and immerse ourself deeply in spiritual training, we will quickly attain our spiritual goal. Training in spiritual paths is like constructing a large building—it demands continuous effort. If we allow our effort to be interrupted by laziness, we will never see the completion of our work.

Our spiritual attainments therefore depend on our own effort. An intellectual understanding of spiritual teachings is not sufficient to carry us to the supreme happiness of liberation—we must overcome our laziness and put our knowledge into practice. Buddha said:

If you have only effort you have all attainments,
But if you have only laziness you have nothing.

A person without great spiritual knowledge who nevertheless applies effort consistently will gradually attain all virtuous qualities. However, someone who knows a great deal and has only one fault—laziness—will not be able to increase his or her good qualities and gain experience of spiritual paths. Understanding all of this, we should apply joyful effort to the study and practice of spiritual teachings in our everyday life.

PART TWO

Progress

Learning to Cherish Others

Learning to Cherish Others

*F*rom the depths of our heart we want to be happy all the time, but we are not usually very concerned with the happiness and freedom of others. In reality, however, our own happiness and suffering are insignificant compared to that of other living beings. Others are countless, while we ourself are just one single person. Understanding this, we must learn to cherish others and accomplish the ultimate, supreme goal of human life.

What is the ultimate, supreme goal of human life? We should ask ourself what we consider to be most important—what do we wish for, strive for, or daydream about? For some people it is material possessions, such as a large house with all the latest luxuries, a fast car, or a well-paid job. For others it is reputation, good looks, power, excitement, or adventure. Many try to find the meaning of their life in relationships with their family and circle of friends. All these things can make us happy for a short while, but they can also cause us much worry and suffering. They can never give us the perfect lasting happiness that all of us, in our heart of hearts, long for. Since we cannot take them with us when we die, if we have made them the principal meaning of our life they will eventually let us down. As an end in themselves worldly attainments are hollow—they are not the real essence of human life.

Of all worldly possessions the most precious is said to be the legendary wish-granting jewel. It is impossible to find such a jewel in these degenerate times, but in the past, when human beings had abundant merit, there used to be magical jewels that had the power to grant wishes. These jewels, however, could only fulfill wishes for contaminated happiness—they could never bestow the pure happiness that comes from a pure mind. Furthermore, a wish-granting jewel only had the power to grant wishes in one life—it could not protect its owner in his or her future lives. Therefore, ultimately even a wish-granting jewel is deceptive.

The only thing that will never deceive us is the attainment of full enlightenment. What is enlightenment? It is omniscient wisdom free from all mistaken appearances. A person who possesses this wisdom is an enlightened being. According to Buddhism, enlightened being and Buddha are synonymous. With the exception of enlightened beings, all beings experience mistaken appearances all the time, day and night, even during sleep.

Whatever appears to us, we perceive as existing from its own side. This is mistaken appearance. We perceive "I" and "mine" as being inherently existent, and we grasp strongly, believing this appearance to be true. Because of this we perform many inappropriate actions that lead us to experience suffering. This is the fundamental reason why we experience suffering. Enlightened beings are completely free from mistaken appearances and the sufferings they produce.

It is only by attaining enlightenment that we can fulfill our deepest wish for pure and lasting happiness, because nothing in this impure world has the power to fulfill this wish. Only when we become a fully enlightened Buddha will we experience the profound and lasting peace that comes from a permanent cessation of all delusions and their imprints. We will be free from all faults and mental obscurations, and possess the qualities needed to help all living beings directly. We will then be an object of refuge for all living beings. Through this understanding, we can clearly see that the attainment of enlightenment is the ultimate, supreme goal and real meaning of our precious human life. Since our main wish is to be happy all the time and to be completely free from all faults and suffering, we must develop the strong intention to attain enlightenment. We should think: "I need to attain enlightenment because in samsara there is no real happiness anywhere."

The main cause of enlightenment is bodhichitta, the spontaneous wish to attain enlightenment that is motivated by compassion for all living beings. A person who possesses this precious mind of bodhichitta is called a *Bodhisattva*. The root of bodhichitta is compassion. Since the development of compassion depends on cherishing others, the first step to the sublime happiness of enlightenment is learning to cherish others. A mother cherishes her children, and we may cherish our friends to a certain degree, but this cherishing is not impartial and is usually mixed with attachment. We need to develop a pure mind that cherishes all living beings without bias or partiality.

Each and every living being has within them the seed or potential to become a fully enlightened being—this is our Buddha nature. In Buddha's teachings, we have found the best method to realize this potential. What we need to do now is to put these teachings into practice. This is something that only human beings can do. Animals can gather resources, defeat their enemies, and protect their families, but they cannot understand or engage in the spiritual path. It would be a great shame if we used our human life to achieve only what animals can also achieve, and thereby wasted this unique opportunity to become a source of benefit for all living beings.

We are faced with a choice: either we can continue to squander our life pursuing worldly enjoyments that give no real satisfaction and disappear when we die, or we can dedicate our life to realizing our full spiritual potential. If we make great effort to practice the instructions contained within this book, we will definitely attain enlightenment, but if we make no effort, enlightenment will never happen naturally, no matter how long we wait. To follow the path to enlightenment, there is no need to change our external lifestyle. We do not need to abandon our family, friends, or enjoyments, and retire to a mountain cave. All we need to do is change the object of our cherishing.

Until now we have cherished ourself above all others, and for as long as we continue to do this our suffering will never end. On the other hand, if we learn to cherish all beings more than ourself, we will soon enjoy the bliss of enlightenment. The path to enlightenment is really very simple—all we need to do is stop cherishing ourself and learn to cherish others. All other spiritual realizations will naturally follow from this.

Our instinctive view is that we are more important than everyone else, while the view of all enlightened beings is that it is others who are more important. Which of these views is more beneficial? In life after life, since beginningless time, we have been slaves to our self-cherishing mind. We have trusted it implicitly and obeyed its every command, believing that the way to solve our problems and find happiness is to put ourself before everyone else. We have worked so hard and so long for our own sake, but what do we have to show for it? Have we solved all our problems and found the lasting happiness we desire? No. It is clear that pursuing our own selfish interests has deceived us. After having indulged our self-cherishing for so many lives, now is the time to realize that it simply does not work. Now is the time to switch the object of our cherishing from ourself to all living beings.

Countless enlightened beings have discovered that by abandoning self-cherishing and cherishing only others they came to experience true peace and happiness. If we practice the methods they taught, there is no reason why we should not be able to do the same. We cannot expect to change our mind overnight, but through patiently and consistently practicing the instructions on cherishing others, while at the same time accumulating merit, purifying negativity, and receiving blessings, we can gradually replace our ordinary self-cherishing attitude with the sublime attitude of cherishing all living beings.

We do not need to change our lifestyle, but we do need to change our views and intentions.

To achieve this we do not need to change our lifestyle, but we do need to change our views and intentions. Our ordinary view is that we are the center of the universe and that other people and things derive their significance principally from the way they affect us. Our car, for example, is important simply because it is *ours*, and our friends are important because they make *us* happy. Strangers, on the other hand, do not seem so important because they do not directly affect our happiness, and if a stranger's car is damaged or stolen we are not that concerned. As we will see in later chapters, this self-centered view of the world is based on ignorance and does not correspond to reality. This view is the source of all our ordinary, selfish intentions. It is precisely because we think, "I am important, I need this, I deserve that," that we engage in negative actions, which result in an endless stream of problems for ourself and others.

By practicing these instructions, we can develop a realistic view of the world, based on an understanding of the equality and interdependence of all living beings. Once we view each and every living being as important, we will naturally develop good intentions toward them. While the mind that cherishes only ourself is the basis for all impure, samsaric experience, the mind that cherishes others is the basis for all the good qualities of enlightenment.

Cherishing others is not so difficult—all we need to do is to understand why we should cherish others and then make a firm decision to do so. Through meditating on this decision, we will develop a deep and powerful feeling of cherishing for all beings. We then carry this special feeling into our daily life.

There are two main reasons why we need to cherish all living beings. The first is that they have shown us immense kindness, and the second is that cherishing them has enormous benefits. These will now be explained.

THE KINDNESS OF OTHERS

We should contemplate the great kindness of all living beings. We can begin by remembering the kindness of our mother of this life; and then, by extension, we can remember the kindness of all other living beings, who, as will be explained below, have been our mothers in previous lives. If we cannot appreciate the kindness of our present mother, how will we ever be able to appreciate the kindness of all our previous mothers?

It is very easy to forget our mother's kindness, or to take it for granted and remember only the times when we think she harmed us; so we need to remember in detail how kind our mother has been to us from the very beginning of this life.

In the beginning our mother was kind in offering us a place of rebirth. Before we were conceived in her womb, we wandered from place to place as a bardo being—a being who is between death and rebirth—with nowhere to rest. We were blown by the winds of our karma without freedom to choose where we would go, and all our acquaintances were fleeting. We experienced great pain and fear, but from this state we were able to enter the safety of our mother's womb. Although we were an uninvited guest, when she knew that we had entered her womb our mother let us stay there. If she had wanted to evict us, she could have done so and we would not be alive today to enjoy all our present opportunities. We are now able to develop the aspiration to attain the supreme happiness of enlightenment only because our mother was kind enough to let us stay in her womb. In winter, when it is cold and stormy outside, if someone invites us into their warm home and entertains us well, we consider this person to be extremely kind. How much kinder is our mother, who let us enter her own body and offered us such good hospitality there!

When we were in our mother's womb she protected us carefully, more carefully than she would guard a priceless jewel. In every situation she thought of our safety. She consulted doctors, exercised, ate special foods, and nurtured us day and night for nine months. She was also mindful not to do anything that might damage our physical or mental development. Because she looked after us so well, we were born with a normal and healthy body that we can use to accomplish so many good things.

At the time of our birth our mother experienced great pain, but when she saw us she felt happier than if someone had presented her with a precious treasure. Even during the agony of childbirth our welfare was foremost in her mind. When we were newly born, even though we looked more like a frog than a human being, our mother loved us dearly. We were completely helpless, even more helpless than a newborn foal, who can at least stand up and feed as soon as it is born. It was as if we were blind, unable to identify our parents, and we could not understand anything. If someone had been preparing to kill us, we would not have known. We had no idea what we were doing. We could not even tell when we were urinating.

Who cared for and protected this barely human thing? It was our mother. She clothed it, cradled it, and fed it with her own milk. She removed the filth from its body without feeling any disgust. Sometimes mothers remove the mucus from their baby's nose by using their own mouths because they do not want to cause the baby any pain by using their rough hands. Even when our mother had problems, she always showed us a loving expression and called us sweet names. While we were small our mother was constantly watchful. If she had forgotten us even for a short time, we might have been killed or disabled for life. Each day of our early childhood our mother rescued us from many disasters, and she always considered things from the point of view of our own safety and well-being.

In the winter she would make sure that we were warm and had good clothing, even when she herself was cold. She always selected the best things for us to eat, taking the worst for herself; and she would rather have been sick herself than see us sick. She would rather have died herself than see us die. Our mother naturally behaves toward us like someone who has gained the realization of exchanging self with others, cherishing us even more than she cherishes herself. She is able to put our welfare before her own, and she does so perfectly and spontaneously. If someone threatened to kill us she would offer herself to the killer instead. She has such compassion for us.

When we were small our mother would not sleep well. She slept lightly, waking every few hours and remaining alert for our cry. As we grew older our mother taught us how to eat, drink, speak, sit, and walk. She sent us to school and encouraged us to do good things in life. If we have any knowledge and skills now, it is mainly as a result of her kindness. When we grew older and became teenagers, we preferred to be with our friends and we would completely forget our mother. While we enjoyed ourself it was as if our mother had ceased to exist, and we would remember her only when we needed something from her. Although we were forgetful and allowed ourself to become completely absorbed in the pleasures we enjoyed with our friends, our mother remained continuously concerned for us. She would often become anxious, and in the back of her mind there was always some worry about us. She had the kind of worry we normally have only for ourself. Even when we are grown up and have a family of our own, our mother does not stop caring for us. She may be old and weak and hardly able to stand on her feet, but she never forgets her children.

By meditating in this way, recalling the kindness of our mother in great detail, we will come to cherish her very dearly. When we have this feeling of cherishing from the depths of our heart, we should extend it to all other living beings, remembering that every one of them has shown us the same kindness.

How are all living beings our mothers? Since it is impossible to find a beginning to our mental continuum it follows that we have taken countless rebirths in the past. And if we have had countless rebirths we must have had countless mothers. Where are all these mothers now? They are all the living beings alive today.

It is incorrect to reason that our mothers of former lives are no longer our mothers just because a long time has passed since they actually cared for us. If our present mother were to die today, would she cease to be our mother? No, we would still regard her as our mother and pray for her happiness. The same is true of all our previous mothers—they died, but they remain our mothers. It is only because of the changes in our external appearance that we do not recognize each other. In our daily life we see many different living beings, both human and non-human. We regard some as friends, some as enemies, and most as strangers. These distinctions are made by our mistaken minds; they are not verified by valid minds.

We can then meditate on the kindness of our mothers when we took other types of rebirth. We can consider, for example, how attentively a mother bird protects her eggs from danger and how she shields her young beneath her wings. When a hunter comes, she does not fly away and leave her babies unprotected. All day long she searches for food to nourish them until they are strong enough to leave the nest.

There was once a robber in Tibet who stabbed a horse who was carrying a foal in her womb. His knife penetrated so deeply into the side of the horse that it cut open her uterus and the foal emerged through its mother's side. As she was dying, the mother spent her last strength licking her offspring with great affection. Seeing this, the robber was filled with remorse. He was amazed to see how, even in the pains of death, this mother had such compassion for her foal and how her only concern was for its welfare. He then ceased his non-virtuous way of life and began to follow spiritual paths purely.

Every single living being has shown us the same selfless concern, the perfect kindness of a mother. Even if we do not consider other living beings as our mother, they have still shown us tremendous kindness. Our body, for example, is the result of the kindness not only of our parents but of countless beings who have provided it with food, shelter, and so forth. It is because we have this present body with human faculties that we are able to enjoy all the pleasures and opportunities of human life. Even simple pleasures such as going for a walk or watching a beautiful sunset can be seen as a result of the kindness of innumerable living beings. Our skills and abilities all come from the kindness of others — we had to be taught how to eat, how to walk, how to talk, and how to read and write. Even the language we speak is not our own invention but the product of many generations. Without it we could not communicate with others or share their ideas. We could not read this book, learn spiritual practices, or even think clearly. All the facilities we take for granted, such as houses, cars, roads, stores, schools, hospitals, and movie theaters, are produced solely through others' kindness. When we travel by bus or car we take the roads for granted, but many people worked very hard to build them and make them safe for us to use.

The fact that some of the people who help us may have no intention of doing so is irrelevant. We receive benefit from their actions, so from our point of view this is a kindness. Rather than focusing on their motivation, which we do not know anyway, we should focus on the practical benefit we receive. Everyone who contributes in any way toward our happiness and well-being deserves our gratitude and respect. If we had to give back everything that others have given us, we would have nothing left at all.

Wherever we look, we find only the kindness of others.

We could argue that we are not given things freely but have to work for them. When we go shopping we have to pay, and when we eat in a restaurant we have to pay. We may have the use of a car, but we had to buy the car, and now we have to pay for gas, tax, and insurance. No one gives us anything for free. But where do we get this money? It is true that generally we have to work for our money, but others employ us or buy our goods and so indirectly they are the ones who provide us with money. In addition, the reason we are able to do a particular job is that we have received the necessary training or education from other people. Wherever we look, we find only the kindness of others. We are all interconnected in a web of kindness from which it is impossible to separate ourself. Everything we have and everything we enjoy, including our very life, is due to the kindness of others. In fact, every happiness in the world arises as a result of others' kindness.

Our spiritual development and the pure happiness of full enlightenment also depend on the kindness of living beings. Our opportunity to read, contemplate, and meditate on spiritual teachings depends entirely on the kindness of others. In addition, as explained later, without living beings to give to, to test our patience, or to develop compassion for, we could never develop the virtuous qualities needed to attain enlightenment.

In short, we need others for our physical, emotional, and spiritual well-being. Without others we are nothing. Our sense that we are an island, an independent, self-sufficient individual, bears no relation to reality. It is closer to the truth to picture ourself as a cell in the vast body of life, distinct yet intimately bound up with all living beings. We cannot exist without others, and they in turn are affected by everything we do. The idea that it is possible to secure our own welfare while neglecting the welfare of others, or even at the expense of others, is completely unrealistic.

Contemplating the countless ways in which others help us, we should make a firm decision: "I must cherish all living beings because they are so kind to me." Based on this determination, we develop a feeling of cherishing—a sense that all living beings are important and that their happiness matters. We try to mix our mind single-pointedly with this feeling and maintain it for as long as we can without forgetting it. When we arise from meditation, we try to maintain this mind of love, so that whenever we meet or remember someone we naturally think: "This person is important, this person's happiness matters." In this way, we can make cherishing living beings our main practice.

THE BENEFITS OF CHERISHING OTHERS

Another reason for cherishing others is that it is the best method to solve our own and others' problems. Problems, worry, pain, and unhappiness are types of mind—they are feelings and do not exist outside the mind. If we cherish everyone we meet or think about, there will be no basis for developing jealousy, anger, or other harmful thoughts, and our mind will be at peace all the time. Jealousy, for example, is a state of mind that cannot bear another's good fortune; but if we cherish someone how can his or her good fortune disturb our mind? How can we wish to harm others if we regard everyone's happiness to be of paramount importance? By genuinely cherishing all living beings, we will always act with loving kindness, in a friendly and considerate way, and they will return our kindness. Others will not act unpleasantly toward us, and there will be no basis for conflict or disputes. People will come to like us, and our relationships will be more stable and satisfying.

Cherishing others also protects us from the problems caused by desirous attachment. We often become strongly attached to another person who we feel will help us overcome our loneliness by providing the comfort, security, or excitement we crave. If we have a loving mind toward everyone, however, we do not feel lonely. Instead of clinging onto others to fulfill our desires, we will want to help them fulfill their needs and wishes. Cherishing all living beings solves all our problems because all our problems come from our mind of self-cherishing. For example, at the moment if our partner left us for someone else we would probably feel very upset, but if we truly cherished him we would want him to be happy, and we would rejoice in his happiness. There would be no basis for us to feel jealous or depressed, so although we might find the situation challenging, it would not be a problem for us. Cherishing others is the supreme protection from suffering and problems, and enables us to remain calm and peaceful all the time.

Cherishing our neighbors and the people in our local area will naturally lead to harmony in the community and society at large, and this will make everyone happier. We may not be a well-known or powerful figure, but if we sincerely cherish everyone we meet we can make a profound contribution to our community. This is true even for those who deny the value of religion. There are some people who do not believe in past or future lives or in holy beings but who nevertheless try to give up self-concern and work for the benefit of others. This is a very positive attitude that will lead to good results. If a schoolteacher cherishes his or her students and is free from self-concern, they will respect him and learn not only the subject he teaches, but also the kind and admirable qualities he demonstrates. Such a teacher will naturally influence those around him in a positive way, and his presence will transform the whole school. It is said that there exists a magic crystal that has the power to purify any liquid it is placed in. Those who cherish all living beings are like this crystal—by their very presence they remove negativity from the world and give back love and kindness.

Even if someone is clever and powerful, if he does not love others, sooner or later he will encounter problems and find it difficult to fulfill his wishes. If the leader of a country does not cherish his or her people but is only concerned with his own interests, he will be criticized and distrusted, and eventually lose his position. If a Spiritual Teacher does not cherish and have a good relationship with his or her students, then he cannot help them and the students will not gain any realizations.

If an employer is concerned only with his own interests and does not look after the welfare of his employees, the employees will be unhappy. They will probably work inefficiently and will certainly not be enthusiastic about fulfilling their employer's wishes. Thus, the employer will suffer from his own lack of consideration toward his employees.

The solution to all the problems of daily life is to cherish others.

Similarly, if the employees are only concerned with what they can get out of the company, this will anger their employer, who may reduce their salary or ask them to leave. The company may even go bankrupt, causing all of them to lose their jobs. In this way, the employees will suffer from their lack of consideration toward their employer. In every field of activity the best way to ensure success is for the people involved to reduce their self-cherishing and to have a greater sense of consideration for others. There may sometimes appear to be short-term advantages to self-cherishing, but in the long term there are always only problems. The solution to all the problems of daily life is to cherish others.

All the suffering we experience is the result of negative karma, and the source of all negative karma is self-cherishing. It is because we have such an exaggerated sense of our own importance that we frustrate other people's wishes in order to fulfill our own. Driven by our selfish desires, we think nothing of destroying others' peace of mind and causing them distress. Such actions only sow the seeds for future suffering. If we sincerely cherish others, we will have no wish to hurt them and will stop engaging in destructive and harmful actions. We will naturally observe pure moral discipline and refrain from killing or being cruel to other living beings, stealing from them, or interfering with their relationships. As a result, we will not have to experience the unpleasant effects of these negative actions in the future. In this way, cherishing others protects us from all future problems caused by negative karma.

By cherishing others we continuously accumulate merit, and merit is the main cause of success in all our activities. If we cherish all living beings we will naturally perform many virtuous and helpful actions. Gradually all our actions of body, speech, and mind will become pure and beneficial, and we will become a source of happiness and inspiration for everyone we meet. We will discover through our own experience that this precious mind of love is the real wish-granting jewel, because it fulfills the pure wishes of both ourself and all living beings.

The mind that cherishes others is extremely precious. Keeping such a good heart will bring only happiness for ourself and all those around us. This good heart is the very essence of the Bodhisattva path and the main cause of great compassion, the wish to protect all living beings from fear and suffering. Through improving our great compassion we will eventually achieve the universal compassion of a Buddha, which has the actual power to protect all living beings from suffering. In this way, cherishing others leads us to the ultimate, supreme goal of human life.

Through contemplating all these advantages of cherishing others, we arrive at the following determination:

I will cherish all living beings without exception because this precious mind of love is the supreme method for solving all problems and fulfilling all wishes. Eventually it will give me the supreme happiness of enlightenment.

We meditate on this determination single-pointedly for as long as possible and develop a strong feeling of cherishing each and every living being. When we arise from meditation, we try to maintain this feeling and put our resolution into practice. Whenever we are with other people, we should be continuously mindful that their happiness and wishes are at least as important as our own. Of course we cannot cherish all living beings right away, but by training our mind in this attitude, beginning with our family and friends, we can gradually extend the scope of our love until it embraces all living beings. When in this way we sincerely cherish all living beings, we are no longer an ordinary person but have become a great being, like a Bodhisattva.

How to Enhance
Cherishing Love

How to Enhance Cherishing Love

The way to deepen our love for others is to familiarize ourself with the practice of cherishing others. To strengthen our determination to cherish all living beings, we need to receive further instructions on enhancing cherishing love.

We all have someone we regard as especially precious, such as our child, our partner, or our mother. This person seems to be imbued with unique qualities that make him or her stand out from others. We treasure and want to take special care of this person. We need to learn to regard all living beings in a similar way, recognizing each and every one as special and uniquely valuable. Although we already cherish our family and close friends, we do not love strangers, and we certainly do not love our enemies. For us the vast majority of living beings are of no particular significance. By practicing the instructions on cherishing others, we can remove this bias and come to treasure each and every living being, just as a mother regards her dearest child. The more we can deepen and enhance our love in this way, the stronger our compassion and bodhichitta will become, and the quicker we will attain enlightenment.

RECOGNIZING OUR FAULTS IN THE MIRROR OF DHARMA

One of the main functions of Buddha's teachings, or Dharma, is to serve as a mirror in which we can see our own faults. For example, when anger arises in our mind, instead of making excuses we need to say to ourself: "This anger is the inner poison of delusion. It has no value or justification—its only function is to harm. I will not tolerate its presence in my mind." We can also use the mirror of Dharma to distinguish between desirous attachment and love. These two are easily confused, but it is vital to discriminate between them, because love will bring us only happiness while the mind of attachment will bring us only suffering and bind us more and more tightly to samsara. The moment we notice attachment arising in our mind, we should be on our guard—no matter how pleasant it may seem to follow our attachment, it is like licking honey off a razor's edge and in the long run invariably leads to more suffering.

The main reason why we do not cherish all living beings is that we are so preoccupied with ourself, and this leaves very little room in our mind to appreciate others. If we wish to cherish others sincerely, we have to reduce our obsessive self-concern. Why do we regard ourself as so precious, but not others? It is because we are so familiar with self-cherishing. Since beginningless time we have grasped at a truly existent I. This grasping at I automatically gives rise to self-cherishing, which instinctively feels, "I am more important than others." For ordinary beings, grasping at one's own I and self-cherishing are like two sides of the same coin: I-grasping grasps at a truly existent I, while self-cherishing feels this I to be precious and cherishes it. The fundamental reason for this is our constant familiarity with our self-cherishing, day and night, even during our sleep.

Since we regard our self or I as so very precious and important, we exaggerate our own good qualities and develop an inflated view of ourself. Almost anything can serve as a basis for this arrogant mind, such as our appearance, possessions, knowledge, experiences, or status. If we make a witty remark we think, "I'm so clever!" or if we have traveled around the world we feel that this automatically makes us a fascinating person. We can even develop pride on the basis of things we should be ashamed of, such as our ability to deceive others, or on qualities that we only imagine we possess. On the other hand, we find it very hard to accept our mistakes and shortcomings. We spend so much time contemplating our real or imagined good qualities that we become oblivious to our faults. In reality our mind is full of gross delusions but we ignore them and may even fool ourself into thinking that we do not have such repulsive minds. This is like pretending that there is no dirt in our house after sweeping it under the rug.

One of the most common ways of not acknowledging our faults is to blame others.

It is often so painful to admit that we have faults that we make all kinds of excuses rather than alter our exalted view of ourself. One of the most common ways of not acknowledging our faults is to blame others. For example, if we have a difficult relationship with someone, we naturally conclude that it is entirely his fault—we are unable to accept that it is at least partly ours. Instead of taking responsibility for our actions and making an effort to change our behavior, we argue with him and insist that it is he who must change. In this way, an exaggerated sense of our own importance leads to a critical attitude toward other people and makes it almost impossible to avoid conflict. The fact that we are oblivious to our faults does not prevent other people from noticing them and pointing them out, but when they do we feel that they are being unfair. Instead of looking honestly at our own behavior to see whether or not the criticism is justified, our self-cherishing mind becomes defensive and retaliates by finding fault with them.

Another reason why we do not regard others as precious is that we pay attention to their faults while ignoring their good qualities. Unfortunately we have become very skilled in recognizing the faults of others, and we devote a great deal of mental energy to listing them, analyzing them, and even meditating on them! With this critical attitude, if we disagree with our partner or colleagues about something, instead of trying to understand their point of view we repeatedly think of many reasons why we are right and they are wrong. By focusing exclusively on their faults and limitations we become angry and resentful, and rather than cherishing them, we develop the wish to harm or discredit them. In this way, small disagreements can easily turn into conflicts that simmer for months.

Nothing positive ever comes from dwelling on our own good qualities and others' faults. All that happens is that we develop a highly distorted, self-important view of ourself, and an arrogant, disrespectful attitude toward others. As the Buddhist Master Shantideva says in *Guide to the Bodhisattva's Way of Life*:

> If we hold ourself in high esteem, we shall be reborn in
> the lower realms
> And later, as a human, experience low status and a foolish
> mind.

As a result of regarding ourself as superior and others as inferior, we perform many negative actions that will later ripen as rebirth in the lower realms. Due to this haughty attitude, even when we finally take rebirth again as a human being we will be of a low social status, living like a servant or slave. Out of pride we may regard ourself as highly intelligent, but in reality our pride makes us foolish and fills our mind with negativity. There is no value in viewing ourself as more important than others and thinking only of our own good qualities. It does not increase our good qualities or reduce our faults, and it does not cause others to share our exalted opinion of ourself.

If we focus instead on the good qualities of others, our deluded pride will decrease and we will come to regard them as more important and precious than ourself. As a result, our love and compassion will increase and we will naturally engage in virtuous actions. Through this we will be reborn in the higher realms, as a human or god, and we will gain the respect and friendship of many people. Only good can come from contemplating the good qualities of others. Therefore, while ordinary beings look for faults in others, Bodhisattvas look only for good qualities.

In *Advice from Atisha's Heart* it says:

Do not look for faults in others, but look for faults in yourself, and purge them like bad blood.

Do not contemplate your own good qualities, but contemplate the good qualities of others, and respect everyone as a servant would.

We need to think about our own faults because if we are not aware of them we will not be motivated to overcome them. It was through constantly examining their minds for faults and imperfections, and then applying great effort to abandon them, that those who are now enlightened were able to release their minds from delusions, the source of all faults. Buddha said that those who understand their own faults are wise, while those who are unaware of their own faults but look for faults in others are fools. Contemplating our own good qualities and others' faults serves only to increase our self-cherishing and diminish our love for others. And yet all enlightened beings agree that self-cherishing is the root of all faults and cherishing others is the source of all happiness. The only people who disagree with this view are those who are still in samsara. We can keep our ordinary view if we wish, or we can adopt the view of all the holy beings. The choice is ours, but we would be wise to adopt the latter if we wish to enjoy real peace and happiness.

Some people argue that one of our main problems is a lack of self-esteem, and that we need to focus exclusively on our good qualities in order to boost our self-confidence. It is true that to make authentic spiritual progress we need to develop confidence in our spiritual potential, and to acknowledge and improve our good qualities. However, we also need a clear and realistic awareness of our present faults and imperfections. If we are honest with ourself, we will recognize that at the moment our mind is filled with defilements such as anger, attachment, and ignorance. These mental diseases will not go away just by our pretending that they do not exist. The only way we can ever get rid of them is by honestly acknowledging their existence and then making the effort to eliminate them.

Although we need to be acutely aware of our faults we should never allow ourself to become overwhelmed or discouraged by them. We may have a lot of anger in our mind but this does not mean that we are an inherently angry person. No matter how many delusions we may have or how strong they are, they are not an essential part of our mind. They are defilements that temporarily pollute our mind but do not soil its pure, essential nature. They are like mud that dirties water but never becomes an intrinsic part of it. Just as mud can always be removed to reveal pure, clear water, similarly delusions can be removed to reveal the natural purity and clarity of our mind. While acknowledging that we have delusions, we should not identify with them by thinking, for example, "I am a selfish, worthless person" or "I am an angry person." Instead, we should identify with our pure potential and develop the wisdom and courage to overcome our delusions.

When we look at external things, we can usually distinguish those that are useful and valuable from those that are not. We must learn to look at our mind in the same way. Although the nature of our root mind is pure and clear, many conceptual thoughts arise from it, like bubbles arising within an ocean or rays of light arising from a single flame. Some of these thoughts are beneficial and lead to happiness both now and in the future, while others lead to suffering and the extreme misery of rebirth in the lower realms. We need to keep a constant watch over our mind and learn to distinguish between the beneficial and harmful thoughts that are arising moment by moment. Those who are able to do this are truly wise.

Once an evil man who had killed thousands of people met a Bodhisattva called King Chandra, who helped him by teaching him Dharma and showing him the error of his ways. The man said, "Having looked into the mirror of Dharma I now understand how negative my actions have been, and I feel great regret for them." Motivated by deep remorse, he engaged sincerely in purification practices and eventually became a highly realized Yogi. This shows that by recognizing one's own faults in the mirror of Dharma and then making a concerted effort to remove them, even the most evil person can become a completely pure being.

In Tibet there was once a famous Dharma practitioner called Geshe Ben Gungyal, who neither recited prayers nor meditated in the traditional meditation posture. His only practice was to observe his mind very attentively and counter delusions as soon as they arose. Whenever he noticed his mind becoming even slightly agitated, he was especially vigilant and refused to follow any negative thoughts. For example, if he felt self-cherishing was about to arise, he would immediately recall its disadvantages and then he would stop this mind from manifesting by applying its opponent, the practice of love. Whenever his mind was naturally peaceful and positive, he would relax and allow himself to enjoy his virtuous states of mind.

To gauge his progress he would put a black pebble down in front of him whenever a negative thought arose, and a white pebble whenever a positive thought arose, and at the end of the day he would count the pebbles. If there were more black pebbles he would reprimand himself and try even harder the next day, but if there were more white pebbles he would praise and encourage himself. At the beginning, the black pebbles greatly outnumbered the white ones, but over the years his mind improved until he reached the point when entire days went by without any black pebbles. Before becoming a Dharma practitioner, Geshe Ben Gungyal had had a reputation for being wild and unruly, but by watching his mind closely all the time, and judging it with complete honesty in the mirror of Dharma, he gradually became a very pure and holy being. Why can't we do the same?

The Kadampa Masters, or Geshes, taught that the function of a Spiritual Guide is to point out his or her disciples' faults, because then the disciples have a clear understanding of these shortcomings and the opportunity to overcome them. These days, however, if a Teacher pointed out his or her disciples' faults they would probably become upset, and might even lose their faith, and so the Teacher usually has to adopt a gentler approach. However, even though our Spiritual Guide may be tactfully refraining from directly pointing out our faults, we still need to become aware of them by examining our mind in the mirror of his or her teachings. By relating our Spiritual Guide's teachings on karma and delusions to our own situation, we can understand what we need to abandon and what we need to practice.

A sick person cannot be cured of his illness just by reading the instructions on a bottle of medicine, but he can be cured by actually taking the medicine. Similarly, Buddha gave Dharma instructions as supreme medicine to cure the inner disease of our delusions, but we cannot cure this disease just by reading or studying Dharma books. We can only solve our daily problems by taking Dharma into our heart and practicing it sincerely.

VIEWING ALL LIVING BEINGS AS SUPREME

The great Bodhisattva Langri Tangpa made the prayer:

> With a perfect intention,
> May I cherish others as supreme.

If we wish to attain enlightenment, or to develop the superior bodhichitta that comes from exchanging self with others, we definitely need to adopt the view that others are more precious than ourself. This view is based on wisdom and leads us to our final goal, while the view that regards ourself as more precious than others is based on self-grasping ignorance and leads us along the paths of samsara.

What exactly does it mean to say that something is precious? If we were asked which was more precious, a diamond or a bone, we would say a diamond. This is because a diamond is more useful to us. However, for a dog a bone would be more precious because he can eat a bone while he cannot do anything with a diamond. This indicates that preciousness is not an intrinsic quality of an object but depends on an individual's needs and wishes, which in turn depend on his or her karma. For someone whose main wish is to achieve the spiritual realizations of love, compassion, bodhichitta, and great enlightenment, living beings are more precious than a universe filled with diamonds or even wish-granting jewels. Why is this? It is because living beings help that person to develop love and compassion and to fulfill their wish for enlightenment, which is something that a whole universe filled with jewels could never do.

No one wants to remain an ordinary, ignorant being forever;

in fact, all of us have the wish to improve ourself and to progress to higher and higher states. The highest state of all is full enlightenment, and the main road leading to enlightenment is the realizations of love, compassion, bodhichitta, and the practice of the six perfections—the perfections of giving, moral discipline, patience, effort, concentration, and wisdom. We can only develop these qualities in dependence upon other living beings. How can we learn to love with no one to love? How can we practice giving with no one to give to, or patience with no one to irritate us? Whenever we see another living being we can increase our spiritual qualities such as love and compassion, and in this way we come closer to enlightenment and the fulfillment of our deepest wishes. How kind living beings are to act as the objects of our love and compassion. How precious they are!

When Atisha was in Tibet he had an Indian assistant who was always criticizing him. When the Tibetans asked him why he kept this assistant when there were many faithful Tibetans who would be more than happy to serve him, Atisha replied, "Without this man, there would be no one I could practice patience with. He is very kind to me. I need him!" Atisha understood that the only way to fulfill his deepest wish to benefit all living beings was to achieve enlightenment, and that to do this he needed to perfect his patience. For Atisha, his bad-tempered assistant was more precious than material possessions, praise, or any other worldly attainment.

Our spiritual realizations are our inner wealth because they help us in all situations and are the only possessions we can take with us when we die. Once we learn to value the inner wealth of patience, giving, love, and compassion above external conditions, we will come to regard each and every living being as supremely precious, no matter how they treat us. This will make it very easy for us to cherish them.

In our meditation session, we contemplate the reasons given above until we reach the following conclusion:

Living beings are extremely precious because without them I cannot gather the inner wealth of spiritual realizations that will eventually bring me the ultimate happiness of full enlightenment. Since without this inner wealth I will have to remain in samsara forever, I will always regard living beings as supremely important.

We meditate on this determination single-pointedly for as long as possible. When we arise from meditation we try to maintain this determination all the time, recognizing how much we need each and every living being for our spiritual practice. By maintaining this recognition, our inner problems of anger, attachment, jealousy, and so forth will subside, and we will naturally come to cherish others. In particular, whenever people interfere with our wishes or criticize us, we should remember that we need these people in order to develop the spiritual realizations that are the true meaning of our human life. If everyone treated us with the kindness and respect our self-cherishing feels we deserve, this would only reinforce our delusions and deplete our merit. Imagine what we would be like if we always got what we wanted! We would be just like a spoiled child who feels that the world revolves around him, and who is unpopular with everyone. In fact, we all need someone like Atisha's assistant, because such people give us the opportunity to destroy our self-cherishing and train our mind, thereby making our life truly meaningful.

Since the above reasoning is the exact opposite of our normal way of thinking, we need to contemplate it very carefully until we are convinced that each and every living being is in fact more precious than any external attainment. In reality Buddhas and living beings are equally precious—Buddhas because they reveal the path to enlightenment, and living beings because they act as the objects of the virtuous minds that we need in order to attain enlightenment. Because their kindness in enabling us to attain our supreme goal, enlightenment, is equal, we should regard Buddhas and living beings as equally important and precious. As Shantideva says in *Guide to the Bodhisattva's Way of Life*:

> Since living beings and enlightened beings are alike
> In that the qualities of a Buddha arise in dependence
>   upon them,
> Why do we not show the same respect to living beings
> As we do to the enlightened beings?

LIVING BEINGS HAVE NO FAULTS

We might object that while it is true that we depend on living beings as the objects of our patience, compassion, and so forth, it is nevertheless impossible to see them as precious when they have so many faults. How can we regard someone as precious whose mind is pervaded by attachment, anger, and ignorance? The answer to this objection is very profound. Although living beings' minds are filled with delusions, living beings themselves are not faulty. We say that sea water is salty, but in fact it is the salt in the water that makes it salty, not the water itself. The real taste of water is not salty. Similarly, all the faults we see in people are actually the faults of their delusions, not of the people themselves. Buddhas see that delusions have many faults but they never see people as faulty, because they distinguish between people and their delusions. If someone is angry we think, "He is a bad and angry person," while Buddhas think, "He is a suffering being afflicted with the inner disease of anger." If a friend of ours were suffering from cancer we would not blame him for his physical disease, and in the same way, if someone is suffering from anger or attachment we should not blame him for the diseases of his mind.

Delusions are the enemies of living beings, and just as we would not blame a victim for the faults of his attacker, why should we blame living beings for the faults of their inner enemies? When someone is temporarily overpowered by the inner enemy of anger it is inappropriate to blame him, because he and the anger in his mind are two separate phenomena. Just as a fault of a microphone is not that of a book, and a fault of a cup is not that of a teapot, so the faults of delusions are not those of a person. The only appropriate response to those who are driven by their delusions to harm others is compassion. Sometimes it is necessary to restrain those who are behaving in very deluded ways, both for their own sake and to protect other people, but it is never appropriate to blame or become angry with them.

We normally refer to our body and mind as "my body" and "my mind," in a similar way to which we refer to our other possessions. This indicates that they are different from our I. The body and mind are the basis upon which we establish our I, not the I itself. Delusions are characteristics of a person's mind, not of the person. Since we can never find faults in living beings themselves, we can say that in this respect living beings are like Buddhas.

Just as we distinguish between a person and his or her delusions, so we should also remember that the delusions are only temporary, adventitious characteristics of that person's mind and not its real nature. Delusions are distorted conceptual thoughts that arise within the mind, like waves on the ocean—just as it is possible for waves to die down without the ocean disappearing, so it is possible for our delusions to end without our mental continuum ceasing.

It is because they distinguish between delusions and persons that Buddhas are able to see the faults of delusions without ever seeing a single fault in any living being. Consequently, their love and compassion for living beings never diminish. We, on the other hand, fail to make this distinction, and so we are constantly finding fault with other people but do not recognize the faults of delusions, even those within our own mind.

There is a prayer that says:

This fault I see is not the fault of the person
But the fault of delusion.
Realizing this, may I never view others' faults,
But see all beings as supreme.

Focusing on other people's faults is the source of much of our negativity and one of the main obstacles to viewing others as supremely precious. If we are genuinely interested in developing cherishing love, we need to learn to discriminate between a person and his or her delusions, and realize that it is the delusions that are to blame for all the faults we perceive.

There may appear to be a contradiction between this and the earlier section where we are advised to recognize our own faults.

We may object, "If we have faults, then so do others." In a sense this is true, because living beings have delusions in their minds and delusions are faults. However, the main issue here is not so much whether or not from their own side living beings have faults, but what is the most beneficial way of viewing them. From a practical point of view, our main spiritual tasks are to remove the delusions from our own mind and to improve our love for other living beings. To accomplish these tasks, there are great benefits in looking at our own faults—our delusions and non-virtuous actions—and great disadvantages in looking at the faults of others. It is only when we have removed our own delusions, and love and respect other people from the depths of our hearts, that we can be truly effective in releasing them from their suffering.

When a mother sees her child throwing a tantrum, she knows that the child is acting in a deluded way, but this does not diminish her love for him or her. Although she is not blind to the anger in her child, this does not lead her to the conclusion that the child is evil or intrinsically angry. Distinguishing between the delusion and the person, she continues to see her child as beautiful and full of potential. In the same way, we should regard all living beings as supremely precious, while clearly understanding that they are afflicted by the sickness of delusion.

We can also apply the above reasoning to ourself, recognizing that our faults are really the faults of our delusions and not of our self. This prevents us from identifying with our faults and thus feeling guilty and inadequate, and it helps us to view our delusions in a realistic and practical way. We need to acknowledge our delusions and take responsibility for overcoming them, but to do this effectively we need to distance ourself from them. For example, we can think: "Self-cherishing is currently in my mind, but it is not me. I can destroy it without destroying myself." In this way, we can be utterly ruthless with our delusions but kind and patient with ourself. We do not need to blame ourself for the many delusions we have inherited from our previous life, but if we wish for our future self to enjoy peace and happiness, it is our responsibility to remove these delusions from our mind.

As mentioned before, one of the best ways to regard others as precious is to remember their kindness. Once again we may object, "How can I see others as kind when they engage in so many cruel and harmful actions?" To answer this we need to understand that when people harm others they are controlled by their delusions. Delusions are like a powerful hallucinogenic drug that forces people to act in ways that are contrary to their real nature. A person under the influence of delusions is not in his right mind, because he is creating terrible suffering for himself and no one in his

We can be utterly ruthless with our delusions but kind and patient with ourself.

right mind would create suffering for himself. All delusions are based on a mistaken way of seeing things. When we see things as they really are, our delusions naturally disappear and virtuous minds naturally manifest. Minds such as love and kindness are based on reality and are an expression of our pure nature. So when we view others as kind, we are seeing beyond their delusions and are relating to their pure nature, their Buddha nature.

Buddha compared our Buddha nature to a gold nugget in dirt, because no matter how disgusting a person's delusions may be, the real nature of their mind remains undefiled, like pure gold. In the heart of even the cruelest and most degenerate person exists the potential for limitless love, compassion, and wisdom. Unlike the seeds of our delusions, which can be destroyed, this potential is utterly indestructible and is the pure, essential nature of every living being. Whenever we meet other people, instead of focusing on their delusions we should focus on the gold of their Buddha nature. This will not only enable us to regard them as special and unique but will also help to bring out their good qualities. Recognizing everyone as a future Buddha, out of love and compassion we will naturally help and encourage this potential to ripen.

Because we are so familiar with cherishing ourself more than others, the view that all living beings are supremely important does not arise easily and we need to train our mind patiently for many years before it becomes natural. Just as an ocean is formed by many tiny drops of water gathering over a long period of time, so the realizations of love and compassion of advanced practitioners are the result of constant training. We should begin by trying to cherish our parents, family, and close friends, and then extend this feeling to the people in our community. Gradually we can increase the scope of our cherishing until it includes all living beings.

It is important to begin with our immediate circle because if we try to love all living beings in a general way, while neglecting to cherish the specific individuals we associate with, our cherishing will be abstract and inauthentic. We may develop some good feelings in meditation, but these will quickly disappear once we arise from meditation, and our mind will remain basically unchanged. However, if at the end of each meditation session we make a special determination to cherish those we are going to spend our time with, and then put this determination into practice, our cherishing will be grounded and sincere. Through making a concerted effort to love our immediate circle, even when they are making life difficult for us, our self-cherishing will be continuously eroded and we will gradually build in our mind a firm foundation of cherishing others. With this foundation it will not be difficult to extend our love to more and more living beings until we develop the universal love and compassion of a Bodhisattva.

Our ability to help others also depends on our karmic connection with them from this and previous lives. We all have a close circle of people with whom we have a special karmic connection in this life. Though we need to learn to cherish all living beings equally, this does not mean that we have to treat everyone in exactly the same way. For example, it would be inappropriate to treat our employer in the same way that we treat our close friends and family. There are also people who just want to be left alone or who dislike any display of affection. Loving others is principally an attitude of mind, and the way in which we express it depends on the needs and wishes of each individual as well as our karmic connection with them. We cannot physically care for everyone, but we can develop a caring attitude toward all beings. This is the main point of training the mind. By training our mind in this way we will eventually become a Buddha with the actual power to protect all living beings.

Through carefully contemplating all the above points, we arrive at the following conclusion:

Because all living beings are very precious for me, I must cherish them and hold them dear.

We should regard this determination as a seed and hold it continuously in our mind, nurturing it until it grows into the spontaneous feeling of cherishing ourself and all living beings equally. This realization is called *equalizing self and others*. Just as we value our own peace and happiness, we should also value the peace and happiness of all living beings. And just as we work to free ourself from suffering and problems, we should also work to free others.

DEVELOPING HUMILITY

Bodhisattva Langri Tangpa said:

Whenever I associate with others,
May I view myself as the lowest of all.

With these words, Langri Tangpa is encouraging us to develop the mind of humility and to see ourself as lower and less precious than others. As mentioned before, preciousness is not an inherent quality of an object but depends on an individual's karma. It is due to a mother's special karmic connection with her children that they naturally appear precious to her. For a practitioner who is seeking enlightenment, all living beings are equally precious, both because they are immensely kind and because they act as supreme objects for developing and increasing his or her spiritual realizations. For such a practitioner, no single being is inferior or less important, not even an insect. We may wonder, if preciousness depends on karma, whether it is because a practitioner seeking enlightenment has a karmic connection with all beings that he sees them as precious? The practitioner develops this special view through contemplating correct reasons that cause his karmic potential to see all beings as his precious mother to ripen. In reality all living beings are our mothers, so of course we have a karmic connection with them. But due to our ignorance we have no idea that they are our precious mothers.

In general, we would all prefer to enjoy high status and a good reputation, and we have little or no interest in being humble. Practitioners like Langri Tangpa are the complete opposite. They actually seek out subordinate positions and wish for others to enjoy the happiness of higher status. There are three reasons why such practitioners strive to practice humility. First, by practicing humility we are not using up our merit on worldly attainments but saving it for the development of internal realizations. We only have a limited supply of merit, so if we waste it on material possessions, reputation, popularity, or power there will not be enough positive energy left in our mind to effect deep spiritual realizations. Second, by practicing humility and wishing for others to enjoy higher status, we accumulate a vast amount of merit. We should understand that now is the time to accumulate merit, not to waste it. Third, we need to practice humility because there is no inherently existent I. We should view our self or I—the object of our self-cherishing—as the lowest of all, as something we need to neglect or forget. In this way our self-cherishing will become weaker and our love for others will increase.

Although many practitioners practice humility, they will nonetheless accept whatever social position enables them to benefit the most living beings. Such a practitioner may become a wealthy, powerful, and respected member of society, but his or her only motivation for doing so would be to benefit others. Worldly attainments do not attract him at all, because he recognizes them as deceptive and a waste of his merit. Even if he became a king he would consider all his wealth as belonging to others and in his heart would continue to view others as supreme. Because he would not grasp at his position or possessions as his own, they would not serve to exhaust his merit.

We need to practice humility even when we associate with those who according to social conventions are equal or inferior to us. Because we cannot see others' minds, we do not know who is actually a realized being and who is not. Someone may not have a high position in society, but if in his heart he maintains loving kindness toward all living beings, in reality he is a realized being.

Humility enables us to learn from everyone.

Moreover, Buddhas are able to manifest in any form to help living beings, and unless we are a Buddha ourself we have no way of knowing who is an emanation of a Buddha and who is not. We cannot say for sure that our closest friend or worst enemy, our mother or even our dog, is not an emanation. Just because we feel we know someone very well and have seen him or her behaving in deluded ways does not mean that he or she is an ordinary person. What we see is a reflection of our own mind. An ordinary, deluded mind will naturally perceive a world filled with ordinary, deluded people.

Only when we purify our mind will we be able to see pure, holy beings directly. Until then we cannot know for sure whether or not someone is an emanation. Perhaps everyone we know is an emanation of a Buddha! This may seem unlikely, but only because we are so used to seeing people as ordinary. We simply do not know. All we can realistically say is that maybe someone is an emanation, or maybe he or she is not. This is a very useful way of thinking, because if we think that someone may be an emanation of a Buddha we will naturally respect him and avoid harming him. From the point of view of the effect it has on our mind, thinking that someone may be a Buddha is almost the same as thinking that he or she is a Buddha. Since the only person we know for sure is not a Buddha is ourself, through training in this way of thinking we will gradually come to regard everyone else as superior to and more precious than ourself.

Viewing ourself as the lowest of all is not easy to accept at first. When we meet a dog, for example, are we supposed to view ourself as lower than the dog? We can consider the story of the Buddhist Master Asanga, who came across a dying dog that in reality turned out to be an emanation of Buddha Maitreya. The dog before us may appear to be an ordinary animal, but the fact is that we do not know its real nature. Perhaps it too has been emanated by Buddha to help us develop compassion. Since we cannot know for sure one way or another, rather than wasting our time speculating whether the dog is an ordinary animal or an emanation, we should simply think, "This dog may be an emanation of Buddha." From this point of view we can think that we are lower than the dog, and this thought will protect us against any feelings of superiority.

One of the advantages of humility is that it enables us to learn from everyone. A proud person cannot learn from other people because he feels he already knows better than they. On the other hand, a humble person who respects everyone and recognizes that they may even be emanations of Buddha has the openness of mind to learn from everyone and every situation. Just as water cannot collect on mountain peaks, so good qualities and blessings cannot gather on the rocky peaks of pride. If, instead, we maintain a humble, respectful attitude toward everyone, good qualities and inspiration will flow into our mind all the time, like streams flowing into a valley.

Exchanging Self with Others

Exchanging Self with Others

*W*hile the two previous chapters explain the practice of what is called *equalizing self and others*—cherishing ourself and all other living beings equally—this chapter shows us how to exchange self with others. This means that we give up our self-cherishing and come to cherish only others. Because the main obstacles to gaining this realization are our delusions, I will now explain how we can overcome our delusions, and in particular our self-cherishing.

Normally we divide the external world into that which we consider to be good or valuable, bad or worthless, or neither. Most of the time these discriminations are incorrect or have little meaning. For example, our habitual way of categorizing people as friends, enemies, and strangers depending on how they make us feel is both incorrect and a great obstacle to developing impartial love for all living beings. Rather than holding so tightly to our discriminations of the external world, it would be much more beneficial if we learned to discriminate between valuable and worthless states of mind.

To overcome a particular delusion, we need to be able to identify it correctly and distinguish it clearly from other states of mind. It is relatively easy to identify delusions such as anger or jealousy and to see how they are harming us. Delusions such as attachment, pride, self-grasping, and self-cherishing, however, are more difficult to recognize and can easily be confused with other states of mind. For example, we have many desires, but not all of these are motivated by desirous attachment. We can have the wish to sleep, to eat, to meet our friends, or to meditate, without being influenced by attachment. A desire that is attachment necessarily disturbs our mind, but since it may affect us in subtle, indirect ways, we may find it difficult to recognize when it arises in our mind.

WHAT IS SELF-CHERISHING?

Of all the innumerable conceptual thoughts that arise from the ocean of our root mind, the most harmful is self-cherishing and the most beneficial is the mind of cherishing others. What exactly is self-cherishing? Self-cherishing is defined as a mind that considers oneself to be supremely important and precious, and that develops from the appearance of true existence of the self. The delusion of self-cherishing is functioning in our mind almost all the time, and is at the very core of our samsaric experience.

It is our self-cherishing that makes us feel that our happiness and freedom are more important than anyone else's, that our wishes and feelings matter more, and that our life and experiences are more interesting. Because of our self-cherishing, we find it upsetting when we are criticized or insulted, but not when our friend is criticized, and we may even feel happy when someone we dislike is insulted. When we are in pain we feel that the most important thing in the world is to stop our pain as quickly as possible, but we are far more patient when someone else is in pain. We are so familiar with self-cherishing that we find it difficult to imagine life without it—for us it is almost as natural as breathing. However, if we check with our wisdom, we will see that self-cherishing is a completely mistaken mind with no basis in reality. There are no valid reasons whatsoever for thinking that we are more important than others. For Buddhas, who have unmistaken minds and see things exactly as they are, all beings are equally important.

Self-cherishing is a wrong awareness because its observed object, the inherently existent self or I, does not exist. If we watch our mind when self-cherishing is manifesting strongly, such as when we are afraid, embarrassed, or indignant, we will notice that we have a very vivid sense of I. Due to self-grasping ignorance, our I appears to us as a solid, real entity, existing from its own side, independently of our body or mind. This independent I is called the *inherently existent I*, and it does not exist at all. The I that we grasp at so strongly, cherish so dearly, and devote our whole life to serving and protecting is merely a fabrication of our ignorance. If we reflect deeply on this point, we will realize how ridiculous it is to cherish something that does not exist. An explanation of how the inherently existent I does not exist is given in the chapter on ultimate truth.

Due to the imprints of self-grasping accumulated since beginningless time, whatever appears to our mind, including our I, appears to be inherently existent. Grasping at our own self as inherently existent, we grasp at the self of others as inherently existent, and then conceive self and others to be inherently different. We then generate self-cherishing, which instinctively feels, "I am supremely important and precious." In summary, our self-grasping apprehends our I to be inherently existent, and our self-cherishing then cherishes that inherently existent I above all others. For ordinary beings, self-grasping and self-cherishing are very closely related and almost mixed together. We can say that they are both types of ignorance because they both mistakenly apprehend a non-existent object, the inherently existent I. Because any action motivated by these minds is a contaminated action that causes us to be reborn in samsara, it is also correct to say that for ordinary beings both self-grasping and self-cherishing are the root of samsara.

There is a more subtle type of self-cherishing, that is not conjoined with self-grasping and that is therefore not a type of ignorance. This type of self-cherishing exists in the minds of Hinayana practitioners who have completely abandoned the ignorance of self-grasping and all other delusions, and achieved nirvana. However, they still have a subtle form of self-cherishing, which arises from the imprints of self-grasping and prevents them from working for the sake of all living beings. An explanation of this type of self-cherishing is not within the scope of this book. Here, self-cherishing refers to the self-cherishing of ordinary beings, which is a deluded mind that cherishes a non-existent self and regards it as supremely important.

THE FAULTS OF SELF-CHERISHING

It is impossible to find a single problem, misfortune, or painful experience that does not arise from self-cherishing. As Bodhisattva Shantideva says:

> All the happiness there is in this world
> Arises from wishing others to be happy,
> And all the suffering there is in this world
> Arises from wishing ourself to be happy.

How should we understand this? As mentioned earlier, all our experiences are the effects of actions we have committed in the past: pleasant experiences are the effects of positive actions, and unpleasant experiences are the effects of negative actions. If we never engaged in negative actions, it would be impossible for us to experience any unpleasant effects. All negative actions are motivated by delusions, which in turn arise from self-cherishing. First we develop the thought, "I am important," and because of this we feel that the fulfillment of our wishes is of paramount importance. Then we desire for ourself that which appears attractive and develop attachment, we feel aversion for that which appears unattractive and develop anger, and we feel indifference toward that which appears neutral and develop ignorance. From these three delusions, all other delusions arise. Self-grasping and self-cherishing are the roots of the tree of suffering, delusions such as anger and attachment are its trunk, negative actions are its branches, and the miseries and pains of samsara are its bitter fruit.

By understanding how delusions develop, we can see that self-cherishing is at the very core of our negativity and suffering. Disregarding the happiness of others and selfishly pursuing our own interests, we perform many non-virtuous actions, the effects of which are only suffering. All the misery of disease, sickness, natural disasters, and war can be traced back to self-cherishing. It is impossible to experience the suffering of sickness or any other misfortune if we have not at some time in the past created its cause, which is necessarily a non-virtuous action motivated by self-cherishing.

We should not think this means that a person's suffering is his own fault and that it is therefore inappropriate to feel compassion for him. Motivated by their delusions, living beings perform negative actions, and whenever they are under the influence of delusions they are not in control of their minds. If a mental patient injured his head by banging it against a wall, the doctors would not refuse to treat him by arguing that it was his own fault. In the same way, if in a previous life someone performed a negative action that has now resulted in his experiencing a serious illness, this is no reason for us not to feel compassion for him. In fact, by understanding that living beings are not free from the delusions that are the cause of all their suffering, our compassion will become much stronger. To be able to help others effectively, we need a profoundly compassionate intention that wishes to free others from their manifest suffering *and* its underlying causes.

It is not difficult to see how the self-cherishing we have in this life causes us suffering. All disharmony, quarreling, and fighting come from the self-cherishing of the people involved. With self-cherishing we hold our opinions and interests very strongly and are not willing to see a situation from another point of view. As a consequence we easily get angry and wish to harm others verbally or even physically. Self-cherishing makes us feel depressed whenever our wishes are not fulfilled, we fail in our ambitions, or our life does not turn out the way we planned. If we examine all the times we have been miserable, we will discover that they are characterized by an excessive concern for our own welfare. If we lose our job, our home, our reputation, or our friends we feel sad, but only because we are so attached to these things. We are not nearly so concerned when other people lose their jobs or are parted from their friends.

In themselves, external conditions are neither good nor bad. For example, wealth is generally thought of as desirable, but if we are strongly attached to wealth it will only cause us to worry and function to deplete our merit. On the other hand, if our mind is governed principally by cherishing others, even losing all our money can be useful, because it gives us the opportunity to understand the suffering of those in similar situations and provides fewer distractions from our spiritual practice. Even if we did fulfill all the wishes of our self-cherishing, there is no guarantee that we would be happy, because every samsaric attainment brings with it new problems and invariably leads to new desires. The relentless pursuit of our selfish desires is like drinking salt water to quench our thirst. The more we indulge our desires, the greater our thirst.

When people kill themselves, it is usually because their wishes were not fulfilled, but this was unbearable to them only because their self-cherishing made them feel that their wishes were the most important thing in the world. It is because of self-cherishing that we take our wishes and plans so seriously and are unable to accept and learn from the difficulties that life brings us. We do not become a better person just by fulfilling our wishes for worldly success; we are as likely to develop the qualities that really matter—such as wisdom, patience, and compassion—through our failures as through our successes.

We often feel that it is someone else who is making us unhappy, and we can become very resentful. If we look at the situation carefully, however, we will find that it is always our own mental attitude that is responsible for our unhappiness. Another person's actions make us unhappy only if we allow them to stimulate a negative response in us. Criticism, for example, has no power from its own side to hurt us; we are hurt only because of our self-cherishing. With self-cherishing we are so dependent on the opinions and approval of others that we lose our freedom to respond and act in the most constructive way.

We sometimes feel that the reason we are unhappy is that someone we love is in trouble. We need to remember that at the moment our love for others is almost invariably mixed with attachment, which is a self-centered mind. The love parents generally feel for their children, for example, is deep and genuine, but it is not always pure love. Mixed with it are feelings such as the need to feel loved and appreciated in return, the belief that their children are somehow part of them, a desire to impress other people through their children, and the hope that their children will in some way fulfill their parents' ambitions and dreams. It is sometimes very difficult to distinguish between our love and our attachment for others, but when we are able to do so, we will see that it is invariably the attachment that is the cause of our suffering. Pure unconditional love never causes any pain or worry but only peace and joy.

All the problems of human society, such as war, crime, pollution, drug addiction, poverty, injustice, and disharmony within families, are the result of self-cherishing. Thinking that human beings alone matter, and that the natural world exists to serve human desires, we have wiped out thousands of animal species and polluted the planet to such an extent that there is great danger it could soon be unfit even for human habitation. If everyone practiced cherishing others, many of the major problems of the world would be solved in a few years.

Self-cherishing is like an iron chain that keeps us locked in samsara. The fundamental reason for our suffering is that we are in samsara, and we are in samsara because we continually create the deluded, self-centered actions that perpetuate the cycle of uncontrolled rebirth. Samsara is the experience of a self-centered mind. The six realms of samsara, from the god realm to the hell realm, are all the dream-like projections of a mind distorted by self-cherishing and self-grasping. By causing us to see life as a constant struggle to serve and protect our own I, these two minds impel us to perform innumerable

The moment we let go of our obsessive concern for our own welfare, our mind naturally relaxes and becomes lighter.

destructive actions that keep us imprisoned in the nightmare of samsara. Until we destroy these two minds, we will never know true freedom or happiness, we will never really be in control of our mind, and we will never be safe from the threat of lower rebirth.

Controlling our self-cherishing is of great value, even temporarily. All worries, anxiety, and sadness are based on self-cherishing. The moment we let go of our obsessive concern for our own welfare, our mind naturally relaxes and becomes lighter. Even if we receive some bad news, if we manage to overcome our normal self-centered reaction our mind will remain at peace. On the other hand, if we fail to subdue our self-cherishing, even the most petty things disturb us. If a friend criticizes us we immediately become upset, and the frustration of even our smallest wishes leaves us dejected. If a Dharma Teacher says something we do not want to hear, we may become upset with him or her, or even lose our faith. Many people can get very agitated just because a mouse comes into their room. Mice do not eat people, so why become upset? It is only the foolish mind of self-cherishing that disturbs us. If we loved the mouse as much as we loved ourself we would welcome the mouse into our room, thinking, "He has as much right to be here as I do!"

For those who aspire to become enlightened, the worst fault is self-cherishing. Self-cherishing is the main obstacle to cherishing others, failing to cherish others is the main obstacle to developing great compassion, and failing to develop great compassion is the main obstacle to developing bodhichitta and entering the path to enlightenment—the Mahayana path. Since bodhichitta is the main cause of great enlightenment, we can see that self-cherishing is also the main obstacle to the attainment of Buddhahood.

Although we might agree that objectively we are no more important than anyone else, and that self-cherishing has many faults, we may still feel that it is nevertheless indispensable. We may think that if we do not cherish and look after ourself, then no one else will. This is a mistaken way of thinking. While it is true that we need to look after ourself, we do not need to be motivated by self-cherishing. We can take care of our health, have a job, and look after our house and possessions solely out of concern for others' welfare. If we view our body as an instrument with which we can benefit others, we can feed it, clothe it, wash it, and rest it—all without self-cherishing. Just as an ambulance driver can take care of his vehicle without regarding it as his own, so we can take care of our body and possessions for the benefit of others. The only way we can ever truly help all living beings is by becoming a Buddha, and the human form is the best possible vehicle for accomplishing this. Therefore, we need to take good care of our body. If we do this with bodhichitta motivation, all our actions of caring for our body become part of the path to enlightenment.

We may sometimes confuse self-cherishing with self-confidence and self-respect, but in reality they are completely unrelated. It is not out of self-respect that we always want the best for ourself, nor is it out of self-respect that we deceive or exploit others, or fail in our responsibilities to them. If we check honestly, we will see that it is our self-cherishing that causes us to act in ways that rob us of our self-respect and destroy our confidence. Some people are driven by their self-cherishing to the depths of alcoholism or drug addiction, completely losing any modicum of self-respect in the process. On the other hand, the more we cherish others and act to benefit them, the greater our self-respect and confidence will become. The Bodhisattva vow, for example, in which the Bodhisattva promises to overcome all faults and limitations, attain all good qualities, and work until all living beings are liberated from the sufferings of samsara, is an expression of tremendous self-confidence, far beyond that of any self-centered being.

We might also ask, "If I had no self-cherishing, wouldn't that mean that I dislike myself? Isn't it necessary to accept and love my-self, because if I cannot love myself then how can I love others?" This is an important point. In *Training the Mind in Seven Points*, Geshe Chekhawa explains a number of commitments that serve as guidelines for practitioners of training the mind. The first of these states: "Do not allow your practice of training the mind to cause inappropriate behavior." This commitment advises practitioners to be happy with themselves. If we are excessively self-critical, we will turn in on ourself and become discouraged, and this will make it very difficult for us to turn our mind to cherishing others. Although it is necessary to be aware of our faults, we should not hate ourself for them. This commitment also advises us to take care of ourself and look after our needs. If we try to live without basic necessities such as sufficient food and shelter we will probably damage our health and undermine our capacity to benefit others. In addition, if people see us behaving in an extreme way, they may conclude that we are unbalanced and consequently will not trust us or believe what we say; and under such circumstances we will not be able to help them. Abandoning self-cherishing completely is not easy and will take a long time. If we are not happy with ourself, or foolishly neglect our own well-being, we will have neither the confidence nor the energy to effect such a radical spiritual transformation.

Once we are free from self-cherishing we do not lose our wish to be happy, but we understand that real happiness is to be found in benefiting others. We have discovered an inexhaustible fountain of happiness within our own mind—our love for others. Difficult external conditions do not depress us and pleasant conditions do not overexcite us, because we are able to transform and enjoy both. Rather than focusing on gathering good external conditions, our desire for happiness is channeled into a determination to attain enlightenment, which we recognize as the only means of achieving pure happiness. Though we long to enjoy the ultimate bliss of full enlightenment, we do so only for the sake of others, because attaining enlightenment is simply the means to fulfill our real wish, which is to bestow the same happiness on all living beings. When we become a Buddha our happiness radiates eternally as compassion, nourishing all living beings and gradually drawing them into the same state.

In short, self-cherishing is an utterly worthless and unnecessary mind. We may be highly intelligent, but if we are only concerned with our own welfare we can never fulfill our basic wish to find happiness. In reality, self-cherishing makes us stupid. It causes us to experience unhappiness in this life, leads us to perform countless negative actions that cause suffering in future lives, binds us to samsara, and blocks the path to enlightenment. Cherishing others has the opposite effects. If we cherish only others we will be happy in this life, we will perform many virtuous actions that lead to happiness in future lives, we will become free from the delusions that keep us in samsara, and we will quickly develop all the qualities needed to attain full enlightenment.

HOW TO DESTROY SELF-CHERISHING

By contemplating the faults of self-cherishing and the benefits of cherishing others, we will develop a strong determination to abandon self-cherishing and to cherish only others. We should hold this determination in meditation for as long as possible. When we arise from meditation, we should try to put our determination into practice and maintain it in all our activities. It is impossible to stop self-cherishing immediately, because it is such a deeply ingrained and all-pervasive mental habit that has been with us since beginningless time. However, through understanding its disadvantages and applying great effort, we can slowly reduce it. We can stop the worst excesses of self-cherishing right now and eliminate the more subtle types of self-cherishing gradually.

Having developed the intention to overcome our self-cherishing, the next step is to recognize it the moment it arises in our mind. To do this we need to examine our mental continuum throughout all our actions. This means that we should practice like Geshe Ben Gungyal and watch our own mind, or mental continuum, in everything we do. Usually we keep an eye on what other people are doing, but it would be much better if we kept an eye on what is going on in our own mind. Whatever actions we are doing, whether working, talking, relaxing, or studying Dharma, one part of our mind should always be watching to check what thoughts are arising. As soon as a delusion is about to arise, we should try to stop it. If we catch a delusion in its early stages, it is quite easy to stop, but if we allow it to develop fully it becomes very difficult to control.

One of our most destructive delusions is anger. Since it is so harmful in our daily life, I give further instructions on how we can deal with the problem of anger in *How to Solve Our Human Problems*. The reason we get angry is that we allow our mind to remain on an object that is likely to stimulate anger. If we catch our mind as soon as it starts to focus on such an object, it is quite easy to prevent anger from arising and to channel our thoughts in a more constructive direction. All we need to do is say to ourself: "This is an inappropriate way of thinking and will soon give rise to anger, which has many faults." However, if we fail to catch the anger early on, and allow it to grow, it will soon become like a raging fire that is very difficult to extinguish. The same is true of all other delusions, including self-cherishing. If we become aware of a selfish train of thought early on, we can easily avert it, but if we allow it to continue, it will gather momentum until it becomes almost impossible to stop.

There are three levels of abandoning delusions. The first is to recognize a particular delusion as it is about to arise, and remembering its disadvantages, prevent it from manifesting. As long as we keep a watch over our mind, this is straightforward and is something we should try to practice all the time, whatever we are doing. In particular, as soon as we notice that our mind is becoming tense or unhappy we should be especially vigilant, because such a mind is a perfect breeding ground for delusions. For this reason, in *Training the Mind in Seven Points* Geshe Chekhawa says: "Always rely upon a happy mind alone."

The second level of abandoning our delusions is to subdue them by applying their specific opponents. For example, to subdue our attachment, we can meditate on the faults of samsara and replace our attachment with the opposite mind of renunciation. Through meditating on the path to enlightenment in a regular, systematic way, we not only prevent deluded patterns of thinking and feeling from arising but we also replace them with strong and stable virtuous patterns, based on wisdom rather than ignorance. In this way, we can prevent most delusions from arising in the first place. For instance, through deep familiarity with the view that others are more important than ourself, self-cherishing will rarely arise.

The third level of abandoning our delusions is to abandon them completely, together with their seeds, by gaining a direct realization of emptiness. In this way we destroy self-grasping, which is the root of all delusions.

In the practice of equalizing self and others that was explained earlier, we think, "Just as my happiness is important, so is the happiness of everyone else," and in this way we share our feeling of cherishing. Because this appeals to our sense of fairness and does not directly challenge our self-cherishing mind, it is easier to accept and practice. We can also reflect that, no matter how much we may suffer, we are only one single person while other living beings are countless, so it is obviously important for them to experience at least some peace and happiness. Although we regard each of our fingers and thumbs as precious, we would be prepared to sacrifice one to save the other nine, while sacrificing nine to save one would be absurd. Similarly, nine people are more important than one, so of course countless living beings are more important than one self alone. It follows that it is logical to cherish others at least as much as we cherish ourself.

Having gained some familiarity with the practice of equalizing self and others, we are ready to confront the self-cherishing mind more directly. Because self-cherishing has so many faults, we should encourage ourself to confront and overcome it the moment it arises in our mind. By keeping a close watch over our mind all the time, we can train ourself to recognize self-cherishing the moment it arises and then immediately recall its disadvantages. Geshe Chekhawa advises us to "Gather all blame into one," by which he means that we should blame self-cherishing for all our problems and suffering. Normally when things go wrong we blame others, but the real cause of our problems is our self-cherishing mind. Once we have correctly identified self-cherishing, we should regard it as our worst enemy and blame it for all our suffering. Although it is good to be tolerant of others and to forgive their weaknesses, we should never tolerate our self-cherishing, because the more lenient we are with it the more it will harm us. It is far better to be utterly ruthless and blame it for everything that goes wrong. If we want to be angry with something, we should be angry with the "demon" of our self-cherishing. In reality, anger directed against self-cherishing is not real anger, because it is based on wisdom rather than ignorance and functions to make our mind pure and peaceful.

To practice in this way, we need to be very skillful. If, as a result of blaming our self-cherishing for all our problems, we find ourself feeling guilty and inadequate, this indicates that we have not made a clear distinction between blaming our self-cherishing and blaming ourself. Although it is true that self-cherishing is to blame for all our problems, this does not mean that we ourself are to blame. Once again, we have to learn to distinguish between ourself and our delusions. If we are attacked it is not our fault but the fault of our self-cherishing. Why? Because it is the karmic effect of a non-virtuous action we performed in a previous life under the influence of self-cherishing. In addition, our attacker harms us only because of his or her self-cherishing, and blaming him will not help, because it will only make us bitter. However, if we place all the blame on our self-cherishing mind and resolve to destroy it, we will not only remain undisturbed but also undermine the basis for all our future suffering.

This teaching on recognizing the faults of our self-cherishing and subsequently developing the desire to overcome it is not easy to put into practice, and so we need to be patient. A practice that is suitable for one person is not necessarily suitable for someone else, and a practice that is appropriate for one person at one time is not necessarily appropriate for that same person at another time. Buddha did not expect us to put all his teachings into practice right away—they are intended for a great variety of practitioners of different levels and dispositions. There are also some instructions that cannot be practiced while we are emphasizing other practices, just as it is not appropriate to drink tea and coffee together at the same time. Dharma instructions are like medicine and need to be administered skillfully, taking into account the nature of the individual and his or her particular needs. For example, to encourage us to develop renunciation, the wish to attain liberation from samsara, Buddha gave extensive teachings on how ordinary life is in the nature of suffering—but not everyone can apply these teachings right away. For some people, meditating on suffering only causes them to become despondent. Instead of developing a joyful mind of renunciation, they just get depressed. For these people it is better for the time being not to meditate on suffering but to come back to it later when their minds are stronger and their wisdom clearer.

If we practice advanced teachings and find that our pride or confusion increase, this indicates that we are not yet ready for such teachings and should first emphasize building a firm foundation of basic practices. If any meditation or practice is not having a good effect on our mind, is making us unhappy, or is increasing our delusions, this is a clear sign that we are practicing incorrectly. Rather than stubbornly pushing at the practice, it may be better to put it to one side for the time being and seek advice from senior practitioners. We can go back to that practice once we understand where we are going wrong and what the correct way of practicing is. What we should never do, however, is reject any Dharma instruction by thinking, "I will never practice this."

When we go shopping, we do not feel impelled to buy everything in the store, but it is useful to remember what the store sells so that we can return later when we need something. In a similar way, when we listen to Dharma teachings, we may not immediately be able to practice all that we hear, but it is still important to remember everything so that we can build up a comprehensive understanding of Dharma. Later, when we are ready, we can put the instructions we have heard into practice. One of the great advantages of the instructions on Lamrim—the stages of the path to enlightenment—is that it gives us a structure, or storehouse, within which we can keep all the Dharma teachings we have heard.

If we only remember those teachings that we are immediately able to apply in our present situation, when our circumstances change we will have nothing to fall back on. However, if we can remember all the teachings we have received, we will have at our disposal a huge range of instructions that we can apply at the appropriate time. A practice that may seem obscure and of little significance to us now may later become an essential part of our spiritual practice.

Expecting quick results is itself based on self-cherishing and is a recipe for disappointment.

What is important is to proceed carefully and at our own pace, otherwise we might feel confused or discouraged and may even end up rejecting Dharma altogether.

There is no greater spiritual practice than recognizing self-cherishing whenever it arises and then blaming it for all our problems. It does not matter how long we spend on this. Even if it takes years or our whole life, we need to continue until our self-cherishing is completely destroyed. We should not be in a hurry to see results but instead practice patiently and sincerely. Expecting quick results is itself based on self-cherishing and is a recipe for disappointment. If we practice with joy and steadfastness, while at the same time purifying negativity, accumulating merit, and receiving blessings, we will definitely succeed in reducing and finally abandoning our self-cherishing.

Even when our meditation is not going well, we can practice mindfulness and alertness in our daily life and stop self-cherishing as soon as it arises. This is a simple practice but it has great results. If we train in it continuously, our problems will disappear and we will naturally be happy all the time. There are people who have succeeded in completely abandoning their self-cherishing and who now cherish only others. As a result, all their problems have disappeared and their minds are always filled with joy. I can guarantee that the less you cherish yourself and the more you cherish others the happier you will become.

We should keep a strong determination in our heart to abandon our self-cherishing mind. If we apply armor-like effort in this determination day by day, year by year, our self-cherishing will gradually diminish and eventually cease altogether. The early Kadampa Geshes would often say that to lead a virtuous life all we need to do is harm our delusions as much as possible and benefit others as much as possible. Understanding this, we should wage continuous warfare against our inner enemy of self-cherishing and strive to cherish and benefit others instead.

To destroy our self-cherishing completely, we need to rely on the practice of exchanging self with others, in which we no longer grasp at our own happiness but instead feel that other people, and their needs and wishes, are of supreme importance. Our only concern is for the well-being of others.

Although someone who has completely exchanged himself with others has no self-cherishing, this does not mean that he does not look after himself. He does look after himself, but for the sake of others. He regards himself as a servant of all living beings and as belonging to them; but even servants need to eat and rest if they are to be effective. It would generally be very foolish, for example, if we gave away all we owned, leaving ourself with nothing to live on or to sustain our spiritual practice. Since our real wish is to benefit all living beings, and the only way we can do this is by becoming a Buddha, we need to protect our spiritual practice by organizing our life so that we are able to practice in the most effective way. In addition, when we help others, we should also make sure that in helping one person we are not undermining our capacity to help many people. Although in our hearts we would gladly give away everything we have to help one person, practically we need to manage our time and resources so that we can be of the greatest benefit to all living beings.

The practice of exchanging self with others belongs to the special wisdom lineage that came from Buddha Shakyamuni through Manjushri and Shantideva to Atisha and Je Tsongkhapa. The bodhichitta that is developed through this method is more profound and powerful than the bodhichitta developed through other methods. Although everyone with an interest in spiritual development can reduce their self-cherishing and learn to cherish others, a complete realization of exchanging self with others is a very profound attainment. To transform our mind in such a radical way, we need deep faith in this practice, an abundance of merit, and powerful blessings from a Spiritual Guide who has personal experience of these teachings. With all these conducive conditions, the practice of exchanging self with others is not difficult.

We may wonder why it is necessary to cherish others more than ourself. Rather than aiming for such high spiritual realizations, wouldn't it be better just to emphasize helping people in a practical way right now? The reason why we need to train our mind in exchanging self with others is because our self-cherishing interferes with both our intention and our ability to benefit others. With self-cherishing, we do not have unbiased, universal love for all living beings, and for as long as our desire to help them is mixed with self-cherishing we can never be sure that our actions will actually benefit them. Although we may genuinely want to help some people, such as our family, our friends, or those in need, we usually expect something back in return and are hurt and disappointed if we do not receive it. Since our wish to benefit is mixed with selfish concerns, our help nearly always comes with the strings of expectation or personal reward. Because our intention is impure, our ability to help lacks power and remains limited.

If, while making no effort to eliminate our self-cherishing, we claim to be working for the benefit of all, our claim is coming from our mouth and not from our heart. Of course we should help others practically whenever we can, but we should always remember that our main intention is to develop our mind. By training in exchanging self with others we will finally experience the ultimate happiness of Buddhahood and possess complete power to benefit all living beings. Only then will we be in a position to say, "I am a benefactor of all living beings." In this way, our training in exchanging self with others accomplishes both our own and others' purpose.

Our most important task at the moment is to train our mind, and in particular to strengthen our intention to be of service to others. In his *Friendly Letter* Nagarjuna says that although we may not have the ability to help others now, if we always keep in mind the intention to do so, our ability to help them will gradually increase. This is because the more we cherish others, the more our merit, wisdom, and capacity to actually benefit them will increase, and opportunities to help in practical ways will naturally present themselves.

HOW IS IT POSSIBLE TO EXCHANGE SELF WITH OTHERS?

Exchanging self with others does not mean that we become the other person—it means that we exchange the object of our cherishing from self to others. To understand how this is possible we should understand that the object of our self-cherishing mind is always changing. When we are young, the object of our self-cherishing is a young girl or boy, but later it changes to a teenager, then to a middle-aged person, and finally to an old person. At the moment, we may cherish ourself as a particular human being called Maria or John, but after we die the object of our cherishing will completely change. In this way, the object of our cherishing is continually changing, both during this life and from one life to the next. Since our cherishing naturally changes from one object to another, it is definitely possible through training in meditation for us to change the object of our cherishing from self to others.

Due to our ignorance we grasp at our body very strongly, thinking, "This is my body." Identifying with this body as "mine," we cherish and love it dearly, feeling that it is our most precious possession. In reality, however, our body belongs to others—we did not bring it with us from our previous life but received it from our parents of this life. At the moment of conception our consciousness entered into the union of our father's sperm and mother's ovum, which gradually developed into our present body. Our mind then identified with this body and we began to cherish it. As Shantideva says in *Guide to the Bodhisattva's Way of Life*, our body is not really our own but belongs to others; it was produced by others, and after our death will be disposed of by others. If we contemplate this carefully, we will realize that we are already cherishing an object that in reality belongs to others, so why can't we cherish other living beings? Furthermore, while cherishing our body only leads to rebirth within samsara, cherishing others is a cause for attaining the nirvana of full enlightenment, the state beyond sorrow.

"Self" and "other" are relative terms, similar to "this mountain" and "that mountain" but not like "donkey" and "horse." When we look at a horse, we cannot say that it is a donkey, and likewise we cannot say that a donkey is a horse. However, if we climb a mountain in the east we call it "this mountain," and we call the mountain to the west "that mountain." But if we climb down the eastern mountain and up the western mountain, we then refer to the western mountain as "this mountain" and to the eastern mountain as "that mountain." "This" and "that" therefore depend on our point of reference. This is also true of self and other. By climbing down the mountain of self, it is possible to ascend the mountain of other, and thereby cherish others as much as we now cherish ourself. We can do this by recognizing that, from another person's point of view, it is he or she who is self while it is we who are other.

Those who are skilled in Secret Mantra, or Tantra, have a profound experience of exchanging self with others. In the Tantric practice of self-generation, we exchange our present self with that of a Tantric Buddha. Suppose there is a Vajrayogini practitioner called Sarah. Whenever she is not engaged in Tantric practice, her ordinary body appears to her and she identifies with it and cherishes it. When she concentrates deeply on self-generation meditation, however, the sense of being Sarah and having Sarah's body completely disappears. Instead of identifying with Sarah's body, the practitioner identifies with the divine body of Buddha Vajrayogini and develops the thought, "I am Vajrayogini." The practitioner has now entirely changed the object of cherishing from the impure body of an ordinary being to the uncontaminated body of an enlightened being, Buddha Vajrayogini. Through training in meditation, the practitioner develops deep familiarity with the body of the Deity and comes to identify with it completely. Because Vajrayogini's body is a pure body, identifying with it and cherishing it is a cause of enlightenment. From this we can see that it is possible to change our basis of identification—it just depends on our motivation and our familiarity. A detailed explanation of Tantric practice can be found in *Guide to Dakini Land* and *Tantric Grounds and Paths*.

THE ACTUAL PRACTICE OF EXCHANGING SELF WITH OTHERS

We think:

I have worked for my own purpose since beginningless time, trying to find happiness for myself and avoid suffering, but what do I have to show for all my efforts? I am still suffering. I still have an uncontrolled mind. I still experience disappointment after disappointment. I am still in samsara. This is the fault of my self-cherishing. It is my worst enemy and a terrible poison that harms both myself and others.

Cherishing others, however, is the basis of all happiness and goodness. Those who are now Buddhas saw the futility of working for their own purpose and decided to work for others instead. As a result, they became pure beings, free from all the problems of samsara, and they attained the lasting happiness of full enlightenment. I must reverse my ordinary childish attitude—from now on I will stop cherishing myself and cherish only others.

This decision will give rise to a deep feeling of cherishing love for all living beings, and we meditate on this feeling for as long as we can.

We try to carry this feeling with us during the meditation break. Whoever we meet, we think: "This person is important. Their happiness and freedom are important." Whenever self-cherishing begins to arise in our mind, we think: "Self-cherishing is poison, I will not allow it in my mind." In this way we can change our object of cherishing from ourself to all living beings. When we have developed a love for all living beings that does not have even the slightest trace of self-concern, we have gained the realization of exchanging self with others.

If our wishes are not fulfilled and we begin to feel unhappy, we should immediately remember that the fault does not lie with the other person or the situation but with our own self-cherishing mind, which instinctively feels, "My wishes are of paramount importance." Remaining continually mindful of the dangers of our self-cherishing will strengthen our resolve to abandon it, and instead of feeling sorry for ourself when we have problems, we can use our own suffering to remind us of the suffering of countless mother beings and develop love and compassion for them.

In *Guide to the Bodhisattva's Way of Life*, Shantideva explains a special method to enhance our experience of exchanging self with others. In meditation we imagine that we exchange places with another person, and we try to see the world from his or her point of view. Normally we develop the thought "I" on the basis of our own body and mind, but now we try to think "I" observing the body and mind of another person. This practice helps us develop a profound empathy with other people, and shows us that they have a self that is also an I, and that is just as important as our own self or I. Because of her ability to identify with the feelings of her baby, a mother is able to understand her child's needs and wishes far better than other people. Similarly, as we become familiar with this meditation, our understanding of and empathy with other people will increase.

This technique is particularly powerful when we apply it to someone we have a difficult relationship with, such as someone we dislike or see as our rival. By imagining we are that person, and seeing the situation from his or her point of view, we will find it difficult to hold onto our deluded attitudes. Understanding the relativity of self and other from our own experience, and learning to see our "self" as "other," we will become far more objective and impartial toward our self, and our sense that we are the center of the universe will be shaken. We will become more open to others' point of view, more tolerant, and more understanding. And we will naturally treat others with greater respect and consideration. More details on this practice are given in *Meaningful to Behold*.

In summary, through practicing the instructions of training the mind, Bodhisattva Langri Tangpa and countless other practitioners of the past have attained profound spiritual realizations, including the complete realization of exchanging self with others. At the beginning, these practitioners were self-centered people just like us, but through constant perseverance they managed to eliminate their self-cherishing completely. If we practice these instructions wholeheartedly and patiently, there is no reason why we too should not attain similar realizations. We should not expect to destroy our self-cherishing immediately, but through patient practice it will gradually become weaker and weaker until eventually it ceases altogether.

Great Compassion

Great Compassion

Having gained some experience of cherishing all living beings, we can now extend and deepen our compassion, and the method for doing so is revealed in this chapter. In general, everyone already has some compassion. We all feel compassion when we see our family or friends in distress, and even animals feel compassion when they see their offspring in pain. Our compassion is our Buddha seed or Buddha nature, our potential to become a Buddha. It is because all living beings possess this seed that they will all eventually become Buddhas.

When a dog sees her puppies in pain, she develops the wish to protect them and free them from pain, and this compassionate wish is her Buddha seed. Unfortunately, however, animals have no ability to train in compassion, and so their Buddha seed cannot ripen. Human beings, though, have a great opportunity to develop their Buddha nature. Through meditation we can extend and deepen our compassion until it transforms into the mind of great compassion—the wish to protect all living beings without exception from their suffering. Through improving this mind of great, or universal, compassion, it will eventually transform into the compassion of a Buddha, which actually has the power to protect all living beings. Therefore, the way to become a Buddha is to awaken our compassionate Buddha nature and complete the training in universal compassion. Only human beings can do this.

Compassion is the very essence of a spiritual life and the main practice of those who have devoted their lives to attaining enlightenment. It is the root of the Three Jewels—Buddha, Dharma, and Sangha. It is the root of Buddha because all Buddhas are born from compassion. It is the root of Dharma because Buddhas give Dharma teachings motivated solely by compassion for others. It is the root of Sangha because it is by listening to and practicing Dharma teachings given out of compassion that we become Sangha, or Superior beings.

WHAT IS COMPASSION?

What exactly is compassion? Compassion is a mind that is motivated by cherishing other living beings and wishes to release them from their suffering. Sometimes out of selfish intention we can wish for another person to be free from their suffering—this is quite common in relationships that are based principally on attachment. If our friend is ill or depressed, for example, we may wish him to recover quickly so that we can enjoy his company again. But this wish is basically self-centered and is not true compassion. True compassion is necessarily based on cherishing others.

Although we already have some degree of compassion, at present it is very biased and limited. When our family and friends are suffering, we easily develop compassion for them, but we find it much more difficult to feel sympathy for people we find unpleasant or for strangers. Furthermore, we feel compassion for those who are experiencing manifest pain, but not for those who are enjoying good conditions, and especially not for those who are engaging in harmful actions. If we genuinely want to realize our potential by attaining full enlightenment we need to increase the scope of our compassion until it embraces all living beings without exception, just as a loving mother feels compassion for all her children regardless of whether they are behaving well or badly. This universal compassion is the heart of Mahayana Buddhism. Unlike our present, limited compassion, which already arises naturally from time to time, universal compassion must first be cultivated through training over a long period of time.

HOW TO DEVELOP COMPASSION

There are two essential stages to cultivating universal compassion. First we need to love all living beings, and then we need to contemplate their suffering. If we do not love someone, we cannot develop real compassion for him even if he is in pain, but if we contemplate the suffering of someone we love, compassion will arise spontaneously. This is why we feel compassion for our friends or relatives but not for people we do not like. Cherishing others is the foundation for developing compassion. The way to develop and enhance our mind of cherishing love has already been explained. Now we need to consider how each and every samsaric being is experiencing suffering.

To begin with, we can think about those who are suffering intense manifest pain right now. There are so many people experiencing terrible mental and physical suffering from illnesses such as cancer, AIDS, and Parkinson's disease. How many people have lost a beloved child or friend through the scourge of AIDS, watching him become weaker and weaker, knowing that there is no cure? Every day, thousands of people experience the agony of dying from illnesses or in accidents. Without choice they are separated forever from everyone they love, and those they leave behind often experience inconsolable grief and loneliness. Imagine an old woman losing her husband and lifelong partner, sadly returning home after the funeral to an empty house to live out the rest of her days alone.

Throughout the world we can see how millions of people are suffering through the horrors of war and ethnic cleansing, from bombing, landmines, and massacres. Suppose it was your child who went out to play in the fields and lost a limb, or even his life, by stepping on a land mine? Hundreds of thousands of refugees throughout the world live in squalid camps, hoping someday to return to their ruined homes, many of them waiting to be reunited with their loved ones, every day not knowing if they are alive or dead.

Every year natural disasters such as floods, earthquakes, and hurricanes devastate whole communities and leave people homeless and hungry. A few short seconds of an earthquake can kill thousands of people, destroy their homes, and bury everything under tons of rubble. How would we feel if this happened to us? Famine and drought are endemic in many countries throughout the world. So many people live on a subsistence diet, barely scraping together one meager meal a day, while others who are less fortunate succumb and die of starvation. Imagine the torment of watching your loved ones slowly waste away, knowing that there is nothing you can do. Whenever we read a newspaper or watch the news on television, we see living beings who are in terrible pain, and we all personally know people who are experiencing immense mental or physical suffering.

We can also consider the plight of countless animals who experience extremes of heat and cold, and suffer great hunger and thirst. Every day, all around us, we can see the suffering of animals. Animals in the wild are in almost constant fear of being prey to others, and in fact many of them are eaten alive by predators. Just think of the terror and pain a field mouse experiences when caught and ripped to shreds by a hawk! Countless animals are kept by humans for labor, food, or entertainment, and often live in disgusting conditions until they are slaughtered, butchered, and packaged for human consumption. Hungry spirits and hell beings have to experience far worse sufferings, for inconceivably long periods of time.

There is no such thing as an ordinary person who has fulfilled all his or her wishes—only those who have transcended selfish minds can do this.

We also need to remember that even those who are not currently experiencing manifest pain still experience other forms of suffering. Everyone in samsara experiences the suffering of not fulfilling their wishes. So many people find it difficult to satisfy even modest desires for adequate shelter, food, or companionship. And even if those desires are fulfilled, we have more to take their place. The more we get what we want, the stronger our attachment becomes; and the stronger our attachment, the more difficult it is to find satisfaction. The desires of samsaric beings are endless. There is no such thing as an ordinary person who has fulfilled all his or her wishes—only those who have transcended selfish minds can do this.

All suffering is the result of negative karma. If we develop compassion for those who are experiencing the effects of their previous negative actions, why can't we also develop compassion for those who are creating the cause to experience suffering in the future? In the long term a torturer is in a worse position than his victim, because his suffering is just beginning. If the victim can accept his or her pain without developing hatred, he will exhaust that particular negative karma and not create any more, and so his suffering has an end in sight. The torturer, on the other hand, will first have to endure many eons in hell, and then, when he is again reborn as a human being, will have to experience pain similar to that which he inflicted on the victim. For this reason it is entirely appropriate to develop strong compassion for such people.

If a child burns himself by putting his hand in a fire, this will not stop his mother from feeling compassion, even if the child has been previously warned about the dangers of fire. No one actually wants to suffer—living beings create the causes of suffering because they are controlled by their delusions. Therefore we should feel equal compassion for all living beings—for those who are creating the causes of suffering, as much as for those who are already suffering the consequences of their unskillful actions. There is not a single living being who is not a suitable object of our compassion.

We may also find it difficult to feel compassion for the rich, healthy, and well respected, who do not appear to be experiencing any manifest pain. In reality, however, they too experience a great deal of mental suffering and find it hard to maintain a peaceful mind. They worry about their money, their bodies, and their reputation. Like all other samsaric beings, they suffer from anger, attachment, and ignorance, and have no choice but to undergo the sufferings of birth, aging, sickness, and death unceasingly and relentlessly, life after life. In addition, their wealth and good conditions are utterly meaningless if, through their ignorance, they use them only to create the cause for future suffering.

If, on the basis of a heartfelt love for all living beings, we contemplate their pain, their inability to fulfill their wishes, how they are sowing the seeds for their future suffering, and their lack of freedom, we will develop deep compassion for them. We need to empathize with them and feel their pain as intensely as we feel our own. To begin with, we can contemplate the suffering of our family and close friends, and then we can extend our mind of compassion until it embraces all living beings. When this feeling of universal compassion arises, we mix our mind with it and try to hold it for as long as we can. In this way, we can familiarize our mind with great compassion. At first we will probably only be able to hold this feeling for a few minutes, but gradually through training we will be able to maintain it for longer and longer periods until it arises spontaneously day and night and permeates all our thoughts. From that point on, everything we do will bring us closer to enlightenment and our whole life will become meaningful.

In summary, everyone who has been reborn in samsara has to experience suffering. Human beings have no choice but to experience human suffering, animals have to experience animal suffering, and hungry spirits and hell beings have to experience all the sufferings of their respective realms. If living beings experienced all this suffering for just one single life it would not be so bad, but the cycle of suffering continues life after life, endlessly. Contemplating this relentless cycle, we develop a strong wish to release all living beings from samsaric rebirth and lead them to a state of permanent liberation, and we meditate on this universal compassion.

THE INNER WEALTH OF COMPASSION

When we arise from meditation, we try to carry our feeling of compassion into the meditation break. Whenever we encounter anyone, we should recall how they are suffering and develop compassion for them. Then, just seeing a living being will be like finding a rare and precious treasure. This is because the compassion we experience when meeting others is a supreme inner wealth that is an inexhaustible source of benefit for us in both this and future lives.

As mentioned earlier, external wealth cannot help us in our future lives, and even in this life it is not certain that it will bring us happiness because it is often the cause of much anxiety and can even endanger our life. Rich people have particular worries that poor people never have. For example, they often worry about thieves, about investments and interest rates, and about losing their money and social status. This is a heavy burden for them. While most people can go out freely whenever they choose, many wealthy and famous people need bodyguards and may even worry about being kidnapped. Rich people have little freedom or independence and can never fully relax. The higher up we are in the world the further we have to fall; it is safer to be nearer the bottom.

No matter how much we succeed in improving our external conditions, they can never bring us pure happiness or provide real protection from suffering. True happiness cannot be found in this impure world. Instead of striving to obtain external wealth, it would be far better if we sought the internal wealth of virtue, because unlike external wealth, this can never deceive us and will definitely bring us the peace and happiness we desire.

If we are skillful, friends can be like treasure chests, from whom we can gain the precious wealth of love, compassion, patience, and so forth. For our friends to function in this way, however, our love for them must be free from attachment. If our love for our friends is mixed with strong attachment, it will be conditional on their behaving in ways that please us, and as soon as they do something we disapprove of, our fondness for them may turn into anger. In fact, the most common objects of our anger are often our friends, not our enemies or strangers!

If we often get angry with our friends, we are transforming them into maras. A mara, or demon, is someone or something that interferes with our spiritual practice. No one is a mara from his or her own side, but if we allow people to stimulate deluded minds in us, such as anger, strong attachment, or self-cherishing, we transform them into maras for us. A mara does not need to have horns and a terrifying expression; someone who appears to be a good friend, who flatters us and leads us into meaningless activities, can be a greater obstacle to our spiritual practice. Whether our friends are precious treasures or maras depends entirely on us; if we are sincerely practicing patience, compassion, and love, they can be like priceless jewels, but if we are often getting angry with them, they can become maras.

We would be delighted to find a treasure chest buried beneath the ground or to win a large amount of money, and would consider ourself very fortunate. However, if we consider the deceptiveness of external wealth and the superiority of the inner wealth of virtue, shouldn't we feel much more fortunate whenever we meet another living being, the potential source of limitless inner wealth? For sincere, compassionate practitioners, just seeing other living beings, speaking with them, or even thinking about them is like finding buried treasure. All their encounters with other people serve to enhance their compassion, and even everyday activities such as shopping or chatting to friends become causes of enlightenment.

Of all virtuous minds, compassion is supreme. Compassion purifies our mind, and when our mind is pure its objects also become pure. There are many accounts of spiritual practitioners who, by developing strong compassion, purified their minds of the negativity that had long been obstructing their spiritual progress. For example, Asanga, a great Buddhist Master who lived in India in the fifth century AD, meditated in an isolated mountain cave in order to gain a vision of Buddha Maitreya. After twelve years he still had not succeeded, and feeling discouraged, abandoned his retreat. On his way down the mountain he came across an old dog lying in the middle of the path. Its body was covered with maggot-infested sores and it seemed close to death. This sight induced within Asanga an overwhelming feeling of compassion for all living beings trapped within samsara. As he was painstakingly removing the maggots from the dying dog, Buddha Maitreya suddenly appeared to him. Maitreya explained that he had been with Asanga since the beginning of his retreat, but due to the impurities in Asanga's mind, Asanga had not been able to see him. It was Asanga's extraordinary compassion that had finally purified the karmic obstructions preventing him from seeing Maitreya. In reality the dog had been an emanation of Buddha Maitreya all along—Maitreya emanated as a suffering dog for the purpose of arousing Asanga's compassion. We can see from this how Buddhas manifest in many different ways to help living beings.

Anyone who dies with a mind of pure compassion will definitely be reborn in a Pure Land, where he or she will never again have to experience the sufferings of samsara. The Bodhisattva Geshe Chekhawa's main wish was to be reborn in hell so that he could help the beings suffering there. As he lay on his deathbed, however, he perceived a vision of the Pure Land and realized that his wish would not be fulfilled. Instead of being reborn in hell, he had no choice but to go to the Pure Land! This was because his compassion had purified his mind to such an extent that, from the point of view of his own experience, impure objects such as hell realms no longer existed—for him everything was pure.

We may find these stories difficult to believe, but this is because we do not understand the relationship between our mind and its objects. We feel that the world exists "out there," independent of the mind that perceives it. But in reality objects are totally dependent on the minds that perceive them. This impure world that we currently experience exists only in relation to our impure mind. Once we have completely purified our mind through training in exchanging self with others, compassion, and so forth, this impure world will disappear and we will perceive a new, pure world. Our sense that things exist separately from our mind, with their own fixed, inherent natures, comes from our ignorance. When we understand the true nature of things, we will see that our world is like a dream, in that everything exists as a mere appearance to mind. We will realize that we can change our world simply by changing our mind, and that if we wish to be free from suffering, all we need to do is purify our mind. Having purified our own mind, we will then be in a position to fulfill our compassionate wish by showing others how to do the same.

Considering all these benefits of compassion, we should resolve to make use of every opportunity to develop it. The most important thing is to put the teachings on compassion into practice, otherwise for us they will remain just empty words.

Pure compassion is a mind that finds the suffering of others unbearable, but it does not make us depressed. In fact, it gives us tremendous energy to work for others and to complete the spiritual path for their sake. It shatters our complacency and makes it impossible to rest content with the superficial happiness of satisfying our worldly desires, but in its place we will come to know a deep inner peace that cannot be disturbed by changing conditions. It is impossible for strong delusions to arise in a mind filled with compassion. If we do not develop delusions, external circumstances alone have no power to disturb us; so when our mind is governed by compassion it is always at peace. This is the experience of all those who have developed their compassion beyond the limited compassion normally felt for a close karmic circle into a selfless compassion for all living beings.

Developing compassion and wisdom and helping those in need is the true meaning of life.

Developing compassion and wisdom, and helping those in need whenever possible, is the true meaning of life. By increasing our compassion we come closer to enlightenment and to the fulfillment of our deepest wishes. How kind living beings are to act as the objects of our compassion. How precious they are! If there were no suffering beings left for us to help, Buddhas would have to emanate them for us! Indeed, if we consider the story of Maitreya and Asanga, we will see that we have no way of knowing for sure whether those we are currently trying to help are not in fact emanations of Buddha, manifested for our benefit. The indication that we have mastered the meditations on cherishing others and compassion is that whenever we meet another person, even someone who is harming us, we genuinely feel as if we had found a rare and precious treasure.

Wishing Love

Wishing Love

*I*n general, there are three types of love: affectionate love, cherishing love, and wishing love. Affectionate love is a mind unmixed with desirous attachment that sees another person as pleasant, likable, or beautiful. For example, when a mother looks at her children she feels great affection for them and perceives them to be beautiful, no matter how they appear to other people. Because of her affectionate love, she naturally feels them to be precious and important—this feeling is cherishing love. Because she cherishes her children, she sincerely wishes for them to be happy—this wish is wishing love. Wishing love arises from cherishing love, which in turn arises from affectionate love. We need to develop these three types of love toward all living beings without exception.

HOW TO DEVELOP WISHING LOVE

The way to develop and enhance our cherishing love has already been explained. Now we need to develop and enhance wishing love by contemplating how these living beings whom we cherish so much lack true happiness. Everyone wants to be happy, but no one in samsara experiences true happiness. In comparison with the amount of suffering they endure, the happiness of living beings is rare and fleeting, and even this is only a contaminated happiness that is in reality the nature of suffering. Buddha called the pleasurable feelings that result from worldly enjoyments *changing suffering* because they are simply the experience of a temporary reduction of manifest suffering. In other words, we experience pleasure due to the relief of our previous pain. For example, the pleasure we derive from eating is really just a temporary reduction of our hunger, the pleasure we derive from drinking is merely a temporary reduction of our thirst, and the pleasure we derive from ordinary relationships is for the most part merely a temporary reduction of our underlying loneliness.

How can we understand this? If we increase the cause of our worldly happiness, our happiness will gradually change into suffering. When we eat our favorite food, it tastes wonderful, but if we were to continue plateful after plateful our enjoyment would soon change into discomfort, disgust, and eventually pain. The reverse, however, does not happen with painful experiences. For instance, hitting our finger with a hammer again and again can never become pleasurable, because it is a true cause of suffering. Just as a true cause of suffering can never give rise to happiness, so a true cause of happiness can never give rise to pain. Since the pleasurable feelings resulting from worldly enjoyments do turn into pain, it follows that they cannot be real happiness. Prolonged indulgence in eating, sports, sex, or any other ordinary enjoyment invariably leads to suffering. No matter how hard we try to find happiness in worldly pleasures, we will never succeed. As mentioned earlier, indulging in samsaric pleasures is like drinking salt water; rather than satisfying our thirst, the more we drink the thirstier we become. In samsara we never reach a point when we can say, "Now I am completely satisfied. I don't need anything else."

Not only is worldly pleasure not true happiness, but it also does not last. People devote their lives to acquiring possessions and social standing, and building up a home, a family, and a circle of friends. But when they die they lose everything. Everything they have worked for suddenly disappears, and they enter their next life alone and empty-handed. They long to form deep and lasting friendships with others, but in samsara this is impossible. The dearest lovers will eventually be torn apart, and when they meet again in a future life they will not recognize each other. We may feel that those who have good relationships and have accomplished their ambitions in life are truly happy, but in reality their happiness is as fragile as a water bubble. Impermanence spares nothing and no one; in samsara all our dreams are broken in the end. As Buddha says in the *Vinaya Sutras*:

The end of collection is dispersion.
The end of rising is falling.
The end of meeting is parting.
The end of birth is death.

The nature of samsara is suffering, so for as long as living beings are reborn in samsara they can never experience true happiness. Buddha compared living in samsara to sitting on top of a pin—no matter how much we try to adjust our position it is always painful. Similarly, no matter how hard we try to adjust and improve our samsaric situation it will always irritate us and give rise to pain. True happiness can only be found by attaining liberation from samsara. Through contemplating this, we will develop a heartfelt desire for all living beings to experience pure happiness by attaining liberation.

We should begin our meditation by focusing on our family and friends, reflecting that for as long as they remain in samsara they will never know true happiness, and that even the limited happiness they now experience will soon be taken away from them.

Love is the great protector. Then we extend this feeling of wishing love to include all living beings, thinking, "How wonderful it would be if all living beings experienced the pure happiness of liberation!" We mix our mind with this feeling of wishing love for as long as possible. Out of meditation, whenever we see or remember any living being, human or animal, we mentally pray: "May they be happy all the time. May they attain the happiness of enlightenment." By constantly thinking like this, we can maintain wishing love day and night, even during sleep.

Meditation on love is very powerful. Even if our concentration is not very strong we accumulate a vast amount of merit. By meditating on love, we create the cause to be reborn as a human or a god, to have a beautiful body in the future, and to be loved and respected by many people. Love is the great protector, protecting us from anger and jealousy and from harm inflicted by spirits. When Buddha Shakyamuni was meditating under the Bodhi Tree, he was attacked by all the terrifying demons of this world, but his love transformed their weapons into a rain of flowers. Ultimately our love will become the universal love of a Buddha, which actually has the power to bestow happiness on all living beings.

Most relationships between people are based on a mixture of love and attachment. This is not pure love because it is based on a desire for our own happiness—we value the other person because they make us feel good. Pure love is unmixed with attachment and stems entirely from a concern for others' happiness. It never gives rise to problems but only to peace and happiness for both ourself and others. We need to remove attachment from our minds, but this does not mean that we have to abandon our relationships. Instead, we should learn to distinguish attachment from love, and gradually try to remove all traces of attachment from our relationships and to improve our love until it becomes pure.

TRANSFORMING ADVERSE CONDITIONS

When things are going well, and people are kind and treating us with respect, it is not so difficult to wish for them to be happy. However, if our love for others diminishes as soon as they cause us problems or fail to appreciate us, this indicates that our love is not pure. For as long as our good feelings for others are conditional upon their treating us well, our love will be weak and unstable and we will not be able to transform it into universal love. It is inevitable that people will sometimes respond to our kindness in ungrateful and negative ways, and so it is essential that we find a way of transforming this experience into the spiritual path.

Whenever anyone harms us, instead of getting angry we should try to see that person as a Spiritual Teacher and generate a mind of gratitude toward him or her. There are various lines of reasoning we can use to develop this special recognition. We can think:

The only reason people harm me is because I have created the cause for them to do so through my previous negative actions. These people are teaching me about the law of karma. By deceiving me and repaying my help with harm, they are reminding me that in the past I deceived and harmed others. They are betraying me only because I betrayed them or others in previous lives. They are encouraging me to purify my negative karma and to refrain from harmful actions in the future. How kind they are! They must be my Spiritual Guide, emanated by Buddha.

By thinking this way, we transform a situation that would normally give rise to anger or self-pity into a powerful lesson in the need for purification and moral discipline.

Alternatively we can think:

This experience shows me that there is no certainty in samsara. Everything changes. Friends become enemies and enemies become friends. Why is this? Because in samsara everyone is controlled by their delusions and no one has any freedom. This situation is encouraging me to abandon samsaric rebirth, so instead of getting angry or discouraged, I must abandon samsaric rebirth and generate the joyful mind of renunciation—a sincere wish to attain the permanent inner peace of liberation. I pray that I may attain liberation from samsara and that all living beings may attain the same state.

By following this line of reasoning, we view the person who is treating us unkindly as a Spiritual Teacher who is encouraging us to leave samsara and experience pure happiness. This skillful way of viewing our difficulty transforms it into an opportunity to progress on the spiritual path. Since this person is teaching us a profound lesson about the nature of samsara, and having such a beneficial effect on our mind, he or she is supremely kind.

We can also think:

This person who is harming or disturbing me is in reality encouraging me to practice patience. And since it is impossible to make progress on the spiritual path without developing the strong mind of patience, he or she is of great benefit to me.

Patience is a mind motivated by a virtuous intention that happily accepts difficulties and harm from others. A person with no patience has no stability of mind and is upset by the slightest obstacle or criticism. In contrast, when we develop real patience, our mind will be as stable as a mountain and as calm as the depths of an ocean. With such a calm, strong mind it will not be difficult to perfect the spiritual realizations of universal love, great compassion, and bodhichitta.

By thinking skillfully in these ways, we can regard even those who harm or deceive us as our Spiritual Teachers. This is a very important point because it means that everyone can be our Teacher. Whether someone is our Spiritual Teacher or an obstacle to our spiritual progress depends entirely on our mind. In many ways, those who harm us are the kindest of all because they shatter our complacent view that sees samsara as a pleasure garden, and like a powerful Spiritual Guide, they inspire us to engage more strongly in spiritual practice. By thinking this way, we can transform the harm we receive into the spiritual path, and instead of being discouraged, we can learn to cherish even those who harm us. It is especially important to have this attitude toward our close friends and family. Since we spend so much time with them, it would be very beneficial if we regarded them as pure Spiritual Teachers! We have great expectations of our friends, hoping that they will be a source of true happiness, but in samsara we can never find such friends. Even if they do not deliberately try to harm us, they will inevitably cause us problems from time to time. We think that if we search long enough we will find the right friend or perfect partner who will never disappoint us, but in samsara there are no perfect friends. Samsaric relationships are by their very nature deceptive. We hope to find a permanently harmonious and satisfying relationship, but somehow it never works out. There is no need to blame the other person for failing to live up to our expectations—it is the fault of samsaric rebirth. Having taken rebirth in samsara, we have to experience unsatisfactory relationships—it is impossible to find pure friends in this impure world. If we really want to enjoy pure, harmonious relationships, we must abandon samsara. Therefore, when our friends let us down, we should not get angry with them. Instead we should regard them as Spiritual Teachers who are showing us the faults of samsara.

Samsaric places are also deceptive by nature. We think that by moving to another house, moving away from the city, or moving to a different country we will find a place where we can be really comfortable and happy, but for as long as we remain in samsara we will never find such a place. We have moved so often, but still we are not satisfied. When we visit a new area it seems so beautiful, and we feel that if we lived there all our problems would be solved; but once we have actually moved, new problems soon begin to surface. There are no places in this world where we will not experience any problems. If we wish to live in a pure environment, or to find a place where we will always feel at home, we need to purify our mind by developing universal love and compassion.

Although we spend our lives searching for happiness in samsara, moving from friend to friend and from place to place, we will never find true happiness. We are like the thief who entered Milarepa's cave one night, looking for something valuable to steal. Hearing him, Milarepa laughed and said, "I cannot find anything during the day, so how do you expect to find anything at night?" How can we expect to find happiness in the empty cave of samsara while obscured by the darkness of our delusions, when all the Buddhas with their omniscient wisdom have been unable to find it? Samsara is a prison that we must escape from, instead of wasting our time in a fruitless search for happiness within it.

By thinking in these ways, we can transform seemingly adverse conditions into opportunities for spiritual growth. There are two ways of transforming adverse conditions into the path: by means of method and by means of wisdom. We have within us the seeds of Buddhahood, but to transform these seeds into the perfect body and mind of a Buddha we need both to nurture them and to free them from any obstructions to their growth. Practices that nurture the growth of Buddha seeds, such as renunciation, compassion, and bodhichitta, are known as *method practices*. And practices that free Buddha seeds from obstructions are known as *wisdom practices*. When we use our adversities to strengthen our experience of renunciation, cherishing others, and so forth, we are transforming adverse conditions into the path by means of method. When we use our adversities to deepen our realization of ultimate truth, or emptiness, we are transforming adverse conditions into the path by means of wisdom. More details can be found in *Universal Compassion*.

Transforming adverse conditions into the path is vital in these degenerate times because we are constantly surrounded by difficulties, like a candle flame exposed to the wind, blown first from this direction, then from that. There is no way of avoiding difficult situations, but if we can change our attitude toward them they will no longer be problems for us. Instead of allowing adversities to make us unhappy and discouraged, we can use them to enhance our experience of the stages of the spiritual path and in this way maintain a pure and peaceful mind all the time.

In *Wheel of Sharp Weapons*, the great Master Dharmarakshita explains that all the difficulties we experience in this life are the result of the negative actions we committed in previous lives or earlier in this life. If we find it difficult to fulfill our wishes, it is because in the past we prevented others from fulfilling theirs. If we are separated from our friends, it is because we interfered with other people's relationships. If we cannot find trustworthy friends, it is because we deceived people. If our body is racked with sickness, it is because we inflicted physical pain on others. If people find us unattractive, it is because we were frequently angry with others. If we are poor, it is because we stole others' possessions. If we have a short lifespan, it is because we killed others. Dharmarakshita lists many such examples of actions and their effects that are explained by Buddha in Sutras such as the *Hundred Actions Sutra* and the *Vinaya Sutras*. If we read these Sutras, we will be able to recognize all the difficulties we experience in our daily lives as a wheel of sharp weapons that returns full circle upon us for the harm we have caused.

It is important to understand the relationship between actions and their effects. Our normal reaction when faced with a problem is to try and find someone to blame, but if we look at the situation with wisdom, we will realize that we created the cause of that problem through our negative actions. The main cause of all our problems is necessarily a negative bodily, verbal, or mental action that we ourself created in the past; other people's actions are only secondary conditions that enable our negative karma to ripen. If they do not provide the conditions for our negative karma to ripen, someone or something else definitely will; because once the main cause has been established, unless we purify it through purification practice, nothing can stop the effect from occurring sooner or later. Instead of blaming others for our problems, we should use our misfortunes to deepen our understanding of karma.

By training our mind to recognize the spiritual lessons in all our experiences, we can come to view everyone and everything as our Spiritual Teacher and we can turn any and every situation to our advantage. This is a very important understanding because it means that no experience is ever wasted. The time we spend listening to Dharma teachings or reading Dharma books is usually quite limited, but if we can recognize the Dharma lessons in everyday life, we will always be in the presence of our Spiritual Guide. As Milarepa said:

I don't need to read books; everything that appears to my mind is a Dharma book. All things confirm the truth of Buddha's teachings and increase my spiritual experience.

It was because Milarepa saw everything as his Spiritual Teacher that he progressed very swiftly along the spiritual path and attained full enlightenment in that one lifetime.

The function of a Buddha is to reveal holy Dharma and to bestow blessings. Because our Spiritual Guide performs these functions, from our point of view he or she is a Buddha. In a similar way, for a qualified Dharma practitioner all living beings are Spiritual Teachers and all situations are Dharma lessons. If we can hold this special recognition with mindfulness, there will no longer be any obstacles to our spiritual practice, because all our daily experiences will become meaningful and will help to increase our good qualities.

If we are skillful, whoever we see can teach us about the law of karma. When we see or hear about poor people, we can reflect that the experience of poverty is the result of not having practiced giving in the past. This will encourage us to practice giving. When we see animals, we can think that they have taken lower rebirth because they did not practice moral discipline, and in this way are teaching me that I must observe pure moral discipline now. In a similar way, those suffering from anger are teaching me how important it is to practice patience. And all those trapped in the prison of samsara are teaching me that I must abandon laziness and apply great effort to attain a permanent cessation of samsaric rebirth and to help everyone else do the same. By thinking in this way, we will gradually gain a deep experience that all living beings are giving us the priceless gift of Dharma teachings. Instead of looking down on those who are experiencing suffering, we will come to respect and value them as our incomparably precious Spiritual Guides.

Accepting Defeat and
Offering the Victory

Accepting Defeat and Offering the Victory

*H*aving gained some experience of love and compassion for all living beings, we now need to put this good heart into practice in our daily life. For example, when someone out of anger or jealousy harms or insults us, with our mind abiding in love and compassion we should happily accept the harm and not retaliate. This is the meaning of accepting defeat and offering the victory to others. This practice of patience directly protects us from discouragement and unhappiness. The sincere practice of patience is the basis for the realization of taking and giving that is explained in the next chapter.

When inanimate objects or other people cause us problems and we have done everything we can to improve the situation, there is nothing to do but bear our suffering patiently, without getting angry or upset. Once the effects of our negative actions have already ripened it is impossible to avoid them, and not even a Buddha can prevent our suffering. The only thing we can do is practice patience and happily accept our difficulties. In this way, we keep our mind in a balanced and positive state, no matter how bad our external circumstances may be. For example, if we practice patience when we are sick, we will be able to remain calm and peaceful, and if we practice patience when someone harms us, we will have the clarity and calmness of mind to respond in a constructive way, without anger or self-pity. Whenever we find ourself in an unpleasant or painful situation, we should think:

This situation is the result of my negative karma. Since the effect has already ripened, it is too late to purify it. There is nothing to do but accept the situation patiently, with a happy mind. I myself created the cause for this problem and so it is my responsibility to accept the result. If I do not experience the results of my negative actions, who else will?

Although the patience of voluntarily enduring our suffering is not in itself the actual practice of taking, if we are able to bear our own suffering courageously we will not find it difficult to take on the suffering of others. Those who are able to practice this patience have very strong minds. They are like real heroes or heroines, undaunted by the sufferings of samsara, and nothing has the power to disturb their minds. As Dharmarakshita says:

A person who accepts samsaric enjoyments but cannot
    accept suffering
Will experience many problems;
But a Bodhisattva who accepts suffering courageously
Will always be happy.

Those who expect only happiness within samsara and find it difficult to bear its sufferings will only heap more misery on themselves. We are suffering because we are in samsara. Samsara is the creation of our impure mind of self-grasping and so its very nature is suffering. For as long as we have the cause in our mind—self-grasping ignorance—we will continue to experience the effect—samsara and all its miseries. Hoping to escape from suffering without purifying our mind of self-grasping reveals a fundamental lack of wisdom. Lacking wisdom, in life after life we have sought freedom from suffering through manipulating our samsaric world while neglecting to purify our mind. Rather than continuing in this way, we should now emulate the wise and courageous attitude of a Bodhisattva and view our suffering and problems as incentives to spur us on in our spiritual practice.

The reason we find it so difficult to accept suffering is that our self-cherishing mind grossly exaggerates the importance of our own happiness. In reality, when we are happy only one person is happy, and when we are suffering only one person is suffering; compared with the suffering of countless living beings, our own suffering is insignificant. Of course, even one living being is important, but if someone asked who is more important, one person or ten people, we would have to answer that ten people are more important. This reasoning is very useful and can help us in our practice of accepting defeat.

However, we need to use our wisdom when engaged in this practice. If our accepting defeat and offering the victory presents a serious obstacle to the fulfillment of our bodhichitta wishes, this will indirectly harm countless living beings, including the person we are offering the victory to. Without wisdom, we might allow someone to destroy our great opportunity to progress toward enlightenment and benefit many living beings. Such compassion would be unskillful and lead to incorrect practice. Suppose there is a practitioner called Maria who has dedicated all her activities to benefiting others. If someone out of jealousy tries to kill her, and in order to fulfill her assailant's wishes Maria allows herself to be killed, this would be crazy compassion. Compassion alone is not enough; we need to balance it with wisdom, because otherwise we will make many mistakes.

A compassionate man once found a large fish still alive on the road, which had fallen from a fisherman's cart. Wanting to save its life, he carefully picked it up and took it to a nearby pond. It was not long, however, before the local people noticed that all the small fish in the pond had disappeared and that only one large fish remained. When they realized that it was the large fish that had eaten all the other fish in the pond, they were very upset and killed it. The man's compassionate action therefore led to the deaths not only of all the fish in the pond but also of the large fish that he had tried to save. This story illustrates that, if we truly wish to help others, we need more than just a compassionate desire to help. We also need to develop our wisdom, because without wisdom our efforts to help can often backfire. In Buddhism, compassion and wisdom are seen as complementary and equally necessary for helping others effectively.

Compassion alone is not enough; we need to balance it with wisdom.

Suppose we have abandoned self-cherishing and someone demands that we give up our life. From our side, we may have the ability to lay down our life without any sense of loss, but before we do so we must ask ourself whether it will really help others. In certain cases it may be the most beneficial thing to do. The Tibetan King Yeshe Ö sacrificed his life to invite the great Indian Buddhist

Master Atisha to teach Dharma in Tibet, and as a result of Yeshe Ö's selfless act of giving, Atisha was so profoundly moved that he accepted the invitation. He was able to teach the rough and unruly Tibetans the precious Kadam Dharma, and they responded with love and gratitude. The pure Buddhadharma he taught flourished throughout Tibet and other countries. Since that time, countless beings have received, and continue to receive, profound benefit from Yeshe Ö's skillful action of voluntarily giving up his life. This story is explained in more detail in *Joyful Path of Good Fortune*.

On the other hand, there are times when giving up our life may please one person but also destroy our opportunity to help many others. If we realize that we can benefit more people by staying alive, we should not give up our life. If one person gets angry and threatens to kill us, we can even fight to protect our life for the sake of the many. Buddha said that it would be a grave mistake to give up our body for an insignificant reason, or to endanger our health unnecessarily, since this would be a great obstacle to our spiritual practice.

Usually we should try to please others by going along with their wishes and accepting any criticism or problems they give us, but there are times when it would be very unskillful to do this, such as when a person's wishes are harmful and will lead to unnecessary suffering. For example, if someone asked us to help him rob a bank, or if our child asked us to buy him a fishing rod or a gun to shoot birds, we should of course refuse. We need to use our wisdom and not just blindly agree to whatever we are asked.

It can also happen that if we spend most of our time complying with others' wishes, we are left with no time for Dharma study, contemplation, and meditation. Also, many people have incorrect wishes and may misuse us. Unless we make some time every day to meditate, we will find it very difficult to maintain peaceful and positive minds in our daily life, and our spiritual practice as a whole will suffer. Since the real purpose of meditation is to increase our capacity to help others, taking time each day to meditate is not selfish. We have to manage our time and energy in such a way that we can be of maximum benefit to others, and to do this effectively we need time alone to recover our strength, collect our thoughts, and see things in perspective.

Once they have been harmed, practitioners of training the mind accept their suffering patiently, but this does not mean that they do not try to prevent themselves from being hurt in the first place. It is a mistake to think that because we are trying to practice patience and destroy our self-cherishing mind we can allow others to harm us. In fact it is our duty to protect ourself from harm because if others succeed in harming us they will have created the cause to experience great suffering in the future. Bodhisattvas use whatever peaceful and wrathful means they have at their disposal to prevent others from harming them, but their only motivation for doing so is to protect others from creating negative karma and to safeguard their own opportunity to benefit others. Although outwardly it may appear as if they are acting out of self-concern, in reality they are protecting their body and life out of compassion for all living beings. In certain extreme circumstances, Bodhisattvas may even fight others in order to protect many living beings.

It is very difficult to judge from someone's outward actions alone whether or not he or she is practicing Dharma purely. Perhaps if we lived with someone for many years we would gradually come to understand his real motivation, but otherwise we cannot know a person's motivation from his external behavior alone.

There is also no point in our enduring suffering needlessly, such as by refusing to accept medical help when we are seriously ill. We may think, "As a practitioner of training the mind I can solve all my problems through my inner strength alone." But in fact by refusing help we are breaking the commitment of training the mind to "Remain natural while changing your aspiration." According to the Kadampa Tradition of Je Tsongkhapa, even if we have high realizations we should observe the conventions of ordinary society. Since it is customary to accept medical treatment when we are sick, we should not attract undue attention to ourself by refusing it if it can help us, even if we are mentally strong enough to bear the pain unaided. Je Tsongkhapa's tradition of outwardly remaining like an ordinary person while inwardly cultivating special minds such as universal compassion and love is very practical and beautiful.

We may think that if we patiently practice accepting defeat all the time, our suffering and problems will multiply and completely overwhelm us. But in fact the practice of patience always reduces our suffering because we do not add mental pain to the difficulties we are having. Because suffering, worry, depression, and pain are feelings, they are types of mind, so it follows that they exist inside and not outside our mind. If, while experiencing adverse conditions, our mind remains calm and happy through the practice of patience, we do not have a problem. We may have a challenging situation, and may even be sick or injured, but we are free from pain. By controlling our mind in this way, we experience a cessation of our pain, worry, and depression, and find true inner peace. Furthermore, by keeping a peaceful mind in difficult situations, we are far more likely to find solutions and respond constructively. The practice of training the mind is very gentle. It does not require physical deprivation and hardship but is mainly concerned with the internal task of controlling and transforming the mind. Once we have learned how to do this we will understand the real meaning of these instructions.

In summary, if we wish to help others effectively, we definitely need to be able to accept our problems without getting angry or discouraged. Helping others is not always easy—it often involves considerable hardship and inconvenience, and going against the wishes of our self-cherishing mind. Unless we are able to accept this, our commitment to benefiting others will be half-hearted and unstable. However, once we develop the ability to accept our own problems patiently, we will have the strength of mind to practice taking on the suffering of others and giving them happiness. Gradually we will develop the inner realization of accepting defeat and offering the victory, and nothing will have the power to discourage us from our beneficial activities.

Taking and Giving

Taking and Giving

Through the practice of taking and giving, we can further improve our love and compassion. In dependence upon this practice we can develop a very special bodhichitta, which is the actual path to enlightenment.

When we first meditate on taking and giving, we cannot actually take on the suffering of others or give them our happiness, but by imagining that we are doing so now, we are training our mind to be able to do so in the future. We do not need to think too much about how it is possible to relieve others' suffering through the power of our imagination alone. Instead, we should simply practice taking and giving with a good motivation, understanding that it is a supreme method for increasing our merit and concentration. This practice also purifies our non-virtues and delusions, especially our self-cherishing, and makes our love and compassion very strong. Through gradual training, our meditation on taking and giving will become so powerful that we will develop the ability to directly take on the suffering of others and give them happiness.

There are many examples of accomplished Buddhist Yogis using their concentration to take on the suffering of other

beings with whom they have a karmic connection. There is
a story of an Indian Buddhist Master called Maitriyogi who
took on the pain of a dog that was being beaten, so that the
wounds appeared on his body instead of the dog's. The great
Tibetan Yogi Milarepa had completely mastered the meditation on taking and giving. On one occasion he took on the
suffering of a sick man, but the man refused to believe that
it was due to Milarepa that he was free from
pain. To prove it, Milarepa returned the pain
to him, and when the pain became too much
Milarepa then transferred the pain to a door,
which started to shake! Faithful Buddhist practitioners believe
that when their Spiritual Guide is ill, in reality he or she is
taking on the suffering of others. Many Christians also believe
that by allowing himself to be crucified Jesus was taking on the
sufferings of human beings. It is quite possible that Jesus was
practicing taking while he was on the cross.

*Faith is the life force
of spiritual practice.*

If Buddhas and high Bodhisattvas have the power to directly
take on the suffering of others and bestow happiness on them,
we might wonder why living beings are still suffering. Because
Buddhas have this power, they are continuously bestowing blessings on all living beings. As a direct result of receiving these
blessings, each and every living being, including animals and hell
beings, occasionally experiences peace of mind, and at these times
they are happy and free from manifest suffering. The only way
living beings can achieve permanent liberation from suffering,
however, is if they actually put Buddha's teachings into practice.
Just as a doctor cannot cure a disease unless the sick person actually takes the medicine that the doctor has prescribed, so Buddhas

cannot cure our inner disease of delusions unless we actually take the medicine of Dharma. In the Sutras it says:

> Buddhas cannot remove living beings' suffering with their
> hands,
> Wash the evil from their minds with water,
> Or give them their realizations like a present;
> But they can lead them to liberation by revealing ultimate
> truth.

Even when the sun is shining, if our house is shuttered only a little light can enter and our house will remain cold and dark; but if we open the shutters, the warm rays of the sun will come pouring in. Similarly, even though the sun of Buddha's blessings is always shining, if our mind is shuttered by our lack of faith, few blessings can enter and our mind will remain cold and dark; but by developing strong faith, our mind will open and the full sun of Buddha's blessings will come pouring in. Faith is the life force of spiritual practice. We need to have unshakeable faith in Buddha's teachings or we will never find the energy to put these teachings into practice.

TAKING BY MEANS OF COMPASSION

For non-humans, such as animals or even gods, suffering only causes them distress and unhappiness, and they cannot learn anything from their pain. By contrast, humans who have met Buddhadharma can learn a great deal from their suffering. For us, suffering can be a great incentive to develop renunciation, compassion, and bodhichitta, and can encourage us to engage in sincere purification practice.

When the Tibetan Lama Je Gampopa was a young lay man he was happily married to a beautiful young woman, but before long she became sick and died. Because of his deep attachment to his wife, Gampopa was grief-stricken, but his loss made him realize that death and impermanence are the very nature of samsara and this encouraged him to seek permanent liberation from samsara through practicing Dharma purely. First he relied on a number of Kadampa Geshes and practiced Kadam Lamrim, and later he met Milarepa and received the Mahamudra instructions. Finally, by sincerely practicing all the teachings he had heard, he became a great Master who led many beings along spiritual paths. From this we can see that, for the qualified Dharma practitioner, suffering has many good qualities. For these practitioners, samsara's sufferings are like a Spiritual Guide who leads them along the path to enlightenment.

Shantideva says:

Moreover, suffering has many good qualities.
Through experiencing it, we can dispel pride,
Develop compassion for those trapped in samsara,
Abandon non-virtue, and delight in virtue.

Understanding the good qualities of suffering, we should develop joy at our opportunity to practice taking by means of compassion.

TAKING ON OUR OWN FUTURE SUFFERING

To prepare ourself for the actual meditation on taking on others' suffering, we can begin by taking on our own future suffering. This meditation is a powerful method for purifying the negative karma that is the main cause of our future suffering. If we remove the cause of our future suffering, there will be no basis to experience the effect. Freedom from future suffering is more important than freedom from present suffering because our future suffering is endless, while our present suffering is just the suffering of one short life. Therefore, while we still have the opportunity to purify the causes of our future suffering, we should train in taking on this suffering. This practice also functions to reduce our self-cherishing, which is the main reason why we find our suffering so difficult to bear, and it also strengthens our patience. When through the practice of patiently accepting our own suffering we can happily endure our adversities, it will not be difficult to take on the suffering of others. In this way, we gain the ability to prevent our own suffering and to benefit others. Understanding this, we make a determination to purify our non-virtues by taking on their effects now.

We imagine that all the sufferings we will experience in the future as a human, god, demi-god, animal, hungry spirit, or hell being gather together in the aspect of black smoke and dissolve into our root mind at our heart. We strongly imagine that this purifies the negative potentialities in our mind, the cause of all our future suffering. We then generate a feeling of joy and meditate on this feeling for as long as possible. We should repeat this meditation on taking on our future suffering many times, until we receive signs that our negative karma has been purified. The joy we experience from engaging in this meditation encourages us to develop a sincere wish to take on the suffering of others by means of compassion.

We can also prepare for the actual meditation on taking others' suffering by making prayers. It is very easy to say prayers, and if we say them with a good heart and strong concentration they are very powerful. While concentrating on the meaning, and believing that the living Buddha Shakyamuni is present in front of us, we pray:

> *Therefore, O Compassionate Venerable Guru, I seek your*
> *   blessings*
> *So that all the suffering, negativities, and obstructions of*
> *   mother sentient beings*
> *Will ripen upon me right now.*

We feel joy at the thought of taking on the suffering of all living beings, and we hold this special feeling for as long as possible. By repeating this prayer day and night, we continually strengthen our sincere wish to take on the suffering of others. We then engage in the actual meditation on taking on others' suffering.

THE BENEFITS OF TAKING ON OTHERS' SUFFERING

The practice of taking on the sufferings of all living beings has five main benefits: (1) our negative karma will be purified, (2) our merit will increase, (3) our compassion will become stronger, (4) we will develop a very strong mind that can bear adversity with courage, and (5) our compassion will eventually transform into the universal compassion of a Buddha.

At present our mind is like an open wound—at the slightest sign of hardship we recoil in fear. With such a weak mind, even minor difficulties interfere with our Dharma practice. By training in taking, however, we can strengthen our mind until it becomes unshakable. The Kadampa Geshes used to pray to develop a mind that is as strong and stable as a blacksmith's anvil, which does not break no matter how hard it is struck. We need a strong and stable mind, one that is undisturbed by any hardship that life throws at us. With such a mind, we are like a hero or heroine, and nothing can interfere with our progress toward enlightenment.

Those with deep experience of the practice of taking can easily fulfill their own and others' wishes. Why is this? It is because they have so much merit and because their wishes are always pure and motivated by compassion. They can even fulfill their wishes by means of prayer or simply by declaring the truth.

There are many stories of Bodhisattvas performing miraculous feats through the power of their declaration of truth. These declarations are very powerful because they are motivated by bodhichitta, and bodhichitta derives its power from great compassion. When I was a young monk at Jampaling Monastery in Western Tibet, I was seriously ill for a few months. When the pain got so bad that I could hardly bear it, my Teacher Geshe Palden came to see me. He had a blessed mala and would often tell us how special it was, but we used to think he was joking. On this occasion, however, he stood by my bedside and said to me, "If it is true that my mala is blessed by the Wisdom Buddha Manjushri, may you soon be cured," and then blessed me by touching my crown with the mala. After this, I recovered completely.

THE ACTUAL MEDITATION ON TAKING

There are two ways of training in taking by means of compassion. The first is to focus on all living beings in general and imagine taking on their suffering, and the second is to focus on an individual living being or a specific group and imagine taking on their particular sufferings.

To practice the first method, we visualize ourself surrounded by all mother living beings. For auspiciousness, and to help us relate to them more easily, we can visualize them all in human aspect, but we should remember that each of them is experiencing the suffering of their own particular realm. It is not necessary to picture them clearly—a rough mental image is sufficient.

We then develop compassion for all these living beings by thinking about their suffering. Human beings experience the sufferings of birth, sickness, aging, and death, of poverty, hunger, and thirst, of meeting adverse conditions and not fulfilling their wishes, and of being separated from their loved ones, as well as countless other sorrows. Animals experience the same sufferings, only far worse. In addition, they suffer from great ignorance, exploitation by humans, and living in constant fear of being killed by other animals. Hungry spirits experience the sufferings of intense hunger and thirst, and hell beings experience unimaginable sufferings of heat and cold. Demi-gods experience the sufferings of jealousy and conflict for long periods of time. Even the gods, who spend most of their lives enjoying the pleasures of samsara, are not free from suffering. Their enjoyments, environments, and bodies are contaminated and in the nature of suffering, and they experience great anguish at the time of death. Because they too are under the control of their delusions, they have no freedom from samsaric rebirth and have to experience samsara's sufferings endlessly, life after life.

Focusing on all living beings of the six realms and contemplating their suffering, we think:

These living beings are my mothers and have shown me great kindness. They are all drowning in the ocean of samsara, experiencing unbearable suffering, life after life. How wonderful it would be if they were free from suffering! May they be free from suffering. I myself will free them.

With this compassionate motivation, we pray:

May the negative karma and suffering of all living beings ripen on me, and through this may they all be freed from suffering and its causes.

With this heartfelt prayer, we imagine that all the suffering, fear, negative karma, and delusions of humans, gods, demi-gods, animals, hungry spirits, and hell beings gather together in the aspect of black smoke and dissolve into our heart. We develop the conviction: "My self-cherishing mind has ceased and all living beings have attained permanent liberation from suffering." We generate joy and meditate on this feeling single-pointedly for as long as possible. Remembering the five main benefits of taking on the suffering of all living beings, we repeat this meditation again and again until we gain a deep experience of it.

We may think that we are just pretending and have not really liberated all living beings from suffering, but there is no point in thinking like this. It is true that at first we do not have the power to take on others' suffering directly, but through repeatedly meditating on the conviction that we have taken on their suffering, we will gradually develop the actual power to do so. This is similar to the Tantric practice of bringing the result into the path, in which, through strongly imagining that we are already a Buddha, we gradually become a Buddha. The fact is that if we cannot even imagine attaining enlightenment, we will never be able to attain it! In the teachings of training the mind, it is said that the practice of taking and giving is similar to the practice of Secret Mantra, or Tantra.

How is it possible for something that exists only in our imagination to become a reality? It is a remarkable quality of the mind that we first create objects with our imagination and then bring them into our everyday reality. In fact, everything starts in the imagination. For example, the house we live in was first created in the imagination of the architect. He or she then made a design on paper, which acted as the blueprint for the actual building. If no one had first imagined our house, it would never have been built. In reality, our mind is the creator of all the things we experience. All external creations such as money, cars, and computers were developed in dependence upon someone's imagination—if no one had imagined them, they would never have been invented. In the same way, all inner creations and all Dharma realizations, even liberation and enlightenment, are developed in dependence upon the imagination. Therefore, for both worldly and spiritual attainments, the imagination is of primary importance.

If we imagine something that could in theory exist, and then familiarize our mind with it for long enough, eventually it will appear directly to our mind, first to our mental awareness and then even to our sense awarenesses. For as long as the object is still just an imagined object, the mind that apprehends it is simply a belief. If the object is a beneficial one it is a correct belief, and if the object stimulates delusions it is an incorrect belief. A belief is a conceptual mind that apprehends its object by means of a generic, or mental, image of that object. If we meditate on a correct belief for long enough, the generic image will become progressively more transparent until eventually it disappears entirely and we perceive the object directly. The imagined object will then have become a real object. By meditating on the beneficial belief that we have liberated all living beings and destroyed our self-cherishing mind, eventually we will actually accomplish this. Our correct belief will have transformed into a valid cognizer, a completely reliable mind.

In the second way of training in taking by means of compassion, we take on the particular sufferings of individuals or groups of people throughout infinite worlds. For example, we focus on all those living beings throughout infinite worlds who are suffering from sickness, and develop compassion, thinking, "How wonderful it would be if these living beings achieved permanent freedom from their suffering." We pray, "May they be free from suffering," and we make the determination, "I myself will free them." We imagine that all their suffering gathers together in the aspect of black smoke and dissolves into our heart. We develop the strong conviction that we have destroyed our self-cherishing and that all living beings have attained permanent liberation from the suffering of sickness. We experience joy, and meditate on this feeling for as long as possible.

In reality, our mind is the creator of all the things we experience.

In the same way, we can focus on all people throughout infinite worlds who are suffering from aging, death, or poverty, or loss of their loved ones, friends, or freedom. With the motivation of compassion, we pray and engage in the meditation on taking on their sufferings. We can also focus on any individual person who is experiencing suffering, and with a mind of compassion, we pray and engage in the meditation on taking on their sufferings.

Whenever we are experiencing a particular problem, whether from sickness, lack of resources, or our delusions, we can think about the countless living beings who are experiencing similar problems, and then with a compassionate motivation we imagine taking on their suffering. This will help us deal with our own problem, and by purifying the negative karma that prolongs the problem, may even free us from it. If we are suffering from strong attachment, for example, we can consider all those who are also suffering from attachment, develop compassion for them, and imagine that we take on all their attachment together with the suffering it causes. This is a powerful method for destroying our own attachment.

Taking motivated by compassion is an extremely pure mind, unstained by self-cherishing. For this reason, if we are able to meditate on taking on others' suffering as we are about to die, we will definitely take a higher rebirth, either in a Pure Land or as a human being with all the conditions needed to continue our spiritual practice.

To conclude our meditation sessions on taking, we dedicate our merit to freeing all living beings from their suffering and problems, and to lasting peace in this world.

GIVING BY MEANS OF LOVE

We focus on all living beings and think:

These mother beings are seeking happiness in life after life. They all want to be happy, but in samsara there is no real happiness anywhere. I will give them the supreme happiness of permanent inner peace right now.

We meditate on this wishing love for a short while, and then imagine that, through our pure mind of wishing love and great accumulation of merit, our body transforms into a wish-fulfilling jewel that has the power to fulfill the wishes of each and every living being. Infinite light rays radiate from our body and pervade the entire universe, reaching the bodies and minds of all living beings and bestowing on them the supreme happiness of permanent inner peace. With the conviction that all living beings are experiencing this inner peace, we develop joy and meditate on this feeling for as long as possible.

If we wish to meditate on giving more extensively, we can imagine that the rays of light we emanate fulfill all the individual needs and wishes of each and every living being. Human beings receive close friends, comfortable houses, good jobs, delicious food, beautiful clothes, and anything else they need or desire. Animals receive food, secure and warm homes, and freedom from fear; hungry spirits receive food and drink; beings in the hot hells receive cooling breezes, and beings in the cold hells receive warm sunshine. The demi-gods receive peace and satisfaction, and the gods receive uncontaminated happiness and a meaningful life. Through enjoying these objects of desire, all living beings are completely satisfied and develop uncontaminated bliss. With the conviction that we have provided all living beings with uncontaminated happiness, we develop joy and meditate on this feeling.

Although we are principally training in the thought of giving, we can also engage in taking and giving in practical ways whenever we have the opportunity. At our stage we cannot take on the suffering of others through the power of our concentration, but we can often be of practical benefit to them. We can ease the pain of sick people by taking good care of them, and we can help others when they are busy or by doing some of the jobs they dislike. Accepting hardship while engaged in helping others is also a form of giving. We can also give material help, our labor, our skills, Dharma teachings, or good advice. When we meet people who are depressed and need cheering up we can give our time and love.

We can also give to animals. Saving insects from drowning or gently picking up worms from the road is an example of giving fearlessness, or protection. Even allowing a mouse to rummage through our wastepaper basket without getting irritated can be a form of giving. Animals want to be happy just as much as we do, and they need our help even more than other humans. Most humans have some power to help themselves, but animals are so deeply enveloped in ignorance that they have no freedom at all to improve their situation. Animals have taken rebirth in a lower state of existence than humans but we should never regard them as less important. Buddhas and Bodhisattvas have complete equanimity and cherish animals and human beings equally.

At the end of our meditation on giving, we dedicate our merit so that all living beings may find true happiness. We can also make specific dedications, praying that the sick be restored to health, the poor obtain wealth, the unemployed find good jobs, the unsuccessful meet with success, the anxious find peace of mind, and so forth. We should especially dedicate our merit for world peace and happiness, and for the elimination of natural disasters, wars, and famine. Through the strength of our pure motivation and the power and blessings of Buddhadharma, our dedications can certainly help, especially if we have a strong karmic link with the people we are praying for. Dedicating our merit to others is itself a form of giving. We can also mentally practice giving in daily life. Whenever we see or read about people who are poor, unhealthy, fearful, unsuccessful, or unhappy, we can increase our wishing love for them and dedicate our merit toward their happiness and freedom from suffering.

MOUNTING TAKING AND GIVING UPON THE BREATH

Once we have become familiar with the meditations on taking and giving, we can combine the two and practice them in conjunction with our breathing. We begin by meditating on compassion and love for all living beings, and developing a strong determination to take on their suffering and give them pure happiness. With this determination, we imagine that we inhale through our nostrils the suffering, delusions, and non-virtues of all living beings in the form of black smoke, which dissolves into our heart and completely destroys our self-cherishing. As we exhale, we imagine that our breath in the aspect of wisdom light, its nature pure uncontaminated happiness, pervades the entire universe. Each and every living being receives whatever they need and desire, and in particular the supreme happiness of permanent inner peace. We practice this cycle of breathing day and night, with each breath taking on the suffering of all living beings and giving them pure happiness, until we gain a deep experience of this practice.

Once we are proficient at this meditation on mounting taking and giving upon the breath, it is very powerful because there is a close relationship between the breath and the mind. The breath is related to the inner energy winds that flow through the channels of our body, and that act as the vehicles, or mounts, for different types of awareness. By harnessing our breath for virtuous purposes, we purify our inner winds, and when pure winds are flowing through our channels, pure minds arise naturally.

Many people practice breathing meditation, but the most widely practiced type consists simply of concentrating on the sensation of the breath entering and leaving the nostrils. This functions to calm the mind temporarily and reduces distracting thoughts, but it does not have the power to effect a deep and lasting transformation of our mind. Combining breathing meditation with the practice of taking and giving, however, has the power to transform our mind from its present miserable and self-centered state into the blissful and altruistic mind of a Bodhisattva. It improves our concentration, makes our love and compassion very strong, and accumulates vast merit. In this way, the simple act of breathing is transformed into a powerful spiritual practice. At first we do this practice only in meditation, but with familiarity we can do it at any time. Through deep familiarity with this practice, our mind will eventually transform into the compassion of a Buddha.

Meditating on taking and giving can also be very effective in curing disease. By taking on the sickness and suffering of others with a mind of compassion, we can purify the negative karma that causes the continuation of our disease. Although we should always seek medical advice when we are sick, there may be times when doctors are unable to help us. There are many stories in Tibet of people curing themselves of otherwise incurable diseases through sincerely meditating on taking and giving. There was a meditator called Kharak Gomchen who contracted a disease that doctors were unable to cure. Thinking that he was going to die, he gave away all his possessions as offerings to Avalokiteshvara, the Buddha of

Compassion, and retired to a cemetery, where he intended to make the last few weeks of his life meaningful by meditating on taking and giving. However, through his practice of taking and giving he purified the karma that was perpetuating his illness, and much to everyone's surprise, returned home completely cured. This shows us how powerful the practice of taking and giving can be.

If we purify our negative karma, it is easy to cure even the heaviest disease. My mother told me about a monk she met who had contracted leprosy. Hoping to purify his sickness, he made a pilgrimage to Mount Kailash in western Tibet, which Tibetans believe to be Buddha Heruka's Pure Land. He was extremely poor and so my mother helped him on his way by giving him food and shelter, which was very kind as most people avoided lepers out of fear of catching leprosy. He stayed around Mount Kailash for about six months, prostrating and circumambulating the holy mountain as his purification practice. Afterwards, while he was sleeping near a lake, he dreamed that many worms crawled out of his body and into the water. When he woke up he felt extremely comfortable, and later discovered that he was completely cured. On his way home, he stopped to see my mother and told her what had happened.

We can reflect that since beginningless time we have had countless lives and countless bodies, but that we have wasted them all in meaningless activities. Now we have the opportunity to derive the greatest meaning from our present body by using it to engage in the path of compassion and wisdom. How wonderful it would be for our world if many modern-day practitioners could emulate the training the mind practitioners of ancient times and become actual Bodhisattvas!

The Supreme Good Heart

The Supreme Good Heart

The supreme good heart in this context is bodhichitta. *Bodhi* is the Sanskrit word for "enlightenment," and *chitta* the word for "mind"—therefore *bodhichitta* literally means "mind of enlightenment." It is defined as a mind, motivated by compassion for all living beings, that spontaneously seeks enlightenment. Bodhichitta is born from great compassion, which itself depends on cherishing love. Cherishing love can be compared to a field, compassion to the seeds, taking and giving to the supreme methods for making the seeds grow, and bodhichitta to the harvest. The cherishing love that is developed through the practice of exchanging self with others is more profound than that developed through other methods, and so the resultant compassion and bodhichitta are also more profound. Without great compassion, the spontaneous wish to protect all living beings from suffering, bodhichitta cannot arise in our mind. But if we have great compassion, especially the great compassion generated through exchanging self with others, bodhichitta will arise naturally. The strength of our bodhichitta depends entirely on the strength of our great compassion.

Of all Dharma realizations, bodhichitta is supreme. This profoundly compassionate mind is the very essence of the

Bodhisattva's training. Developing the good heart of bodhichitta enables us to perfect all our virtues, solve all our problems, fulfill all our wishes, and develop the power to help others in the most appropriate and beneficial ways. Bodhichitta is the best friend we can have and the highest quality we can develop. We generally consider someone who is kind to his or her friends, takes care of his parents, and gives freely to worthwhile causes to be a good person. But how much more praiseworthy is a person who has dedicated his or her whole life to relieving the suffering of each and every living being? Atisha had many Teachers, but the one he revered above all was Guru Serlingpa. Whenever he heard Serlingpa's name, he would prostrate. When Atisha's disciples asked him why he respected Serlingpa more than his other Teachers, he replied, "It is due to the kindness of Guru Serlingpa that I have been able to develop the good heart of bodhichitta." Through the power of his bodhichitta, Atisha was able to bring great joy and happiness to everyone he met, and whatever he did was of benefit to others.

Our mental attitude transforms a situation into either a problem or an opportunity.

How does bodhichitta solve all our problems and fulfill all our wishes? As already explained, problems do not exist outside of the mind—it is our mental attitude that transforms a situation into either problem or an opportunity. If we have bodhichitta, negative states of mind such as attachment, anger, and jealousy have no power over us. If we cannot find a well-paid job, a comfortable home, or good friends, we will not be upset. Instead we will think: "My main wish is to attain enlightenment. It does not matter if I cannot obtain these worldly enjoyments, which only serve to bind me to samsara." With such a pure mind, there will be no basis for self-pity or blaming others, and nothing will be able to obstruct our progress toward enlightenment. Furthermore, with the supremely altruistic mind of bodhichitta we will create a vast amount of merit because we engage in all our actions for the benefit of others. With such an accumulation of merit, our wishes will easily be fulfilled, we will develop a tremendous capacity to benefit others, and all our Dharma activities will be successful.

We need to contemplate the benefits of bodhichitta until we are deeply inspired to develop this rare and precious mind. An extensive presentation of these benefits can be found in *Meaningful to Behold* and *Joyful Path of Good Fortune*.

At the moment we have a very special opportunity to develop bodhichitta. However, we do not know how long our good fortune will last, and if we waste this opportunity it will not arise again. If we wasted an opportunity to make a lot of money, or to get a good job or an attractive partner, we would probably feel strong regret, but in reality we would not have lost much. These things are not so difficult to find, and even when found they do not bring us real happiness. Not taking advantage of this unique opportunity to develop bodhichitta, however, is an irretrievable loss. Humans have the greatest opportunity for spiritual development, and of all the possible types of rebirth we could have taken we have been born human. These days most humans have no interest in spiritual development, and of those who do, only a few have met Buddhadharma. If we contemplate this carefully we will realize how very fortunate we are to have this precious opportunity to attain the supreme happiness of Buddhahood.

DEVELOPING BODHICHITTA

Although we have developed superior great compassion—the spontaneous wish to take the sufferings of all living beings upon ourself—we understand that, despite our strong desire to protect all living beings, we do not have the power to do so at present. Just as one drowning person cannot save another, no matter how fervently he or she may wish to do so, likewise it is only when we have freed ourself from suffering and mental limitations that we are able to free others. If we ask ourself who has the actual power to protect all living beings, we will realize that only a Buddha does. Only a Buddha is free from all faults and limitations, and has both the omniscient wisdom and the skill to help each and every living being in accordance with his or her individual needs and dispositions. Only a Buddha has reached the shore of enlightenment and is in a position to release all mother beings from the cruel ocean of samsara. If we consider this deeply, bodhichitta will arise naturally in our mind. We contemplate:

I want to protect all living beings from suffering, but in my present, limited state I have no power to do this. Because only a Buddha has such power, I must become a Buddha as quickly as possible.

We meditate on this determination again and again until it arises spontaneously.

When we want a cup of tea, our main wish is to drink tea, but to fulfill this wish we naturally develop the secondary wish to find a cup. In a similar way, the main wish of those who have great compassion is to protect all living beings from their suffering; but to fulfill this wish they know that they must first attain Buddhahood themselves, and so they naturally develop the secondary wish to attain enlightenment. Just as finding a cup is the way to accomplish our goal of drinking tea, so attaining enlightenment is the way to accomplish our ultimate goal of benefiting all living beings.

At first our bodhichitta will be artificial, or fabricated, bodhichitta, arising only when we make a specific effort to generate it. The best way to transform this into spontaneous bodhichitta is to gain deep familiarity with it through continual practice. Since most of our time is spent out of meditation, it is vital that we make use of every opportunity to improve our virtuous minds during our daily life. We need to make our meditation sessions and meditation breaks mutually supportive. During our meditation session, we may experience a peaceful state of mind and develop many virtuous intentions; but if we forget them all as soon as we arise from meditation we will not be able to solve our daily problems of anger, attachment, and ignorance, or make progress in our spiritual practice. We must learn to integrate our spiritual practice into our daily activities so that day and night we can maintain the peaceful states of mind and pure intentions that we developed in meditation.

At the moment we may find that our meditations and our daily life are pulling in different directions. In meditation we try to generate virtuous minds, but because we cannot stop thinking about our other activities, our concentration is very weak. The virtuous feelings we do manage to develop are then quickly dissipated in the busyness of daily life, and we return to our meditation seat tired, tense, and filled with distracting thoughts.

We can overcome this problem by transforming all our daily activities and experiences into the spiritual path by developing special ways of thinking. Activities such as cooking, working, talking, and relaxing are not intrinsically mundane; they are mundane only if done with a mundane mind. By doing exactly the same actions with a spiritual motivation, they become pure spiritual practices. For example, when we talk to our friends our motivation is usually mixed with self-cherishing and we say whatever comes into our head, regardless of whether or not it is beneficial. We can, however, talk to others with the sole purpose of benefiting them, encouraging them to develop positive states of mind and being careful not to say anything that will upset them. Instead of thinking about how we can impress people, we should think about how we can help them, recalling how they are trapped in samsara and lack pure happiness. In this way, talking with our friends can become a means of improving our love, compassion, and other realizations. If we can skillfully transform all our daily activities in this way, instead of feeling drained and tired when we sit down to meditate we will feel joyful and inspired, and it will be easy to develop pure concentration.

Developing great compassion is the main, or substantial, cause of generating bodhichitta—it is like the seed of bodhichitta. To enable this seed to grow, we also need the cooperative conditions of accumulating merit, purifying negativity, and receiving the blessings of the Buddhas and Bodhisattvas. If we gather all these causes and conditions together, it is not difficult to develop bodhichitta. To fulfill the wishes of our compassionate mind of bodhichitta, we need to engage sincerely in the practices of giving, moral discipline, patience, effort, concentration, and wisdom. When these practices are motivated by bodhichitta, they are called *the six perfections*. We especially need to apply great effort to training in the wisdom that realizes ultimate truth, emptiness.

Ultimate Truth

Ultimate Truth

Ultimate truth, or emptiness, is the principal object of ultimate bodhichitta. Ultimate bodhichitta is a direct realization of ultimate truth that is held by conventional bodhichitta. It is a wisdom of meditative equipoise completely mixed with emptiness, and it is known as *ultimate bodhichitta* because it is a principal cause of enlightenment that focuses on ultimate truth. Conventional bodhichitta is the spontaneous wish to attain enlightenment for the sake of all living beings.

The main difference between the two bodhichittas is that the observed object of conventional bodhichitta is conventional truth, while the observed object of ultimate bodhichitta is ultimate truth. Conventional bodhichitta is the gateway to the Bodhisattva's path in general, and is possessed by all Bodhisattvas. Ultimate bodhichitta is the gateway to the superior Bodhisattva paths, and is possessed only by Superior Bodhisattvas and Buddhas. A superior path is a spiritual realization of a Superior being, a person who has gained a direct realization of emptiness.

Conventional bodhichitta and ultimate bodhichitta are like the two wings of a bird, because just as a bird needs both wings to fly, we need both bodhichittas to fly to the state of full enlightenment.

Conventional bodhichitta is the main method for ripening the potentiality of our Buddha nature—it functions to accumulate merit, and is the main cause of attaining the Form Body of a Buddha. Ultimate bodhichitta is the direct method for releasing our Buddha nature from ignorance and mistaken appearance, and is the main cause of attaining the Truth Body of a Buddha, known as the *Dharmakaya*.

Emptiness is not nothingness but is the real nature of phenomena. Since it is a very profound subject, you will need to read the following explanation carefully, with a positive mind, and think about it deeply. It may seem very technical at first but please be patient and do not waste this precious opportunity to understand such a meaningful subject. Until we abandon our self-grasping ignorance, we will have no real happiness because self-grasping destroys our inner peace, or mental peace. The only direct method for eliminating this ignorance is the realization of emptiness.

Emptiness is not nothingness but is the real nature of phenomena.

Ultimate truth, emptiness, and ultimate nature of phenomena are the same. We should know that all our problems arise because we do not realize ultimate truth. The reason we remain in samsara's prison is that due to our delusions we continue to engage in contaminated actions. All our delusions stem from self-grasping ignorance. Self-grasping ignorance is the source of all our negativity and problems, and the only way to eradicate it is to realize emptiness. Emptiness is not easy to understand, but it is extremely important that we make the effort. Ultimately our efforts will be rewarded by the permanent cessation of all suffering and the everlasting bliss of full enlightenment.

THE PURPOSE OF MEDITATING ON EMPTINESS

The purpose of understanding and meditating on emptiness is to release our mind from wrong conceptions and mistaken appearances so that we will become a completely pure, or enlightened, being. In this context, *wrong conception* refers to the mind of self-grasping ignorance—a conceptual mind that grasps objects as truly existent; and *mistaken appearance* refers to the appearance of truly existent objects. The former are the obstructions to liberation and the latter are the obstructions to omniscience. Only a Buddha has abandoned both obstructions.

There are two types of self-grasping: self-grasping of persons and self-grasping of phenomena. The first grasps our own or others' self, or I, as truly existent, and the second grasps any phenomenon other than our own or others' self as truly existent. Minds that grasp our body, our mind, our possessions, and our world as truly existent are all examples of self-grasping of phenomena.

The main point of meditating on emptiness is to reduce and finally to eliminate both types of self-grasping. Self-grasping is the source of all our problems—the extent to which we suffer is directly proportional to the intensity of our self-grasping. For example, when our self-grasping is very strong, we feel a sharp mental pain when others simply tease us in a friendly way, while at times when our self-grasping is weak we just laugh with them. Once we completely destroy our self-grasping, all our problems will naturally disappear. Even temporarily, meditating on emptiness is very helpful for overcoming anxiety and worry.

If during the meditation session we come to a clear understanding and firm realization that all phenomena lack inherent existence, this will strongly influence our mind during the meditation break. Even though the things we see around us appear to exist inherently, we will immediately remember from our own experience during meditation that they do not exist in that way. We will be like a magician who immediately realizes that his magical creations are just illusions.

We can check to see if our meditation on emptiness is working by observing whether or not our self-grasping is becoming weaker. If after studying, contemplating, and meditating for several months or even years our self-grasping is just as strong as it was before, we can be sure that our understanding or our meditation is faulty. We have suffered from self-grasping since beginningless time and we cannot expect to eliminate it overnight, but if we meditate on emptiness regularly we should notice a gradual reduction in its strength. If by contemplating emptiness we are able to subdue our delusions—for example, overcoming our anger by reflecting how the object of our anger does not exist from its own side, or reducing the intensity of our attachment by realizing that the object of our attachment is not inherently desirable—this is proof that our understanding of emptiness is correct.

The extent to which we are able to solve our inner problems by meditating on the true nature of things depends on two factors: the accuracy of our understanding, and our familiarity with this knowledge. Therefore, first we need to study emptiness in order to gain an intellectual understanding, and then we need to meditate on this understanding over and over again in order to deepen our familiarity.

When our body is sick, we immediately try to find a cure, but there are no hospitals or medicines that can cure the mental sickness of our delusions. We consider a disease such as cancer to be a terrible thing, but in reality cancer is not so bad. Cancer is just a temporary sickness that will end the moment this present body disintegrates at death. Much worse than any physical illness is the internal sickness of our delusions, because there is no end to the suffering this can cause us. Because of our attachment to the fulfillment of our own wishes, we experience continual mental pain, life after life. It can lead to conflict, murder, and even suicide, and it forces us to act in ways that lead to immense suffering in future lives. Similarly, anger, jealousy, and other delusions continually cause us harm. It does not matter whether we are healthy or unhealthy, rich or poor, successful or unsuccessful, popular or unpopular, we are never free from the threat of delusions. We might be quietly reading a book when suddenly, for no apparent reason, we remember an insult or an object of attachment and become unhappy. It is rare to enjoy even one hour of mental peace undisturbed by delusions.

We have endured the internal sickness of delusions since beginningless time. We brought it with us from our previous lives, suffer from it throughout this life, and will take it with us into our future lives. Doctors cannot cure it, and it will never end by itself. The only medicine with the power to cure our inner sickness is the medicine of Buddha's teachings, and especially the teachings on emptiness. All Buddha's teachings are methods to cure our inner sickness. For example, by putting Buddha's teachings on love and patience into practice we will gain some respite from the sickness of anger, and by putting his teachings on impermanence and the disadvantages of samsara into practice we will find some relief from the sickness of attachment. However, the only way that we can ever completely cure all our mental sicknesses is by gaining a direct realization of emptiness.

Once we realize emptiness directly, we have complete freedom. We can even control our death and choose our rebirth. Right now we may be making plans for our next vacation or our retirement, but we cannot be sure that we will even be alive for our next meal. After we die, there is no certainty where we will be reborn; just because we are human now is no guarantee that in our next life we will not take rebirth as an animal. Even if we are reborn human, there is no real happiness. We are born amid blood and screams, and are completely unable to comprehend anything that is happening to us. The possessions, knowledge, and friends that we worked so hard to accumulate in our previous life are all lost, and we come into the world empty-handed, confused, and alone. As we grow older we have to experience all the sufferings of human life, such as aging, sickness, hunger, thirst, fighting, having to part with what we like, having to encounter what we do not like, and failing to satisfy our desires. This does not happen in just this one life, but in life after life, over and over again. If we had to experience this suffering for just one or several lives, maybe we could just accept it. But this suffering will be repeated over and over again, without end. How can we bear this?

We should contemplate these points until we reach a definite conclusion:

I cannot bear this meaningless cycle of suffering one moment longer. I must escape from samsara. Before I die, I must attain a deep experience of emptiness.

We then turn our attention to other living beings by thinking:

To remain in the prison of samsara myself is unbearable, yet all other living beings are in exactly the same situation. In addition, when I suffer, only one person suffers, but when others suffer, countless living beings suffer. How can I bear the thought of countless living beings experiencing suffering without end? I must liberate them all from suffering. To free all living beings from suffering I must become a Buddha, and to become a Buddha I must realize ultimate truth, emptiness.

If we meditate on emptiness with this motivation, we are training in ultimate bodhichitta.

When we study emptiness, it is important to do so with the right motivation. There is little benefit in studying emptiness if we just approach it as an intellectual exercise. Emptiness is difficult enough to understand, but if we approach it with an incorrect motivation this will obscure the meaning even more. However, if we study with a good motivation, faith in Buddha's teachings, and the understanding that a knowledge of emptiness can solve all our problems and enable us to help everyone else solve theirs, we will receive Buddha's wisdom blessings and understand emptiness more easily. Even if we cannot understand all the technical reasoning, we will get a feeling for emptiness, and we will be able to subdue our delusions and solve our daily problems through contemplation and meditation on emptiness. Gradually our wisdom will increase until it transforms into the wisdom of superior seeing and finally into a direct realization of emptiness.

Through training in the practices of equalizing and exchanging self with others we will gain the ability to recognize self-cherishing whenever it arises, which will make it much easier to recognize the inherently existent I that we cherish day and night. Having in this way clearly identified the object of negation through our own experience, the reasoning refuting it will not be so hard to follow. In addition, as our merit increases through our increased good heart and dedication, our meditation on emptiness will become more effective, until eventually it becomes so powerful that we destroy our self-grasping. There is no greater method for experiencing peace of mind and happiness than to meditate on emptiness. Since it is self-grasping that keeps us bound to samsara and is the source of all our suffering, meditation on emptiness is the universal solution to all problems. It is the medicine that cures all mental and physical diseases, and the nectar that bestows the everlasting happiness of enlightenment.

WHAT IS EMPTINESS?

Emptiness is the way things really are. It is the way things exist as opposed to the way they appear. We naturally believe that the things we see around us, such as tables, chairs, and houses are truly existent, because we believe that they exist in exactly the way that they appear. However, the way things appear to our senses is deceptive and completely contradictory to the way in which they actually exist. Things appear to exist from their own side, without depending on our mind. This book that appears to our mind, for example, seems to have its own independent, objective existence. It seems to be "outside" while our mind seems to be "inside." We feel that the book can exist without our mind; we do not feel that our mind is involved in any way in bringing the book into existence. This way of existing independent of our mind is variously called *true existence, inherent existence, existence from its own side,* and *existence from the side of the object.*

Although things appear directly to our senses to be truly, or inherently, existent, in reality all phenomena lack, or are empty of, true existence. This book, our body, our friends, we ourself, and the entire universe are in reality just appearances to mind, like things seen in a dream. If we dream of an elephant, the elephant appears vividly in all its detail—we can see it, hear it, smell it, and touch it—but when we wake up we realize that it was just an appearance to mind. We do not wonder, "Where is the elephant now?" because we understand that it

Meditation on emptiness is the universal solution to all problems.

was simply a projection of our mind and had no existence outside our mind. When the dream awareness that apprehended the elephant ceased, the elephant did not go anywhere—it simply disappeared, because it was just an appearance to the mind and did not exist separately from the mind. Buddha said that the same is true for all phenomena—they are mere appearances to mind, totally dependent on the minds that perceive them.

The world we experience when we are awake and the world we experience when we are dreaming are very similar, because both are mere appearances to mind that arise from our karma. If we want to say that the dream world is false, we also have to say that the waking world is false; and if we want to say that the waking world is true, we also have to say that the dream world is true. The only difference between them is that the dream world is an appearance to our subtle dreaming mind while the waking world is an appearance to our gross waking mind. The dream world exists only for as long as the dream awareness to which it appears exists, and the waking world exists only for as long as the waking awareness to which it appears exists. When we die, our gross waking minds dissolve into our very subtle mind and the world we experienced when we were alive simply disappears. The world as others perceive it will continue, but our personal world will disappear as completely and irrevocably as the world of last night's dream.

Buddha said that all phenomena are like illusions. There are many different types of illusion, such as mirages, rainbows, or drug-induced hallucinations. In ancient times, there used to be magicians who would cast a spell over their audience, causing them to see objects, such as a piece of wood, as something else, such as a tiger. Those deceived by the spell would see what appeared to be a real tiger and develop fear, but those who arrived after the spell had been cast would see only a piece of wood. What all illusions have in common is that the way they appear does not coincide with the way they exist. Buddha compared all phenomena to illusions, because through the force of the imprints of self-grasping ignorance accumulated since beginningless time, whatever appears to our mind naturally appears to be truly existent and we instinctively assent to this appearance, but in reality everything is totally empty of true existence. Like a mirage that appears to be water but is not actually water, things appear in a deceptive way. Not understanding their real nature, we are fooled by appearances, and grasp at books and tables, bodies and worlds as truly existent. The result of grasping at phenomena in this way is that we develop self-cherishing, attachment, hatred, jealousy, and other delusions, our mind becomes agitated and unbalanced, and our inner peace is destroyed. We are like travelers in a desert who exhaust themselves running after mirages, or like someone walking down a road at night mistaking the shadows of the trees for criminals or wild animals waiting to attack.

THE EMPTINESS OF OUR BODY

To understand how phenomena are empty of true, or inherent, existence, we should consider our own body. Once we have understood how our body lacks true existence, we can easily apply the same reasoning to other objects.

In *Guide to the Bodhisattva's Way of Life*, Bodhisattva Shantideva says:

> Therefore, there is no body,
> But, because of ignorance, we perceive a body within the
>   hands and so forth,
> Just like a mind mistakenly apprehending a person
> When observing the shape of a pile of stones at dusk.

On one level we know our body very well—we know whether it is healthy or unhealthy, beautiful or ugly, and so forth. However, we never examine it more deeply, asking ourself: "What precisely is my body? Where is my body? What is its real nature?" If we did examine our body in this way, we would not be able to find it—instead of finding our body the result of this examination would be that our body disappears. The meaning of the first part of Shantideva's verse, "Therefore, there is no body," is that if we search for our "real" body, there is no body; and also there is no body within our hands and so forth. Our body exists only if we do not search for a real body behind its mere appearance.

There are two ways of searching for an object. An example of the first way, which we can call a "conventional search," is searching for our car in a parking lot. The conclusion of this type of search is that we find the car, in the sense that we see the thing that everyone agrees is our car. Having located our car in the parking lot, however, suppose that we are still not satisfied with the mere appearance of the car and we want to determine what exactly is the car. We might then engage in what we can call an "ultimate search" for the car, in which we look within the object itself to find something that is the object. To do this we ask ourself: "Are any of the individual parts of the car, the car? Are the wheels the car? Is the engine the car? Is the chassis the car?" and so forth. When conducting an ultimate search for our car we are not satisfied with just pointing to the hood, wheels, and so forth and then saying "car"; we want to know what the car really is. Instead of just using the word "car" as ordinary people do, we want to know what the word really refers to. We want to mentally separate the car from all that is not car, so that we can say: "This is what the car really is; this is the truly existent car."

To understand Shantideva's claim that in reality there is no body, we need to conduct an ultimate search for our body. If we are ordinary beings, all objects, including our body, appear to exist inherently. As mentioned above, objects seem to be independent of our mind and independent of other phenomena. The universe appears to consist of discrete objects that have an existence from their own side. These objects appear to exist in themselves as stars, planets, mountains, people, and so forth, "waiting" to be experienced by conscious beings. Normally it does not occur to us that we are involved in any way in the existence of these phenomena. For example, we feel that our body exists in its own right and does not depend on our mind, or anyone else's, to bring it into existence. However, if our body did exist in the way that we instinctively grasp it—as an external object rather than just a projection of mind—we should be able to point to our body without pointing to any phenomenon that is not our body. We should be able to find it among its parts or outside its parts. Since there is no third possibility, if our body cannot be found either among its parts or outside its parts we must conclude that our body does not exist as an objective entity.

It is not difficult to understand that the individual parts of our body are not our body—it is absurd to say that our back, our legs, or our head are our body. If one of the parts, say our back, is our body, then the other parts are equally our body, and it would follow that we have many bodies. Furthermore, our back, legs, and so forth cannot be our body because they are parts of our body. The body is the part-possessor, and the back, legs, and so forth are the possessed parts; and possessor and possessed cannot be one and the same.

Some people, including even followers of some schools of Buddhist philosophy, believe that although none of the individual parts of the body is the body, the collection of all the parts assembled together is the body. According to these schools, it is possible to find our body when we search for it analytically because the collection of all the parts of our body is our body. However, followers of the highest school of Buddhist philosophy, the Madhyamika-Prasangika school, refute this assertion with many logical reasons. The force of these reasons may not be immediately obvious to us, but if we contemplate them carefully with a calm and positive mind we will come to appreciate their validity.

Since none of the individual parts of our body is our body, how can the collection of all the parts be our body? For example, a collection of dogs cannot be a human being, because none of the individual dogs is human. Since each individual member is "non-human," how can this collection of non-humans magically transform into a human? Similarly, since the collection of the parts of our body is a collection of things that are not our body, it cannot be our body. Just as the collection of dogs remains simply dogs, so the collection of all the parts of our body remains simply parts of our body—it does not magically transform into the part-possessor, our body.

We may find this point difficult to understand, but if we think about it for a long time with a calm and positive mind, and discuss it with more experienced practitioners, it will gradually become clearer. We can also consult authentic books on the subject, such as *Heart of Wisdom*.

There is another way in which we can know that the collection of the parts of our body is not our body. If we can point to the collection of the parts of our body and say that this is, in itself, our body, then the collection of the parts of our body must exist independently of all phenomena that are not our body. Therefore, it would follow that the collection of the parts of our body exists independently of the parts themselves. This is clearly absurd—if it were true, we could remove all the parts of our body and the collection of the parts would remain. We can therefore conclude that the collection of the parts of our body is not our body.

Since the body cannot be found within its parts, either as an individual part or as the collection, the only possibility that remains is that it exists separately from its parts. If this is the case, it should be possible mentally or physically to remove all the parts of our body and still be left with the body. However, if we remove our arms, our legs, our head, our trunk, and all the other parts of our body, no body is left. This proves that there is no body separate from its parts. Whenever we point to our body, we are pointing only to a part of our body, which is not our body.

We have now searched in every possible place and have been unable to find our body either among its parts or anywhere else. We can find nothing that corresponds to the vividly appearing body that we normally grasp at. We are forced to agree with Shantideva that, when we search for our body, there is no body to be found. This clearly indicates that our body does not exist from its own side, independently of mind. It is almost as if our body does not exist. In fact, the only sense in which we can say that our body does exist is if we are satisfied with the mere name "body" and do not expect to find a real body behind the name. If we try to find, or point to, a real body to which the name "body" refers, we will not find anything at all. Instead of finding a truly existent body, we will perceive the non-existence, or emptiness, of such a body. We will realize that the body we normally perceive, grasp at, and cherish does not exist at all. This non-existence of the body we normally grasp at is the true, or ultimate, nature of our body.

The term *true nature* is very meaningful. Not being satisfied with the mere appearance and name "body," we examined our body to discover its true nature. The result of this examination was a definite non-finding of our body. Where we expected to find a truly existent body, we discovered the utter non-existence of that truly existent body. This non-existence, or emptiness, is the true nature of our body. Aside from the mere absence of a truly existent body, there is no other true nature of our body—every other attribute of the body is just part of its deceptive nature. Since this is the case, why do we spend so much time focusing on the deceptive nature of our body? At present we ignore the true nature of our body and other phenomena, and concentrate only on their deceptive nature. Yet the result of concentrating all the time on deceptive objects is that our mind becomes disturbed and we remain in samsara. If we wish to experience pure peace, we must familiarize our mind with the truth. Instead of wasting our energy focusing only on meaningless, deceptive objects, we should focus on the true nature of things.

If we wish to experience pure peace, we must familiarize our mind with the truth.

Although it is impossible to find our body when we search for it analytically, when we do not engage in analysis our body appears very clearly. Why is this? Shantideva says that due to ignorance we see a body within the hands and other parts of our body. It is ignorance, not wisdom, that makes us see a body within its parts. In reality, there is no body within its parts. Just as at dusk we might see a pile of stones as a man even though there is no man within the stones, so in the same way our ignorance sees a body within the collection of arms, legs, and so forth, even though no body exists there. The body we see within the collection of arms and legs is simply a hallucination of our ignorant mind. Not recognizing it as this, however, we grasp at it very strongly, cherish it, and exhaust ourself in trying to protect it from any discomfort.

The way to familiarize our mind with the true nature of the body is to use the above reasoning to search for our body and then, when we have searched in every possible place and not found it, to concentrate on the space-like emptiness that is the mere absence of the truly existent body. This space-like emptiness is the true nature of our body. Although it resembles empty space, it is a meaningful emptiness. Its meaning is the utter non-existence of the truly existent body that we grasp at so strongly and have cherished all our life.

Through becoming familiar with the experience of the space-like ultimate nature of the body, our grasping at our body will be reduced. As a result we will experience far less suffering, anxiety, and frustration in relation to our body. Our physical tension will diminish and our health will improve, and even when we do become sick our physical discomfort will not disturb our mind. Those who have a direct experience of emptiness do not feel any pain even if they are beaten or shot. Knowing that the real nature of their body is like space, for them being beaten is like space being beaten and being shot is like space being shot. In addition, good and bad external conditions no longer have the power to disturb their mind, because they realize them to be like a magician's illusion, with no existence separate from the mind. Instead of being pulled here and there by changing conditions like a puppet on a string, their minds remain free and tranquil in the knowledge of the equal and unchanging ultimate nature of all things. In this way, a person who directly realizes the true nature of phenomena experiences peace day and night, life after life.

We need to distinguish between the conventionally existent body that does exist and the inherently existent body that does not exist. But we need to be careful not to be misled by the words into thinking that the conventionally existent body is anything more than a mere appearance to mind. It may be less confusing just to say that for a mind that directly sees the truth, or emptiness, there is no body. A body exists only for a mind to which a body appears.

Shantideva advises us that unless we wish to understand emptiness we should not examine conventional truths such as our body, possessions, places, and friends, but instead be satisfied with their mere names, just as worldly people are. Once a worldly person knows an object's name and purpose he is satisfied that he knows the object and does not investigate further. We must do the same, unless we want to meditate on emptiness. However, we should remember that if we did examine objects more closely we would not find them, because they would simply disappear, just like a mirage disappears if we try to look for it.

The same reasoning that we have used to prove the lack of true existence of our body can be applied to all other phenomena. This book, for example, seems to exist from its own side, somewhere within its parts. But when we examine the book more precisely we discover that none of the individual pages is the book and the collection of the pages is not the book, yet without them there is no book. Instead of finding a truly existent book, we are left beholding an emptiness that is the non-existence of the book we previously held to exist. Due to our ignorance the book appears to exist separately from our mind, as if our mind were inside and the book outside, but through analyzing the book we discover that this appearance is completely false. There is no book outside the mind. There is no book "out there," within the pages. The only way the book exists is as a mere appearance to mind, a mere projection of the mind.

All phenomena exist by way of convention; nothing is inherently existent. This applies to mind, to Buddha, and even to emptiness itself. Everything is merely imputed by mind. All phenomena have parts—physical phenomena have physical parts, and non-physical phenomena have various parts, or attributes, that can be distinguished by thought. Using the same type of reasoning as above, we can realize that any phenomenon is not one of its parts, not the collection of its parts, and not separate from its parts. In this way, we can realize the emptiness of all phenomena.

It is especially helpful to meditate on the emptiness of objects that arouse strong delusions in us like attachment or anger. By analyzing correctly we will realize that the object we desire, or the object we dislike, does not exist from its own side. Its beauty or ugliness, and even its very existence, are imputed by mind. By thinking in this way, we will discover that there is no basis for attachment or anger.

THE EMPTINESS OF OUR MIND

In *Training the Mind in Seven Points*, after outlining how to engage in analytical meditation on the emptiness of inherent existence of outer phenomena such as our body, Geshe Chekhawa continues by saying that we should then analyze our own mind to understand how it lacks inherent existence.

Our mind is not an independent entity, but an ever-changing continuum that depends on many factors, such as its previous moments, its objects, and the inner energy winds that our minds are mounted on. Like everything else, our mind is imputed on a collection of many factors and therefore lacks inherent existence. A primary mind, or consciousness, for example, has five parts or *mental factors*: feeling, discrimination, intention, contact, and attention. Neither the individual mental factors nor the collection of these mental factors is the primary mind itself, because they are mental factors and therefore parts of the primary mind. However, there is no primary mind that is separate from these mental factors. A primary mind is merely imputed on the mental factors that are its basis of imputation, and therefore it does not exist from its own side.

Having identified the nature of our primary mind, which is a formless continuum that perceives objects, we then search for it within its parts—feeling, discrimination, intention, contact, and attention—until finally we realize its unfindability. This unfindability is its ultimate nature, or emptiness. We then think:

Everything that appears to my mind is the nature of my mind.
My mind is the nature of emptiness.

In this way, we feel that everything dissolves into emptiness. We perceive only the emptiness of our mind and we meditate on this emptiness. This way of meditating on the emptiness of our mind is more profound than the meditation on the emptiness of our body. Gradually our experience of emptiness will become clearer and clearer until finally we gain an undefiled wisdom that directly realizes the emptiness of our mind.

THE EMPTINESS OF OUR I

The object we grasp at most strongly is our self or I. Due to the imprints of self-grasping ignorance accumulated over time without beginning, our I appears to us as inherently existent, and our self-grasping mind automatically grasps at it in this way. Although we grasp at an inherently existent I all the time, even during sleep, it is not easy to identify how it appears to our mind. To identify it clearly, we must begin by allowing it to manifest strongly by contemplating situations in which we have an exaggerated sense of I, such as when we are embarrassed, ashamed, afraid, or indignant. We recall or imagine such a situation and then, without any comment or analysis, try to gain a clear mental image of how the I naturally appears at such times. We have to be patient at this stage because it may take many sessions before we gain a clear image. Eventually we will see that the I appears to be completely solid and real, existing from its own side without depending on the body or the mind. This vividly appearing I is the inherently existent I that we cherish so strongly. It is the I that we defend when we are criticized and that we are so proud of when we are praised.

Once we have an image of how the I appears in these extreme circumstances, we should try to identify how it appears normally, in less extreme situations. For example, we can observe the I that is now reading this book and try to discover how it appears to our mind. Eventually we will see that although in this case there is not such an inflated sense of I, nevertheless the I still appears to be inherently existent, existing from its own side without depending on the body or the mind. Once we have an image of the inherently existent I, we focus on it for a while with single-pointed concentration. Then in meditation we proceed to the next stage, which is to contemplate logical reasons to prove that the inherently existent I we are grasping at does not in fact exist.

If the I exists in the way that it appears, it must exist in one of four ways: as the body, as the mind, as the collection of the body and mind, or as something separate from the body and mind;

there is no other possibility. We contemplate this carefully until we become convinced that this is the case and then we proceed to examine each of the four possibilities:

1. If the I is the body, there is no sense in saying "my body," because the possessor and the possessed are identical.

   If the I is the body, there is no rebirth because the I ceases when the body dies.

   If the I and the body are identical, then since we are capable of developing faith, dreaming, solving mathematical puzzles, and so on, it follows that flesh, blood, and bones can do the same.

   Since none of this is true, it follows that the I is not the body.

2. If the I is the mind, there is no sense in saying "my mind," because the possessor and the possessed are identical; but usually when we focus on our mind we say "my mind." This clearly indicates that the I is not the mind.

   If the I is the mind, then since each person has many types of mind, such as the six consciousnesses, conceptual minds, and non-conceptual minds, it follows that each person has just as many I's. Since this is absurd, the I cannot be the mind.

3. Since the body is not the I and the mind is not the I, the collection of the body and mind cannot be the I. The collection of the body and mind is a collection of things that are not the I, so how can the collection itself be the I? For example, in a herd of cows none of the animals is

a sheep, therefore the herd itself is not sheep. In the same way, in the collection of the body and mind, neither the body nor the mind is the I, therefore the collection itself is not the I.

4. If the I is not the body, not the mind, and not the collection of the body and mind, the only possibility that remains is that it is something separate from the body and mind. If this is the case, we must be able to apprehend the I without either the body or the mind appearing, but if we imagine that our body and our mind were to disappear completely, there would be nothing remaining that could be called the I. Therefore, it follows that the I is not separate from the body and mind.

We should imagine that our body gradually dissolves into thin air, and then our mind dissolves, our thoughts scatter with the wind, our feelings, wishes, and awareness melt into nothingness. Is there anything left that is the I? There is nothing. Clearly the I is not something separate from the body and mind.

We have now examined all four possibilities and have failed to find the I. Since we have already decided that there is no fifth possibility, we must conclude that the truly existent, or inherently existent, I that normally appears so vividly does not exist at all. Where there previously appeared an inherently existent I, there now appears an absence of that I. This absence of an inherently existent I is emptiness, ultimate truth.

We contemplate in this way until there appears to our mind a generic, or mental, image of the absence of an inherently existent I. This image is our object of placement meditation. We try to become completely familiar with it by concentrating on it single-pointedly for as long as possible.

Because we have grasped at an inherently existent I since beginningless time, and have cherished it more dearly than anything else, the experience of failing to find the I in meditation can be quite shocking at first. Some people develop fear, thinking that they have become completely non-existent. Others feel great joy, as if the source of all their problems is vanishing. Both reactions are good signs and indicate correct meditation. After a while these initial reactions will subside and our mind will settle into a more balanced state. Then we will be able to meditate on emptiness in a calm, controlled manner.

We should allow our mind to become absorbed in space-like emptiness for as long as possible. It is important to remember that our object is emptiness, the absence of an inherently existent I, not mere nothingness. Occasionally we should check our meditation with alertness. If our mind has wandered to another object, or if we have lost the meaning of emptiness and are focusing on mere nothingness, we should return to the contemplations to bring emptiness clearly to mind once again.

We may wonder: "If there is no truly existent I, then who is meditating? Who will get up from meditation, speak to others, and reply when my name is called?" Though there is nothing within the body and mind, or separate from the body and mind, that is the I, this does not mean that the I does not exist at all. Although the I does not exist in any of the four ways mentioned above, it does exist conventionally. The I is merely a designation imputed by conceptual mind on the collection of the body and mind. As long as we are satisfied with the mere designation "I," there is no problem. We can think, "I exist," "I am going to town," and so on. The problem arises only when we look for an I other than the mere conceptual imputation "I." The self-grasping mind grasps at an I that ultimately exists, independent of conceptual imputation, as if there were a "real" I existing behind the

The direct realization of emptiness will be our first completely non-mistaken awareness, or undefiled mind.

label. If such an I existed, we would be able to find it, but we have seen that the I cannot be found upon investigation. The conclusion of our search was a definite non-finding of the I. This unfindability of the I is the emptiness of the I, the ultimate nature of the I. The I that exists as mere imputation is the conventional nature of the I.

When we first realize emptiness, we do so conceptually, by means of a generic image. By continuing to meditate on emptiness over and over again, the generic image gradually becomes more and more transparent until it disappears entirely and we see emptiness directly. This direct realization of emptiness will be our first completely non-mistaken awareness, or undefiled mind. Until we realize emptiness directly, all our minds are mistaken awarenesses, because due to the imprints of self-grasping or true-grasping ignorance, their objects appear as inherently existent.

Most people veer toward the extreme of existence, thinking that if something exists it must exist inherently, thus exaggerating the way in which things exist without being satisfied with them as mere name. Others may veer toward the extreme of non-existence, thinking that if phenomena do not exist inherently they do not exist at all, thus exaggerating their lack of inherent existence. We need to realize that although phenomena lack any trace of existence from their own side, they do exist conventionally as mere appearances to a valid mind.

The conceptual minds grasping at the I and other phenomena as being truly existent are wrong awarenesses and should therefore be abandoned, but I am not saying that all conceptual thoughts are wrong awarenesses and should therefore be abandoned. There are many correct conceptual minds that are useful in our day-to-day lives, such as the conceptual mind remembering what we did yesterday or the conceptual mind understanding how to make a cup of tea. There are also many conceptual minds that need to be cultivated on the spiritual path. For example, conventional bodhichitta in the mental continuum of a Bodhisattva is a conceptual mind because it apprehends its object, great enlightenment, by means of a generic image. Moreover, before we can realize emptiness directly with a non-conceptual mind, we need to realize it by means of an inferential cognizer, which is a conceptual mind. Through contemplating the reasons that refute inherent existence, there appears to our mind a generic image of the absence, or emptiness, of inherent existence. This is the only way that emptiness of inherent existence can initially appear to our mind. We then meditate on this image with stronger and stronger concentration until we finally perceive emptiness directly.

There are some people who say that the way to meditate on emptiness is simply to empty our mind of all conceptual thoughts, arguing that just as white clouds obscure the sun as much as black clouds, so positive conceptual thoughts obscure our mind as much as negative conceptual thoughts. This view is completely mistaken, because if we make no effort to gain a conceptual understanding of emptiness, but try instead to suppress all conceptual thoughts, actual emptiness will never appear to our mind. We may achieve a vivid experience of a space-like vacuity, but this is just the absence of conceptual thought—it is not emptiness, the true nature of phenomena. Meditation on this vacuity may temporarily calm our mind, but it will never destroy our delusions or liberate us from samsara.

If all the necessary atmospheric causes and conditions come together, clouds will appear. If these are absent, clouds cannot form. The clouds are completely dependent on causes and conditions for their development; without these they have no power to develop. The same is true for mountains, planets, bodies, minds, and all other produced phenomena. Because they depend on factors outside themselves for their existence, they are empty of inherent, or independent, existence and are mere imputations of the mind.

Contemplating the teachings on karma can help us to understand this. Where do all our good and bad experiences come from? According to Buddhism, they are the result of the positive and negative karma we created in the past. As a result of positive karma, attractive and agreeable people appear in our life, pleasant material conditions arise, and we live in a beautiful environment. But as a result of negative karma unpleasant people and things appear. This world is the effect of the collective karma created by the beings who inhabit it. Because karma originates in the mind—specifically in our mental intentions—we can see that all worlds arise from the mind. This is similar to the way in which appearances arise in a dream. Everything we perceive when we are dreaming is the result of the ripening of karmic potentials in our mind and has no existence outside our mind. When our mind is calm and pure, positive karmic imprints ripen and pleasant dream appearances arise. But when our mind is agitated and impure, negative karmic imprints ripen and unpleasant, nightmarish appearances arise. In a similar way, all the appearances of our waking world are simply the ripening of positive, negative, or neutral karmic imprints in our mind.

Once we understand how things arise from their inner and outer causes and conditions and have no independent existence, then just seeing or thinking about the production of phenomena will remind us of their emptiness. Instead of reinforcing our sense of the solidity and objectivity of things, we will begin to see things as manifestations of their emptiness, with no more concrete existence than a rainbow arising out of an empty sky.

Just as the production of things depends on causes and conditions, so too does the disintegration of things. Therefore, neither production nor disintegration can be truly existent. For example, if our new car was destroyed we would feel unhappy because we grasp at both the car and the disintegration of the car as truly existent. But if we understood that our car is merely an appearance to our mind, like a car in a dream, its destruction would not disturb us. This is true for all objects of our attachment; if we realize that both objects and their cessations lack true existence, there is no basis for becoming upset if we are separated from them.

All functioning things—our environments, enjoyments, body, mind, and self—change from moment to moment. They are impermanent in the sense that they do not last for a second moment.

The book you are reading in this moment is not the same book that you were reading a moment ago, and it could only come into existence because the book of a moment ago ceased to exist. When we understand subtle impermanence—that our body, mind, self, and so forth do not abide for a second moment—it is not difficult to understand that they are empty of inherent existence.

Even though we may agree that impermanent phenomena are empty of inherent existence, we might think that because permanent phenomena are unchanging and do not arise from causes and conditions, they must exist inherently. However, even permanent phenomena such as emptiness and unproduced space—the mere absence of physical obstruction—are dependent-related phenomena because they depend on their parts, their bases, and the minds that impute them; and therefore they are not inherently existent. Although emptiness is ultimate reality, it is not independent or inherently existent for it too depends on its parts, its bases, and the minds that impute it. Just as a gold coin does not exist separately from its gold, so the emptiness of our body does not exist separately from our body, because it is simply our body's lack of inherent existence.

Whenever we go anywhere, we develop the thought, "I am going," and grasp at an inherently existent act of going. In a similar way, when someone comes to visit us we think, "They are coming," and we grasp at an inherently existent act of coming. Both these conceptions are self-grasping and wrong awarenesses. When someone goes away, we feel that a truly existent person has truly left, and when they come back we feel that a truly existent person has truly returned. However, the coming and going of people is like the appearance and disappearance of a rainbow in the sky. When the causes and conditions for a rainbow to appear are assembled, a rainbow appears; and when the causes and conditions for the continued appearance of the rainbow disperse, the rainbow disappears. But the rainbow does not come from anywhere nor does it go anywhere.

When we observe one object, such as our I, we feel strongly that it is a single, indivisible entity, and that its singularity is inherently existent. In reality, however, our I has many parts, such as the parts that look, listen, walk, and think, or the parts that are, for example, a teacher, a mother, a daughter, and a wife. Our I is imputed onto the collection of all these parts. As with each individual phenomenon it is a singularity, but its singularity is merely imputed, like an army that is merely imputed onto a collection of soldiers or a forest that is imputed onto a collection of trees.

When we see more than one object, we regard the multiplicity of these objects to be inherently existent. However, just as singularity is merely imputed, likewise plurality is just an imputation by mind and does not exist from the side of the object. For example, instead of looking at a collection of soldiers or trees from the point of view of the individual soldiers or trees, we could look at them as an army or a forest, that is, as a singular collection or whole, in which case we would be looking at a singularity rather than a plurality.

In summary, singularity does not exist from its own side because it is just imputed on a plurality—its parts. In the same way, plurality does not exist from its own side because it is just imputed on a singularity—the collection of its parts. Therefore, singularity and plurality are mere imputations by conceptual mind and they lack true existence. If we realize this clearly, there is no basis for developing attachment and anger toward objects, either singular or plural. We tend to project the faults or qualities of the few onto the many, and then develop hatred or attachment on the basis of, for example, race, religion, or country. Contemplating the emptiness of singularity and plurality can be helpful in reducing such hatred and attachment.

Although production, disintegration, and so forth do exist, they do not exist inherently or truly, and the conceptual minds that grasp them as truly existent are instances of self-grasping ignorance. These conceptions grasp at the eight extremes: truly existent production, truly existent disintegration, truly existent impermanence, truly existent permanence, truly existent going, truly existent coming, truly existent singularity, and truly existent plurality. Although these extremes do not exist, due to our ignorance we are always grasping them. The conceptions of these extremes lie at the root of all delusions, and because delusions give rise to contaminated actions that keep us trapped in samsara, these conceptions are the root of samsara.

The subject of the eight extremes is profound and requires detailed explanation and lengthy study. Buddha explains them in detail in the *Perfection of Wisdom Sutras*. And in *Fundamental Wisdom*, a commentary to the *Perfection of Wisdom Sutras*, Nagarjuna also uses many profound and powerful reasons to prove that the eight extremes do not exist by showing how all phenomena are empty of inherent existence. Through analyzing conventional truths, he establishes their ultimate nature, and shows why it is necessary to understand both the conventional and ultimate natures of an object in order to understand that object fully.

CONVENTIONAL AND ULTIMATE TRUTHS

Whatever exists is either a conventional truth or an ultimate truth, and since ultimate truth refers just to emptiness, everything except emptiness is a conventional truth. The things that we see directly, such as houses, cars, and tables, are all conventional truths.

All conventional truths are false objects because the way they appear and the way they exist do not correspond. If someone appears to be friendly and kind, but his real intention is to gain our confidence in order to rob us, we would say that he is false or deceptive because there is a discrepancy between the way he appears and his real nature. Similarly, objects such as forms and sounds are false or deceptive because they appear to exist inherently but in reality are completely devoid of inherent existence. Because the way they appear does not coincide with the way they exist, conventional truths are known as *deceptive phenomena*. A cup, for example, appears to exist independently of its parts, its causes, and the mind that apprehends it, but in reality it totally depends on these things. Because the way the cup appears to our mind and the way it exists do not correspond, the cup is a false object.

Although conventional truths are false objects, nevertheless they actually exist because a mind directly perceiving a conventional truth is a valid mind, a completely reliable mind. For example, an eye consciousness directly perceiving a cup on the table is a valid mind because it will not deceive us—if we reach out to pick up the cup we will find it where our eye consciousness sees it. In this respect, an eye consciousness perceiving a cup on the table is different from an eye consciousness mistaking a cup reflected in a mirror for a real cup, or an eye consciousness seeing a mirage as water. Even though a cup is a false object, for practical purposes the eye consciousness that directly perceives it is a valid, reliable mind. However, although it is a valid mind, it is nevertheless mistaken insofar as the cup appears to that mind to be truly existent. It is valid and non-deceptive with respect to the conventional characteristics of the cup—its position, size, color, and so forth—but mistaken with respect to its ultimate nature.

To summarize, conventional objects are false because although they appear to exist from their own side, in reality they are mere appearances to mind, like things seen in a dream. Within the context of a dream, however, dream objects have a relative validity, and this distinguishes them from things that do not exist at all. Suppose in a dream we steal a diamond and someone then asks us whether we were the one who stole it. Even though the dream is merely a creation of our mind, if we answer "yes" we are telling the truth while if we answer "no" we are telling a lie. In the same way, even though in reality the whole universe is just an appearance to mind, within the context of the experience of ordinary beings we can distinguish between relative truths and relative falsities.

Conventional truths can be divided into gross conventional truths and subtle conventional truths. We can understand how all phenomena have these two levels of conventional truth by considering the example of a car. The car itself, the car depending on its causes, and the car depending on its parts are all gross conventional truths of the car. They are called "gross" because they are relatively easy to understand. The car depending on its basis of imputation is quite subtle and is not easy to understand, but it is still a gross conventional truth. The basis of imputation of the car is the parts of the car. To apprehend car, the parts of the car must appear to our mind; without the parts appearing, there is no way to develop the thought "car." For this reason, the parts are the basis of imputation of the car. We say, "I see a car," but strictly speaking all we ever see is parts of the car. However, when we develop the thought "car" by seeing its parts, we see the car. There is no car other than its parts, there is no body other than its parts, and so on. The car existing merely as an imputation by thought is the subtle conventional truth of the car. We have understood this when we realize that the car is nothing more than a mere imputation by a valid mind. We cannot understand subtle conventional truths unless we have understood emptiness. When we thoroughly realize subtle conventional truth, we have realized both conventional truth and ultimate truth.

Only emptiness is true because only emptiness exists in the way that it appears.

Strictly speaking, truth, ultimate truth, and emptiness are synonymous because conventional truths are not real truths but false objects. They are true only for the minds of those who have not realized emptiness. Only emptiness is true because only emptiness exists in the way that it appears. When the mind of any living being directly perceives conventional truths, such as forms, they appear to exist from their own side. When the mind of a Superior being directly perceives emptiness, however, nothing appears other than emptiness; this mind is totally mixed with the mere absence of true existence. The way in which emptiness appears to the mind of a non-conceptual direct perceiver corresponds exactly to the way in which emptiness exists.

It should be noted that although emptiness is ultimate truth it is not inherently existent. Emptiness is not a separate reality existing behind conventional appearances but is the real nature of those appearances. We cannot talk about emptiness in isolation, because emptiness is always the mere lack of inherent existence *of* something. For example, the emptiness of our body is the lack of inherent existence of our body, and without our body as its basis this emptiness cannot exist. Because emptiness necessarily depends on a basis, it lacks inherent existence.

In *Guide to the Bodhisattva's Way of Life*, Shantideva defines ultimate truth as a phenomenon that is true for the uncontaminated mind of a Superior being. An uncontaminated mind is a mind that realizes emptiness directly. This mind is the only unmistaken awareness and is possessed exclusively by Superior beings. Because uncontaminated minds are completely unmistaken, anything directly perceived by them to be true is necessarily an ultimate truth. In contrast, anything that is directly perceived to be true by the mind of an ordinary being is necessarily not an ultimate truth, because all minds of ordinary beings are mistaken, and mistaken minds can never directly perceive the truth.

Due to the imprints of conceptual thoughts that grasp at the eight extremes, everything that appears to the minds of ordinary beings appears to be inherently existent. Only the wisdom of meditative equipoise that directly realizes emptiness is undefiled by the imprints, or stains, of these conceptual thoughts. This is the only wisdom that has no mistaken appearance.

When a Superior Bodhisattva meditates on emptiness, his or her mind mixes with emptiness completely, with no appearance of inherent existence. He develops a completely pure, uncontaminated wisdom that is ultimate bodhichitta. When he arises from meditative equipoise, however, due to the imprints of true-grasping, conventional phenomena again appear to his mind as inherently existent, and his uncontaminated wisdom becomes temporarily non-manifest. Only a Buddha can manifest uncontaminated wisdom at the same time as directly perceiving conventional truths. An uncommon quality of a Buddha is that a single moment of a Buddha's mind realizes both conventional truth and ultimate truth directly and simultaneously. There are many levels of ultimate bodhichitta. For example, the ultimate bodhichitta attained through Tantric practice is more profound than that developed through Sutra practice alone, and the supreme ultimate bodhichitta is that of a Buddha.

If through valid reasoning we realize the emptiness of the first extreme, the extreme of production, we will easily be able to realize the emptiness of the remaining seven extremes. Once we have realized the emptiness of the eight extremes we have realized the emptiness of all phenomena. Having gained this realization, we continue to contemplate and meditate on the emptiness of produced phenomena and so forth, and as our meditations deepen we will feel all phenomena dissolving into emptiness. We will then be able to maintain a single-pointed concentration on the emptiness of all phenomena.

To meditate on the emptiness of produced phenomena we can think:

There is an I or self that is reborn again and again within samsara. This I is a produced phenomenon because its existence depends on causes and conditions, such as its previous continuum and our karma, and therefore it lacks true existence. If we search for our I within our body and mind, or separate from our body and mind, we cannot find it; and instead of a truly existent I appearing to our mind, a space-like emptiness appears.

We feel that our mind enters into this space-like emptiness and remains there single-pointedly. In this way, we try to continuously maintain the appearance of the emptiness of inherent existence of the I. What appears to our mind is just a space-like emptiness, but we understand this emptiness to be the non-existence of the truly existent I. We need to maintain both the appearance of emptiness and the special understanding of the meaning of this emptiness. This meditation is called *space-like meditative equipoise on emptiness.*

Just as eagles soar through the vast expanse of the sky without meeting any obstructions, needing only minimal effort to maintain their flight, so advanced meditators concentrating on emptiness can meditate on emptiness for a long time with little effort. Their minds soar through space-like emptiness, undistracted by any other phenomenon. When we meditate on emptiness, we should try to emulate these meditators. Once we have found our object of meditation, the mere absence of the inherently existent I, we should refrain from further analysis and simply rest our mind in the experience of this emptiness. From time to time we should check to make sure that we have not lost either the clear appearance of emptiness or the recognition of its meaning, but we should not check too forcefully because this will disturb our concentration. Our meditation should not be like the flight of a small bird, which never stops flapping its wings and is always changing direction, but like the flight of an eagle, which soars gently with only occasional adjustments to its wings. Through meditating in this way, we will feel our mind dissolving into and becoming one with emptiness.

If we are successful in doing this, then during our meditation we are free from manifest self-grasping. If on the other hand, we spend all our time checking and analyzing, never allowing our mind to relax into the space of emptiness, we will never gain this experience and our meditation will not function to reduce our self-grasping.

In general we need to improve our understanding of emptiness through extensive study, approaching it from many angles and using many different lines of reasoning. It is also important to become thoroughly familiar with one complete meditation on emptiness through continuous contemplation, understanding exactly how to use the reasoning to lead to an experience of emptiness. We can then concentrate on emptiness single-pointedly and try to mix our mind with it, like water mixing with water.

THE UNION OF THE TWO TRUTHS

The union of the two truths means that conventional truths, such as our body, and ultimate truths, such as the emptiness of our body, are the same nature. The main purpose of understanding and meditating on this union is to prevent dualistic appearances—appearances of inherent existence to the mind that is meditating on emptiness—and thereby enable our mind to dissolve into emptiness. Once we can do this, our meditation on emptiness will be very powerful in eliminating our delusions. If we correctly identify and negate the inherently existent body, and meditate on the mere absence of such a body with strong concentration, we will feel our normal body dissolving into emptiness. We will understand that the real nature of our body is emptiness and that our body is merely a manifestation of emptiness.

Emptiness is like the sky and our body is like the blue of the sky. Just as the blue is a manifestation of the sky itself and cannot be separated from it, so our blue-like body is simply a manifestation of the sky of its emptiness and cannot be separated from it. If we realize this, when we focus on the emptiness of our body we feel that our body itself dissolves into its ultimate nature. In this way, we can easily overcome the conventional appearance of the body in our meditations, and our mind naturally mixes with emptiness.

In the *Heart Sutra*, Bodhisattva Avalokiteshvara says, "Form is not other than emptiness." This means that conventional phenomena, such as our body, do not exist separately from their emptiness. When we meditate on the emptiness of our body with this understanding, we know that the emptiness appearing to our mind is the very nature of our body, and that apart from this emptiness there is no body. Meditating in this way will greatly weaken our self-grasping mind. If we really believed that our body and its emptiness were the same nature, our self-grasping would definitely become weaker.

Although we can divide emptinesses from the point of view of their bases, and speak of the emptiness of the body, the emptiness of the I, and so forth, in truth all emptinesses are the same nature. If we look at ten bottles, we can distinguish ten different spaces inside the bottles, but in reality these spaces are the same nature. And if we break the bottles the spaces become indistinguishable. In the same way, although we can speak of the emptiness of the body, the mind, the I, and so forth, in reality they are the same nature and indistinguishable. The only way in which they can be distinguished is by their conventional bases.

There are two principal benefits of understanding that all emptinesses are the same nature: in the meditation session our mind will mix with emptiness more easily, and in the meditation break we will be able to see all appearances as equal manifestations of their emptiness.

For as long as we feel that there is a gap between our mind and emptiness—that our mind is "here" and emptiness is "there"—our mind will not mix with emptiness. Knowing that all emptinesses are the same nature helps to close this gap. In ordinary life we experience many different objects—good, bad, attractive, unattractive—and our feelings toward them differ. Because we feel that the differences exist from the side of the objects, our mind is unbalanced and we develop attachment to attractive objects, aversion to unattractive objects, and indifference to neutral objects. It is very difficult to mix such an uneven mind with emptiness. To mix our mind with emptiness we need to know that, although phenomena appear in many different aspects, in essence they are all empty. The differences we see are just appearances to mistaken minds; from the point of view of ultimate truth all phenomena are equal in emptiness. For a qualified meditator single-pointedly absorbed in emptiness, there is no difference between production and disintegration, impermanence and permanence, going and coming, singularity and plurality—everything is equal in emptiness and all problems of attachment, anger, and self-grasping ignorance are solved. In this experience, everything becomes very peaceful and comfortable, balanced and harmonious, joyful and wonderful. There is no heat, no cold, no lower, no higher, no here, no there, no self, no other, no samsara—everything is equal in the peace of emptiness. This realization is called the *yoga of equalizing samsara and nirvana*, and is explained in detail in both the Sutras and Tantras.

Since all emptinesses are the same nature, the ultimate nature of a mind that is meditating on emptiness is the same nature as the ultimate nature of its object. When we first meditate on emptiness, our mind and emptiness appear to be two separate phenomena, but when we understand that all emptinesses are the same nature, we will know that this feeling of separation is simply the experience of a mistaken mind. In reality our mind and emptiness are ultimately of one taste. If we apply this knowledge in our meditations, it will help to prevent the appearance of the conventional nature of our mind and allow our mind to dissolve into emptiness.

Having mixed our mind with emptiness, when we arise from meditation we will experience all phenomena equally as manifestations of their emptiness. Instead of feeling that the attractive, unattractive, and neutral objects we see are inherently different, we will know that in essence they are the same nature. Just as both the gentlest and most violent waves in an ocean are equally water, likewise both attractive forms and repulsive forms are equally manifestations of emptiness. Realizing this, our mind will become balanced and peaceful. We will recognize all conventional appearances as the magical play of the mind, and we will not grasp strongly at their apparent differences.

When Milarepa once taught emptiness to a woman he compared emptiness to the sky and conventional truths to clouds and told her to meditate on the sky. She followed his instructions with great success, but she had one problem—when she meditated on the sky of emptiness, everything disappeared and she could not understand how phenomena could exist conventionally. She said to Milarepa, "I find it easy to meditate on the sky but difficult to establish the clouds. Please teach me how to meditate on the clouds." Milarepa replied, "If your meditation on the sky is going well, the clouds will not be a problem. Clouds simply appear in the sky—they arise from the sky and dissolve back into the sky. As your experience of the sky improves, you will naturally come to understand the clouds."

In Tibetan, the word for both sky and space is *namkha*, although space is different from sky. There are two types of space, produced space and unproduced space. Produced space is the visible space we can see inside a room or in the sky. This space may become dark at night and light during the day, and because it undergoes change in this way it is an impermanent phenomenon. The characteristic property of produced space is that it does not obstruct objects—if there is space in a room we can place objects there without obstruction. Similarly, birds are able to fly through the space of the sky because it lacks obstruction, but they cannot fly through a mountain! Therefore, it is clear that produced space lacks, or is empty of, obstructive contact. This mere lack, or emptiness, of obstructive contact is unproduced space.

Because unproduced space is the mere absence of obstructive contact, it does not undergo momentary change and is therefore a permanent phenomenon. Whereas produced space is visible and quite easy to understand, unproduced space is a mere absence of obstructive contact and is somewhat more subtle. Once we understand unproduced space, however, we will find it easier to understand emptiness.

The only difference between emptiness and unproduced space is their object of negation. The object of negation of unproduced space is obstructive contact while the object of negation of emptiness is inherent existence. Because unproduced space is the best analogy for understanding emptiness, it is used in the Sutras and in many scriptures. Unproduced space is a non-affirming negative phenomenon—a phenomenon that is realized by a mind that merely eliminates its negated object without realizing another positive phenomenon. Produced space is an affirmative, or positive, phenomenon—a phenomenon that is realized without the mind explicitly eliminating a negated object. More details on these two types of phenomenon can be found in *Heart of Wisdom* and *Ocean of Nectar*.

THE PRACTICE OF EMPTINESS IN OUR DAILY ACTIVITIES

In our daily activities, we should regard all appearances as illusory. Although things appear to us as inherently existent we should remember that these appearances are deceptive and that in reality things lack true existence. When a magician creates an illusory tiger, a tiger appears very clearly to his mind but he knows that it is just an illusion. In fact, the very appearance of the tiger reminds him that there is no tiger. In the same way, when we are very familiar with emptiness, the very fact that things appear to be truly existent will remind us that they are not truly existent. We should therefore recognize that whatever appears to us in our daily life is like an illusion and lacks true existence. In this way our wisdom will increase day by day, and our self-grasping ignorance and other delusions will naturally diminish.

Between meditation sessions we should be like an actor. When an actor plays the part of a king, he dresses, speaks, and acts like a king, but he knows all the time that he is not a real king. In the same way, we should live and function in the conventional world yet always remember that we ourself, our environment, and the people around us are not the truly existent entities they seem to be. They are merely projections of our mind, and their real nature is just emptiness.

If we think like this, we will be able to live in the conventional world without grasping at it. We will treat it lightly and have the flexibility of mind to respond to every situation in a constructive way. Knowing that whatever appears to our mind is mere appearance, when attractive objects appear we will not grasp at them and develop attachment, and when unattractive objects appear we will not grasp at them and develop aversion or anger.

In *Training the Mind in Seven Points*, Geshe Chekhawa says: "Think that all phenomena are like dreams." Some of the things we see in our dreams are beautiful and some are ugly, but they are all mere appearances to our dreaming mind. They do not exist from their own side, and are empty of inherent existence. It is the same with the objects we perceive when we are awake—they too are mere appearances to mind and lack inherent existence.

All phenomena lack inherent existence. When we look at a rainbow it appears to occupy a particular location in space, and it seems that if we searched we would be able to find where the rainbow touches the ground. We know, however, that no matter how hard we search we will never be able to find the end of the rainbow, because as soon as we arrive at the place where we saw the rainbow touch the ground, the rainbow will have disappeared. If we do not search for it the rainbow appears clearly, but when we look for it, it is not there. All phenomena are like this. If we do not analyze them they appear clearly, but when we search for them analytically, trying to isolate them from everything else, they are not there.

If something did exist inherently, and we investigated it by separating it from all other phenomena, we would be able to find it. However, all phenomena are like rainbows—if we search for them we will never find them. At first we might find this idea very uncomfortable and difficult to accept, but this is quite natural. With greater familiarity we will find this reasoning more acceptable, and eventually we will realize that it is true.

> *All phenomena are like rainbows—if we search for them we will never find them.*

It is important to understand that emptiness does not mean nothingness. Although things do not exist from their own side, independent of the mind, they do exist in the sense that they are understood by a valid mind. The world we experience when we are awake is similar to the world we experience when we are dreaming. We cannot say that dream things do not exist, but if we believe that they exist as more than mere appearances to the mind, existing "out there," then we are mistaken, as we will discover when we wake up.

As mentioned before, there is no greater method for experiencing peace of mind and happiness than to understand and meditate on emptiness. Since it is our self-grasping that keeps us bound to the prison of samsara and is the source of all our suffering, meditation on emptiness is the universal solution to all our problems. It is the medicine that cures all mental and physical diseases and the nectar that bestows the everlasting happiness of nirvana and enlightenment.

Dedication

Through the virtues I have collected by writing this book, may everyone be happy and free from misery. May all living beings find the opportunity to practice the instructions given in *Transform Your Life*, and may they attain the supreme inner peace of enlightenment.

Liberating Prayer

PRAISE TO BUDDHA SHAKYAMUNI

and

Prayers for Meditation

BRIEF PREPARATORY PRAYERS FOR MEDITATION

Liberating Prayer

and

Prayers for Meditation

Liberating Prayer

PRAISE TO BUDDHA SHAKYAMUNI

O Blessed One, Shakyamuni Buddha,
Precious treasury of compassion,
Bestower of supreme inner peace,

You, who love all beings without exception,
Are the source of happiness and goodness;
And you guide us to the liberating path.

Your body is a wishfulfilling jewel,
Your speech is supreme, purifying nectar,
And your mind is refuge for all living beings.

With folded hands I turn to you,
Supreme unchanging friend,
I request from the depths of my heart:

Please give me the light of your wisdom
To dispel the darkness of my mind
And to heal my mental continuum.

Please nourish me with your goodness,
That I in turn may nourish all beings
With an unceasing banquet of delight.

Through your compassionate intention,
Your blessings and virtuous deeds,
And my strong wish to rely upon you,

May all suffering quickly cease
And all happiness and joy be fulfilled;
And may holy Dharma flourish for evermore.

Colophon: This prayer was composed by Venerable Geshe Kelsang Gyatso. It is recited regularly at the beginning of sadhanas in Kadampa Buddhist Centers throughout the world.

Prayers for Meditation

Going for refuge

I and all sentient beings, until we achieve enlightenment,
Go for refuge to Buddha, Dharma, and Sangha.

(3x, 7x, 100x, or more)

Generating bodhichitta

Through the virtues I collect by giving and other perfections,
May I become a Buddha for the benefit of all. (3x)

Generating the four immeasurables

May everyone be happy,
May everyone be free from misery,
May no one ever be separated from their happiness,
May everyone have equanimity, free from hatred and attachment.

Visualizing the Field for Accumulating Merit

In the space before me is the living Buddha Shakyamuni surrounded by all the Buddhas and Bodhisattvas, like the full moon surrounded by stars.

Prayer of seven limbs

With my body, speech, and mind, humbly I prostrate,
And make offerings both set out and imagined.
I confess my wrong deeds from all time,
And rejoice in the virtues of all.
Please stay until samsara ceases,
And turn the Wheel of Dharma for us.
I dedicate all virtues to great enlightenment.

Offering the mandala

The ground sprinkled with perfume and spread with flowers,
The Great Mountain, four lands, sun and moon,
Seen as a Buddha Land and offered thus,
May all beings enjoy such Pure Lands.

I offer without any sense of loss
The objects that give rise to my attachment, hatred, and confusion,
My friends, enemies, and strangers, our bodies and enjoyments;
Please accept these and bless me to be released directly from the three
 poisons.

IDAM GURU RATNA MANDALAKAM NIRYATAYAMI

Prayer of the Stages of the Path

The path begins with strong reliance
On my kind Teacher, source of all good;
O Bless me with this understanding
To follow him with great devotion.

This human life with all its freedoms,
Extremely rare, with so much meaning;
O Bless me with this understanding
All day and night to seize its essence.

My body, like a water bubble,
Decays and dies so very quickly;
After death come results of karma,
Just like the shadow of a body.

With this firm knowledge and remembrance
Bless me to be extremely cautious,
Always avoiding harmful actions
And gathering abundant virtue.

Samsara's pleasures are deceptive,
Give no contentment, only torment;
So please bless me to strive sincerely
To gain the bliss of perfect freedom.

O Bless me so that from this pure thought
Come mindfulness and greatest caution,
To keep as my essential practice
The doctrine's root, the Pratimoksha.

Just like myself all my kind mothers
Are drowning in samsara's ocean;
O So that I may soon release them,
Bless me to train in bodhichitta.

But I cannot become a Buddha
By this alone without three ethics;
So bless me with the strength to practice
The Bodhisattva's ordination.

By pacifying my distractions
And analyzing perfect meanings,
Bless me to quickly gain the union
Of special insight and quiescence.

When I become a pure container
Through common paths, bless me to enter
The essence practice of good fortune,
The supreme vehicle, Vajrayana.

The two attainments both depend on
My sacred vows and my commitments;
Bless me to understand this clearly
And keep them at the cost of my life.

By constant practice in four sessions,
The way explained by holy Teachers,
O Bless me to gain both the stages,
Which are the essence of the Tantras.

May those who guide me on the good path,
And my companions all have long lives;
Bless me to pacify completely
All obstacles, outer and inner.

May I always find perfect Teachers,
And take delight in holy Dharma,
Accomplish all grounds and paths swiftly,
And gain the state of Vajradhara.

Receiving blessings and purifying

From the hearts of all the holy beings, streams of light and nectar flow down, granting blessings and purifying.

At this point we begin the actual contemplation and meditation. After the meditation we dedicate our merit while reciting the following prayers:

Dedication prayers

Through the virtues I have collected
By practicing the stages of the path,
May all living beings find the opportunity
To practice in the same way.

May everyone experience
The happiness of humans and gods,
And quickly attain enlightenment,
So that samsara is finally extinguished.

Colophon: These prayers were compiled from traditional sources by Venerable Geshe Kelsang Gyatso.

APPENDIX II

What is Meditation?

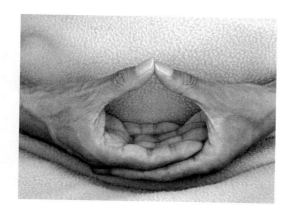

What is Meditation?

What is Meditation?

*M*editation is a mind that concentrates on a virtuous object, and a mental action that is the main cause of mental peace. Whenever we meditate, we are performing an action that will cause us to experience inner peace in the future. Normally, throughout our life, we experience delusions day and night, and these are the opposite of mental peace. Sometimes, however, we naturally experience inner peace because in our previous lives we concentrated on virtuous objects. A virtuous object is one that causes us to develop a peaceful mind when we concentrate on it. If we concentrate on an object that causes us to develop an unpeaceful mind, such as anger or attachment, this indicates that for us the object is non-virtuous. There are also many neutral objects that are neither virtuous nor non-virtuous.

There are two types of meditation: analytical meditation and placement meditation. Analytical meditation involves contemplating the meaning of a spiritual instruction that we have heard or read. By contemplating such instructions deeply, eventually we will reach a definite conclusion, or cause a specific virtuous state of mind to arise. This is the object of placement meditation. We then concentrate single-pointedly on this conclusion or virtuous state of mind for as long as possible to become deeply familiar with it. This single-pointed concentration is placement meditation. Analytical meditation is often called contemplation, and placement meditation is often called meditation. Placement meditation depends on analytical meditation, and analytical meditation depends on listening to or reading spiritual instructions.

THE BENEFITS OF MEDITATION

The purpose of meditation is to make our mind calm and peaceful. As mentioned earlier, if our mind is peaceful we will be free from worries and mental discomfort, and so we will experience true happiness. But if our mind is not peaceful, we will find it very difficult to be happy, even if we are living in the very best conditions. If we train in meditation, our mind will gradually become more and more peaceful, and we will experience a purer and purer form of happiness. Eventually we will be able to stay happy all the time, even in the most difficult circumstances.

Usually we find it difficult to control our mind. It seems as if our mind is like a balloon in the wind—blown here and there by external circumstances. If things go well, our mind is happy, but if they go badly, it immediately becomes unhappy. For example, if we get what we want, such as a new possession, a new position, or a new partner, we become overly excited and cling to them tightly. But since we cannot have everything we want, and since we will inevitably be separated from the friends, position, and possessions we currently enjoy, this mental stickiness, or attachment, only causes us pain. On the other hand, if we do not get what we want, or if we lose something we like, we become despondent or irritated. For example, if we are forced to work with a colleague we dislike, we will probably become irritated and feel aggrieved, with the result that we will not be able to work with him or her efficiently and our time at work will become stressful and unrewarding.

Such fluctuations of mood arise because we are too closely involved in the external situation. We are like a child making a sandcastle who is excited when it is first made, but who becomes upset when it is destroyed by the incoming tide. By training in meditation, we create an inner space and clarity that enable us to control our mind regardless of the external circumstances. Gradually we develop mental equilibrium, a balanced mind that is happy all the time, rather than an unbalanced mind that oscillates between the extremes of excitement and despondency.

If we train in meditation systematically, we will eventually be able to eradicate the delusions from our mind that are the causes of all our problems and suffering. In this way, we will come to experience permanent inner peace. Then day and night, in life after life, we will experience only peace and happiness.

At the beginning, even if our meditation does not seem to be going well, we should remember that simply by applying effort to training in meditation, we are creating the mental karma to experience inner peace in the future. The happiness of this life and of our future lives depends on the experience of inner peace, which in turn depends on the mental action of meditation. Since inner peace is the source of all happiness, we can see how important meditation is.

HOW TO BEGIN MEDITATION

The first stage of meditation is to stop distractions and make our mind clearer and more lucid. This can be accomplished by practicing a simple breathing meditation. We choose a quiet place to meditate and sit in a comfortable position. We can sit in the traditional cross-legged posture or in any other position that is comfortable. If we wish, we can sit in a chair. The most important thing is to keep our back straight to prevent our mind from becoming sluggish or sleepy.

We sit with our eyes partially closed and turn our attention to our breathing. We breathe naturally, preferably through the nostrils, without attempting to control our breath, and we try to become aware of the sensation of the breath as it enters and leaves the nostrils. This sensation is our object of meditation. We should try to concentrate on it to the exclusion of everything else.

At first our mind will be very busy, and we might even feel that the meditation is making our mind busier, but in reality we are just becoming more aware of how busy our mind actually is. There will be a great temptation to follow the different thoughts as they arise, but we should resist this and remain focused single-pointedly on the sensation of the breath. If we discover that our mind has wandered and is following our thoughts, we should immediately return it to the breath. We should repeat this as many times as necessary until the mind settles on the breath.

If we practice patiently in this way, gradually our distracting thoughts will subside and we will experience a sense of inner peace and relaxation. Our mind will feel lucid and spacious and we will feel refreshed. When the sea is rough, sediment is churned up and the water becomes murky, but when the wind dies down the mud gradually settles and the water becomes clear. In a similar way, when the otherwise incessant flow of our distracting thoughts is calmed through concentrating on the breath, our mind becomes unusually lucid and clear. We should stay with this state of mental calm for a while.

Even though breathing meditation is only a preliminary stage of meditation, it can be quite powerful. We can see from this practice that it is possible to experience inner peace and contentment just by controlling the mind, without having to depend at all on external conditions. When the turbulence of distracting thoughts subsides and our mind becomes still, a deep happiness and contentment naturally arise from within. This feeling of contentment and well-being helps us cope with the busyness and difficulties of daily life. So much of the stress and tension we normally experience comes from our mind, and many of the problems we experience, including poor health, are caused or aggravated by this stress. Just by doing breathing meditation for ten or fifteen minutes each day, we will be able to reduce this stress. We will experience a calm, spacious feeling in the mind, and many of our usual problems will disappear. Difficult situations will become easier to deal with, we will naturally feel warm and friendly toward other people, and our relationships with others will gradually improve.

We should train in this preliminary meditation until we reduce our gross distractions, and then we can train in the actual meditations explained in *Transform Your Life*. When we do these meditations we should begin by calming the mind with breathing meditation, and then proceed to the stages of analytical and placement meditation according to the specific instructions for each meditation.

The Kadampa Way of Life

THE ESSENTIAL PRACTICE
OF KADAM LAMRIM

The Kadampa Way of Life

Introduction

This essential practice of Kadam Lamrim, known as *The Kadampa Way of Life*, contains two texts: *Advice from Atisha's Heart* and Je Tsongkhapa's *The Three Principal Aspects of the Path*. The first encapsulates the way of life of the early Kadampa practitioners, whose example of purity and sincerity we should all try to emulate. The second is a profound guide to meditation on the stages of the path, Lamrim, which Je Tsongkhapa composed based on the instructions he received directly from the Wisdom Buddha Manjushri.

If we try our best to put Atisha's advice into practice, and to meditate on Lamrim according to Je Tsongkhapa's instructions, we will develop a pure and happy mind and gradually progress toward the ultimate peace of full enlightenment. As Bodhisattva Shantideva says:

> By depending upon this boat-like human form,
> We can cross the great ocean of suffering.
> Since such a vessel will be hard to find again,
> This is no time to sleep, you fool!

Practicing in this way is the very essence of the Kadampa way of life.

Advice from Atisha's Heart

When Venerable Atisha came to Tibet, he first went to Ngari, where he remained for two years giving many teachings to the disciples of Jangchub Ö. After two years had passed, he decided to return to India, and Jangchub Ö requested him to give one last teaching before he left. Atisha replied that he had already given them all the advice they needed, but Jangchub Ö persisted in his request and so Atisha accepted and gave the following advice.

How wonderful!

Friends, since you already have great knowledge and clear understanding, whereas I am of no importance and have little wisdom, it is not suitable for you to request advice from me. However because you dear friends, whom I cherish from my heart, have requested me, I shall give you this essential advice from my inferior and childish mind.

Friends, until you attain enlightenment the Spiritual Teacher is indispensable, therefore rely upon the holy Spiritual Guide.

Until you realize ultimate truth, listening is indispensable, therefore listen to the instructions of the Spiritual Guide.

Since you cannot become a Buddha merely by understanding Dharma, practice earnestly with understanding.

Avoid places that disturb your mind, and always remain where your virtues increase.

Until you attain stable realizations, worldly amusements are harmful, therefore abide in a place where there are no such distractions.

Avoid friends who cause you to increase delusions, and rely upon those who increase your virtue. This you should take to heart.

Since there is never a time when worldly activities come to an end, limit your activities.

Dedicate your virtues throughout the day and the night, and always watch your mind.

Because you have received advice, whenever you are not meditating, always practice in accordance with what your Spiritual Guide says.

If you practice with great devotion, results will arise immediately, without your having to wait for a long time.

If from your heart you practice in accordance with Dharma, both food and resources will come naturally to hand.

Friends, the things you desire give no more satisfaction than drinking sea water, therefore practice contentment.

Avoid all haughty, conceited, proud, and arrogant minds, and remain peaceful and subdued.

Avoid activities that are said to be meritorious, but which in fact are obstacles to Dharma.

Profit and respect are nooses of the maras, so brush them aside like stones on the path.

Words of praise and fame serve only to beguile us, therefore blow them away as you would blow your nose.

Since the happiness, pleasure, and friends you gather in this life last only for a moment, put them all behind you.

Since future lives last for a very long time, gather up riches to provide for the future.

You will have to depart leaving everything behind, so do not be attached to anything.

Generate compassion for lowly beings, and especially avoid despising or humiliating them.

Have no hatred for enemies, and no attachment for friends.

Do not be jealous of others' good qualities, but out of admiration adopt them yourself.

Do not look for faults in others, but look for faults in yourself, and purge them like bad blood.

Do not contemplate your own good qualities, but contemplate the good qualities of others, and respect everyone as a servant would.

See all living beings as your father or mother, and love them as if you were their child.

Always keep a smiling face and a loving mind, and speak truthfully without malice.

If you talk too much with little meaning, you will make mistakes, therefore speak in moderation, only when necessary.

If you engage in many meaningless activities, your virtuous activities will degenerate, therefore stop activities that are not spiritual.

It is completely meaningless to put effort into activities that have no essence.

If the things you desire do not come, it is due to karma created long ago, therefore keep a happy and relaxed mind.

Beware, offending a holy being is worse than dying, therefore be honest and straightforward.

Since all the happiness and suffering of this life arise from previous actions, do not blame others.

All happiness comes from the blessings of your Spiritual Guide, therefore always repay his kindness.

Since you cannot tame the minds of others until you have tamed your own, begin by taming your own mind.

Since you will definitely have to depart without the wealth you have accumulated, do not accumulate negativity for the sake of wealth.

Distracting enjoyments have no essence, therefore sincerely practice giving.

Always keep pure moral discipline for it leads to beauty in this life and happiness hereafter.

Since hatred is rife in these impure times, don the armor of patience, free from anger.

You remain in samsara through the power of laziness, therefore ignite the fire of the effort of application.

Since this human life is wasted by indulging in distractions, now is the time to practice concentration.

Being under the influence of wrong views, you do not realize the ultimate nature of things, therefore investigate correct meanings.

Friends, there is no happiness in this swamp of samsara, so move to the firm ground of liberation.

Meditate according to the advice of your Spiritual Guide and dry up the river of samsaric suffering.

You should consider this well because it is not just words from the mouth, but sincere advice from the heart.

If you practice like this, you will delight me, and you will bring happiness to yourself and others.

I who am ignorant request you to take this advice to heart.

This is the advice that the holy being Venerable Atisha gave to Venerable Jangchub Ö.

The Three Principal Aspects
of the Path

Homage to the venerable Spiritual Guide.

I shall explain to the best of my ability
The essential meaning of all the Conqueror's teachings,
The path praised by the holy Bodhisattvas,
And the gateway for fortunate ones seeking liberation.

You who are not attached to the joys of samsara,
But strive to make your freedom and endowment meaningful,
O Fortunate Ones who apply your minds to the path that
    pleases the Conquerors,
Please listen with a clear mind.

Without pure renunciation, there is no way to pacify
Attachment to the pleasures of samsara;
And since living beings are tightly bound by desire for samsara,
Begin by seeking renunciation.

Freedom and endowment are difficult to find, and there is no
time to waste.
By acquainting your mind with this, overcome attachment to
this life;
And by repeatedly contemplating actions and effects
And the sufferings of samsara, overcome attachment to future
lives.

When, through contemplating in this way, the desire for the
pleasures of samsara
Does not arise, even for a moment,
But a mind longing for liberation arises throughout the day and
the night,
At that time, renunciation is generated.

However, if this renunciation is not maintained
By completely pure bodhichitta,
It will not be a cause of the perfect happiness of unsurpassed
enlightenment;
Therefore, the wise generate a supreme bodhichitta.

Swept along by the currents of the four powerful rivers,
Tightly bound by the chains of karma, so hard to release,
Ensnared within the iron net of self-grasping,
Completely enveloped by the pitch-black darkness of ignorance,

Taking rebirth after rebirth in boundless samsara,
And unceasingly tormented by the three sufferings—
Through contemplating the state of your mothers in conditions
such as these,
Generate a supreme mind [of bodhichitta].

But, even though you may be acquainted with renunciation and
    bodhichitta,
If you do not possess the wisdom realizing the way things are,
You will not be able to cut the root of samsara;
Therefore, strive in the means for realizing dependent
    relationship.

Whoever negates the conceived object of self-grasping
Yet sees the infallibility of cause and effect
Of all phenomena in samsara and nirvana,
Has entered the path that pleases the Buddhas.

Dependent-related appearance is infallible
And emptiness is inexpressible;
For as long as the meaning of these two appear to be separate,
You have not yet realized Buddha's intention.

When they arise as one, not alternating but simultaneous,
From merely seeing infallible dependent relationship
Comes certain knowledge that destroys all grasping at objects.
At that time, the analysis of view is complete.

Moreover, when the extreme of existence is dispelled by
    appearance,
And the extreme of non-existence is dispelled by emptiness,
And you know how emptiness is perceived as cause and effect,
You will not be captivated by extreme views.

When, in this way, you have correctly realized the
    essential points
Of the three principal aspects of the path,
Dear One, withdraw into solitude, generate strong effort,
And quickly accomplish the final goal.

Colophon: Both texts were translated under the compassionate
guidance of Venerable Geshe Kelsang Gyatso.

Glossary

Alertness A mental factor that is a type of wisdom that examines our activity of body, speech, and mind and knows whether or not faults are developing. See *Understanding the Mind*.

Asanga A great Indian Buddhist Yogi and scholar of the fifth century, author of *Compendium of Abhidharma*. See *Living Meaningfully, Dying Joyfully*.

Atisha (AD 982-1054) A famous Indian Buddhist scholar and meditation master. He was Abbot of the great Buddhist monastery of Vikramashila at a time when Mahayana Buddhism was flourishing in India. He was later invited to Tibet and his arrival there led to the re-establishment of Buddhism in Tibet. He is the author of the first text on the stages of the path, *Lamp for the Path*. His tradition later became known as the *Kadampa Tradition*. See *Joyful Path of Good Fortune*.

Attachment A deluded mental factor that observes a contaminated object, regards it as a cause of happiness, and wishes for it. See *Understanding the Mind*.

Attention A mental factor that functions to focus the mind on a particular attribute of an object. See *Understanding the Mind*.

Basis of imputation All phenomena are imputed on their parts. Therefore any of the individual parts, or the entire collection of the parts, of any phenomenon is its basis of imputation. A phenomenon is imputed by mind in dependence upon its basis of imputation appearing to that mind. See *Heart of Wisdom*.

Beginningless time According to the Buddhist world view, there is no beginning to mind and so no beginning to time. Therefore all living beings have taken countless previous rebirths.

Blessing (*Jin gyi lob* in Tibetan.) The transformation of our mind from a negative state to a positive state, from an unhappy state to a happy state, or from a state of weakness to a state of strength, through the inspiration of holy beings such as our Spiritual Guide, Buddhas, and Bodhisattvas.

Buddha's bodies A Buddha has four bodies—the Wisdom Truth Body, the Nature Body, the Enjoyment Body, and the Emanation Body. The first is Buddha's omniscient mind. The second is the emptiness, or ultimate nature, of his or her mind. The third is his subtle Form Body. The fourth, of which each Buddha manifests a countless number, are gross Form Bodies that are visible to ordinary beings. The Wisdom Truth Body and the Nature Body are both included within the Truth Body, and the Enjoyment Body and the Emanation Body are both included within the Form Body. See *Joyful Path of Good Fortune*.

Channels Subtle inner passageways of the body through which subtle drops flow, moved by inner winds. See *Mahamudra Tantra* and *Clear Light of Bliss*.

Channel wheel (*Chakra* in Sanskrit.) A focal center where secondary channels branch out from the central channel. Meditating on these points can cause the inner winds to enter the central channel. See *Mahamudra Tantra* and *Clear Light of Bliss*.

Chekhawa, Geshe (AD 1102-1176) A great Kadampa Bodhisattva who composed the text *Training the Mind in Seven Points*, a commentary to Geshe Langri Tangpa's *Eight Verses of Training the Mind*. He spread the study and practice of training the mind throughout Tibet. See *Universal Compassion*.

Clear light A manifest very subtle mind that perceives an appearance like clear, empty space. See *Clear Light of Bliss* and *Mahamudra Tantra*.

Commitments Promises and pledges taken when engaging in certain spiritual practices.

Concentration A mental factor that makes its primary mind remain on its object single-pointedly. See *Joyful Path of Good Fortune*.

Conceptual thought/mind A thought that apprehends its object through a generic, or mental, image. See *Understanding the Mind*.

Contact A mental factor that functions to perceive its object as pleasant, unpleasant, or neutral. See *Understanding the Mind*.

Contentment Being satisfied with one's inner and outer conditions, motivated by a virtuous intention.

Degenerate times A period when spiritual activity degenerates.

Deity (*Yidam* in Tibetan.) A Tantric enlightened being.

Desire realm The environment of hell beings, hungry spirits, animals, human beings, demi-gods, and the gods who enjoy the five objects of desire.

Dharma Buddha's teachings and the inner realizations that are attained in dependence upon practicing them. *Dharma* means "protection." By practicing Buddha's teachings, we protect ourself from suffering and problems.

Direct perceiver A cognizer that apprehends its manifest object. See *Understanding the Mind*.

Discrimination A mental factor that functions to apprehend the uncommon sign of an object. See *Understanding the Mind*.

Elements, four Earth, water, fire, and wind. All matter can be said to be composed of a combination of these elements. There are four inner elements (those that are conjoined with the continuum of a person), and four outer elements (those that are not conjoined with the continuum of a person). These four elements are not the same as the earth of a field, the water of a river, and so forth. Instead, the elements of earth, water, fire, and wind in broad terms are the properties of solidity, liquidity, heat, and movement respectively.

Emanation Animate or inanimate form manifested by Buddhas or high Bodhisattvas to benefit others.

Feeling A mental factor that functions to experience pleasant, unpleasant, or neutral objects. See *Understanding the Mind*.

Foe Destroyer (*Arhat* in Sanskrit.) A practitioner who has abandoned all delusions and their seeds by training on the spiritual paths and who will never again be reborn in samsara. In this context, the term *Foe* refers to the delusions.

Form Body The Enjoyment Body and the Emanation Body of a Buddha. See also *Buddha's bodies*.

Form realm The environment of the gods who possess form.

Formless realm The environment of the gods who do not possess form.

Functioning thing A phenomenon that is produced and disintegrates within a moment. Synonymous with impermanent phenomenon, thing, and product. See also *Impermanence*.

Generation stage A realization of a creative yoga prior to attaining the actual completion stage, which is attained through the practice of bringing the three bodies into the path, in which one mentally generates oneself as a Tantric Deity and one's surroundings as the Deity's mandala. Meditation on generation stage is called a *creative yoga* because its object is created, or generated, by correct imagination. See *Tantric Grounds and Paths* and *Mahamudra Tantra*.

Generic image The appearing object of a conceptual mind. A generic image, or mental image, of an object is like a reflection of that object. Conceptual minds know their object through the appearance of a generic image of that object, not by seeing the object directly. See *Understanding the Mind*.

Geshe A title given by Kadampa monasteries to accomplished Buddhist scholars. A contracted form of the Tibetan *ge wai she nyen*, literally meaning "virtuous friend."

Guide to the Bodhisattva's Way of Life A classic Mahayana Buddhist text composed by the great Indian Buddhist Yogi and scholar Shantideva, which presents all the practices of a Bodhisattva from the initial generation of bodhichitta through to the completion of the practice of the six perfections. For a translation, see *Guide to the Bodhisattva's Way of Life*. For a full commentary, see *Meaningful to Behold*.

Guru See *Spiritual Guide*.

Heart Sutra One of several *Perfection of Wisdom Sutras* that Buddha taught. Although much shorter than the other *Perfection of Wisdom Sutras*, it contains explicitly or implicitly their entire meaning. For a full commentary, see *Heart of Wisdom*.

Heruka A principal Deity of Mother Tantra, who is the embodiment of indivisible bliss and emptiness. See *Essence of Vajrayana*.

Hinayana Sanskrit word for "Lesser Vehicle." The Hinayana goal is to attain merely one's own liberation from suffering by completely abandoning delusions. See *Joyful Path of Good Fortune*.

Holy being A being who is worthy of devotion.

Impermanence Phenomena are either permanent or impermanent. *Impermanent* means "momentary," thus an impermanent phenomenon is a phenomenon that is produced and disintegrates within a moment. Synonyms of impermanent phenomenon are functioning thing, thing, and product. There are two types of impermanence: gross and subtle. Gross impermanence is any impermanence that can be seen by an ordinary sense awareness—for example the aging and death of a living being. Subtle impermanence is the momentary disintegration of a functioning thing. See *Heart of Wisdom.*

Inferential cognizer A completely reliable cognizer whose object is realized in direct dependence upon a conclusive reason. See *Understanding the Mind.*

Inner winds Special subtle winds related to the mind that flow through the channels of our body. Our body and mind cannot function without these winds. See *Mahamudra Tantra* and *Clear Light of Bliss.*

Intention A mental factor that functions to move its primary mind to the object. It functions to engage the mind in virtuous, non-virtuous, and neutral objects. All bodily and verbal actions are initiated by the mental factor intention. See *Understanding the Mind.*

Je Tsongkhapa (AD 1357-1419) An emanation of the Wisdom Buddha Manjushri, whose appearance in fourteenth-century Tibet as a monk, and the holder of the lineage of pure view and pure deeds, was prophesied by Buddha. He spread a very pure Buddhadharma throughout Tibet, showing how to combine the practices of Sutra and Tantra, and how to practice pure Dharma during degenerate times. His tradition later became known as the *Gelug,* or *Ganden Tradition.* See *Heart Jewel* and *Great Treasury of Merit.*

Kadampa A Tibetan word in which *Ka* means "word" and refers to all Buddha's teachings, *dam* refers to Atisha's special Lamrim instructions known as the "stages of the path to enlightenment," and *pa* refers to a follower of Kadampa Buddhism who integrates all the teachings of Buddha that they know into their Lamrim practice.

Kadampa Buddhism A Mahayana Buddhist school founded by the great Indian Buddhist Master Atisha (AD 982-1054).

Kadampa Geshe See *Geshe.*

Kadampa Tradition The pure tradition of Buddhism established by Atisha. Followers of this tradition up to the time of Je Tsongkhapa are known as *Old Kadampas*, and those after the time of Je Tsongkhapa are known as *New Kadampas.*

Lama See *Spiritual Guide.*

Lamrim A Tibetan term, literally meaning "stages of the path." A special arrangement of all Buddha's teachings that is easy to understand and put into practice. It reveals all the stages of the path to enlightenment. For a full commentary, see *Joyful Path of Good Fortune.*

Langri Tangpa, Geshe (AD 1054-1123) A great Kadampa Bodhisattva who was famous for his realization of exchanging self with others. He composed *Eight Verses of Training the Mind*. See *Eight Steps to Happiness.*

Lineage A line of instruction that has been passed down from Spiritual Guide to disciple, with each Spiritual Guide in the line having gained personal experience of the instruction before passing it on to others.

Living being Synonymous with sentient being (*sem chen* in Tibetan). Any being who possesses a mind that is contaminated by delusions or their imprints. Both *living being* and *sentient being* are terms used to distinguish beings whose minds are contaminated by either of these two obstructions from Buddhas, whose minds are completely free from these obstructions.

Lojong See *Training the mind.*

Lord of Death Although the mara of uncontrolled death is not a sentient being, it is personified as the Lord of Death, or *Yama.* The Lord of Death is depicted in the diagram of the Wheel of Life clutching the wheel between his claws and teeth. See *Joyful Path of Good Fortune.*

Madhyamika A Sanskrit term, literally meaning "Middle Way." The higher of the two schools of Mahayana tenets. The Madhyamika view was taught by Buddha in the *Perfection of Wisdom Sutras* during the second turning of the Wheel of Dharma and was subsequently elucidated by Nagarjuna and his followers. There are two divisions of this school, Madhyamika-Svatantrika and Madhyamika-Prasangika, of which the latter is Buddha's final view. See *Meaningful to Behold* and *Ocean of Nectar.*

Mahamudra A Sanskrit word, literally meaning "great seal." According to Sutra, this refers to the profound view of emptiness. Since emptiness is the nature of all phenomena it is called a "seal," and since a direct realization of emptiness enables us to accomplish the great purpose—complete liberation from the sufferings of samsara—it is also called "great." According to Secret Mantra, great seal is the union of spontaneous great bliss and emptiness. See *Mahamudra Tantra, Great Treasury of Merit* and *Clear Light of Bliss.*

Mahayana A Sanskrit word for "Great Vehicle," the spiritual path to great enlightenment. The Mahayana goal is to attain Buddhahood for the benefit of all living beings by completely abandoning delusions and their imprints. See *Joyful Path of Good Fortune.*

Maitreya The embodiment of the loving kindness of all the Buddhas. At the time of Buddha Shakyamuni he manifested as a Bodhisattva disciple in order to show Buddha's disciples how to be perfect Mahayana disciples. In the future, he will manifest as the fifth founding Buddha.

Mala A rosary used to count recitations of prayers or mantras, usually with one hundred and eight beads.

Manjushri The embodiment of the wisdom of all the Buddhas. See *Great Treasury of Merit* and *Heart Jewel.*

Mantra A Sanskrit word, literally meaning "mind protection." Mantra protects the mind from ordinary appearances and conceptions. See *Tantric Grounds and Paths.*

Mara/Demon A Sanskrit term for "demon," referring to anything that obstructs the attainment of liberation or enlightenment. There are four principal types of mara: the mara of the delusions, the mara of contaminated aggregates, the mara of uncontrolled death, and the Devaputra maras. Of these, only the last are actual living beings. See *Heart of Wisdom*.

Mental continuum The continuum of a mind that has no beginning and no end.

Mental factor A cognizer that principally apprehends a particular attribute of an object. There are fifty-one specific mental factors. Each moment of mind comprises a primary mind and various mental factors. See *Understanding the Mind*.

Mere appearance All phenomena are mere appearance because they are imputed by mind in dependence upon a suitable basis of imputation appearing to mind. The word *mere* excludes any possibility of inherent existence. See *Ocean of Nectar*.

Merit The good fortune created by virtuous actions. It is the potential power to increase our good qualities and produce happiness.

Milarepa (AD 1040-1123) A great Tibetan Buddhist meditator and disciple of Marpa, celebrated for his beautiful songs of realization.

Mindfulness A mental factor that functions not to forget the object realized by the primary mind. See *Understanding the Mind*.

Nagarjuna A great Indian Buddhist scholar and meditation master who revived the Mahayana in the first century AD by bringing to light the teachings on the *Perfection of Wisdom Sutras*. See *Ocean of Nectar*.

Object of negation An object explicitly negated by a mind realizing a negative phenomenon. In meditation on emptiness, or lack of inherent existence, it refers to inherent existence. Also known as *negated object*.

Observed object Any object on which the mind is focused. See *Understanding the Mind.*

Obstructions to liberation Obstructions that prevent the attainment of liberation. All delusions, such as ignorance, attachment, and anger, together with their seeds, are obstructions to liberation. Also called *delusion-obstructions.*

Obstructions to omniscience The imprints of delusions, which prevent simultaneous and direct realization of all phenomena. Only Buddhas have overcome these obstructions.

Ordinary being Anyone who has not realized emptiness directly.

Perfection of Wisdom Sutras Sutras of the second turning of the Wheel of Dharma, in which Buddha revealed his final view of the ultimate nature of all phenomena—emptiness of inherent existence. See *Heart of Wisdom* and *Ocean of Nectar.*

Primary mind A cognizer that principally apprehends the mere entity of an object. Synonymous with consciousness. There are six primary minds: eye consciousness, ear consciousness, nose consciousness, tongue consciousness, body consciousness, and mental consciousness. Each moment of mind comprises a primary mind and various mental factors. A primary mind and its accompanying mental factors are the same entity but have different functions. See *Understanding the Mind.*

Pure Land A pure environment in which there are no true sufferings. There are many Pure Lands. For example, Tushita is the Pure Land of Buddha Maitreya, Sukhavati is the Pure Land of Buddha Amitabha, and Dakini Land (or Keajra) is the Pure Land of Buddha Vajrayogini and Buddha Heruka. See *Living Meaningfully, Dying Joyfully.*

Purification Generally, any practice that leads to the attainment of a pure body, speech, or mind. More specifically, a practice for purifying negative karma by means of the four opponent powers. See *Joyful Path of Good Fortune* and *The Bodhisattva Vow.*

Realization A stable and non-mistaken experience of a virtuous object that directly protects us from suffering.

Refuge Actual protection. To go for refuge to Buddha, Dharma, and Sangha means to have faith in these Three Jewels and to rely on them for protection from all fears and suffering. See *Joyful Path of Good Fortune*.

Root mind The very subtle mind located at the center of the heart channel wheel. It is known as the "root mind" because all other minds arise from it and dissolve back into it. See *Mahamudra Tantra*.

Secret Mantra Synonymous with Tantra. Secret Mantra teachings are distinguished from Sutra teachings in that they reveal methods for training the mind by bringing the future result, or Buddhahood, into the present path. Secret Mantra is the supreme path to full enlightenment. The term *Mantra* indicates that it is Buddha's special instruction for protecting our mind from ordinary appearances and conceptions. Practitioners of Secret Mantra overcome ordinary appearances and conceptions by visualizing their body, environment, enjoyments, and deeds as those of a Buddha. The term *Secret* indicates that the practices are to be done in private, and that they can be practiced only by those who have received a Tantric empowerment. See *Tantric Grounds and Paths* and *Mahamudra Tantra*.

Sentient being See *Living being*.

Shantideva (AD 687-763) A great Indian Buddhist scholar and meditation master. He composed *Guide to the Bodhisattva's Way of Life*. See *Meaningful to Behold* and *Guide to the Bodhisattva's Way of Life*.

Spiritual Guide (*Guru* in Sanskrit, and *Lama* in Tibetan.) A Teacher who guides us along the spiritual path. See *Joyful Path of Good Fortune* and *Great Treasury of Merit*.

Stages of the path See *Lamrim*.

Subtle impermanence See *Impermanence*.

Superior being (*Arya* in Sanskrit.) A being who has a direct realization of emptiness. There are Hinayana Superiors and Mahayana Superiors.

Superior seeing A special wisdom that sees its object clearly, and that is maintained by tranquil abiding and the special suppleness that is induced by investigation. See *Joyful Path of Good Fortune*.

Sutra The teachings of Buddha that are open to everyone to practice without the need for an empowerment. These include Buddha's teachings of the three turnings of the Wheel of Dharma.

Tantra See *Secret Mantra*.

Training the mind (*Lojong* in Tibetan.) A special lineage of instructions that came from Buddha Shakyamuni through Manjushri and Shantideva to Atisha and the Kadampa Geshes, which emphasizes the generation of bodhichitta through the practices of equalizing and exchanging self with others combined with taking and giving.

Training the Mind in Seven Points A commentary to *Eight Verses of Training the Mind*, composed by Geshe Chekhawa. For a full commentary, see *Universal Compassion*.

True suffering A contaminated object produced by delusions and karma. See *Joyful Path of Good Fortune*.

Truth Body The Nature Body and the Wisdom Truth Body of a Buddha. See also *Buddha's bodies*.

Vajrayogini A female Highest Yoga Tantra Deity who is the embodiment of indivisible bliss and emptiness. She is the same nature as Heruka. See *Guide to Dakini Land*.

Valid cognizer/mind A cognizer that is non-deceptive with respect to its engaged object. There are two types: inferential valid cognizers and direct valid cognizers. See *Understanding the Mind*.

Very subtle mind There are different levels of mind: gross, subtle, and very subtle. Subtle minds manifest when the inner winds gather and dissolve within the central channel. See *Mahamudra Tantra* and *Clear Light of Bliss*.

Vinaya Sutras Sutras in which Buddha principally explains the practice of moral discipline, and in particular the Pratimoksha moral discipline.

Vow A virtuous determination to abandon particular faults that is generated in conjunction with a traditional ritual. The three sets of vows are the Pratimoksha vows of individual liberation, the Bodhisattva vows, and the Secret Mantra vows. See *The Bodhisattva Vow* and *Tantric Grounds and Paths*.

Wisdom A virtuous, intelligent mind that makes its primary mind realize its object thoroughly. A wisdom is a spiritual path that functions to release our mind from delusions or their imprints. An example of wisdom is the correct view of emptiness.

Worldly concerns, eight The objects of the eight worldly concerns are happiness and suffering, wealth and poverty, praise and criticism, and good reputation and bad reputation. These are called *worldly concerns* because worldly people are constantly concerned with them, wanting some and trying to avoid others. See *Universal Compassion* and *Joyful Path of Good Fortune*.

Yogi/Yogini Sanskrit words usually referring to a male or a female meditator who has attained the union of tranquil abiding and superior seeing.

Bibliography

*G*eshe Kelsang Gyatso is a highly respected meditation master and scholar of the Mahayana Buddhist tradition founded by Je Tsongkhapa. Since arriving in the West in 1977, Geshe Kelsang has worked tirelessly to establish pure Buddhadharma throughout the world. Over this period he has given extensive teachings on the major scriptures of the Mahayana. These teachings are currently being published and provide a comprehensive presentation of the essential Sutra and Tantra practices of Mahayana Buddhism.

Books

The following books by Geshe Kelsang are all published by Tharpa Publications.

The Bodhisattva Vow. A practical guide to helping others.
(2nd. ed., 1995)
Clear Light of Bliss. A Tantric meditation manual. (2nd. ed., 1992)
Eight Steps to Happiness. The Buddhist way of loving kindness. (2000)
Essence of Vajrayana. The Highest Yoga Tantra practice of Heruka body mandala. (1997)
Great Treasury of Merit. The practice of relying upon a Spiritual Guide. (1992)

Guide to Dakini Land. The Highest Yoga Tantra practice of Buddha Vajrayogini. (2nd. ed., 1996)

Guide to the Bodhisattva's Way of Life. How to enjoy a life of great meaning and altruism. (A translation of Shantideva's famous verse masterpiece.) (2002)

Heart Jewel. The essential practices of Kadampa Buddhism. (2nd. ed., 1997)

Heart of Wisdom. An explanation of the *Heart Sutra.* (4th. ed., 2001)

How to Solve Our Human Problems. The four noble truths. (2007)

Introduction to Buddhism. An explanation of the Buddhist way of life. (2nd. ed., 2001)

Joyful Path of Good Fortune. The complete Buddhist path to enlightenment. (2nd. ed., 1995)

Living Meaningfully, Dying Joyfully. The profound practice of transference of consciousness. (1999)

Mahamudra Tantra. The supreme Heart Jewel nectar. (2005)

Meaningful to Behold. The Bodhisattva's way of life. (4th. ed., 1994)

The New Meditation Handbook. Meditations to make our life happy and meaningful. (2003)

Ocean of Nectar. The true nature of all things. (1995)

Tantric Grounds and Paths. How to enter, progress on, and complete the Vajrayana path. (1994)

Transform Your Life. A blissful journey. (2007)

Understanding the Mind. The nature and power of the mind. (2nd. ed., 1997)

Universal Compassion. Inspiring solutions for difficult times. (4th. ed., 2002)

Sadhanas

Geshe Kelsang has also supervised the translation of a collection of essential sadhanas, or prayer booklets.

Avalokiteshvara Sadhana. Prayers and requests to the Buddha of Compassion.

The Bodhisattva's Confession of Moral Downfalls. The purification practice of the *Mahayana Sutra of the Three Superior Heaps.*

Condensed Essence of Vajrayana. Condensed Heruka body mandala self-generation sadhana.

Dakini Yoga. Six-session Guru yoga combined with self-generation as Vajrayogini.

Drop of Essential Nectar. A special fasting and purification practice in conjunction with Eleven-faced Avalokiteshvara.

Essence of Good Fortune. Prayers for the six preparatory practices for meditation on the stages of the path to enlightenment.

Essence of Vajrayana. Heruka body mandala self-generation sadhana according to the system of Mahasiddha Ghantapa.

Feast of Great Bliss. Vajrayogini self-initiation sadhana.

Great Compassionate Mother. The sadhana of Arya Tara.

Great Liberation of the Father. Preliminary prayers for Mahamudra meditation in conjunction with Heruka practice.

Great Liberation of the Mother. Preliminary prayers for Mahamudra meditation in conjunction with Vajrayogini practice.

The Great Mother. A method to overcome hindrances and obstacles by reciting the *Essence of Wisdom Sutra* (the *Heart Sutra*).

Heartfelt Prayers. A funeral service for cremations and burials.

Heart Jewel. The Guru yoga of Je Tsongkhapa combined with the condensed sadhana of his Dharma Protector.

The Kadampa Way of Life. The essential practice of Kadam Lamrim.

Liberation from Sorrow. Praises and requests to the Twenty-one Taras.

Mahayana Refuge Ceremony and Bodhisattva Vow Ceremony.

Medicine Buddha Prayer. A method for benefiting others.

Medicine Buddha Sadhana. A method for accomplishing the attainments of Medicine Buddha.

Meditation and Recitation of Solitary Vajrasattva.

Melodious Drum Victorious in all Directions. The extensive fulfilling and restoring ritual of the Dharma Protector, the great king Dorje Shugdän, in conjunction with Mahakala, Kalarupa, Kalindewi, and other Dharma Protectors.

Offering to the Spiritual Guide (Lama Chöpa). A special way of relying upon a Spiritual Guide.

Path of Compassion for the Deceased. Powa sadhana for the benefit of the deceased

Pathway to the Pure Land. Training in powa—the transference of consciousness.

Powa Ceremony. Transference of consciousness for the deceased.

Prayers for Meditation. Brief preparatory prayers for meditation.

A Pure Life. The practice of taking and keeping the eight Mahayana precepts.

Quick Path to Great Bliss. Vajrayogini self-generation sadhana.

Treasury of Wisdom. The sadhana of Venerable Manjushri.

Union of No More Learning. Heruka Body Mandala self-initiation sadhana.

Vajra Hero Yoga. A brief essential practice of Heruka body mandala self-generation, and condensed six-session yoga.

The Vows and Commitments of Kadampa Buddhism.

Wishfulfilling Jewel. The Guru yoga of Je Tsongkhapa combined with the sadhana of his Dharma Protector.

The Yoga of Buddha Amitayus. A special method for increasing life-span, wisdom, and merit.

The Yoga of Buddha Vajrapani. The self-generation sadhana of Buddha Vajrapani.

The Yoga of White Tara, Buddha of Long Life.

A full catalog of all our books, audio books, and artwork is available online at www.tharpa.com, which includes books in English, Spanish, and many other languages. Or you can receive a mail order catalog, including English and Spanish books, by contacting us:

Tharpa Publications USA
47 Sweeney Road
Glen Spey, NY 12737
USA

Phone: 845-856-5102 or
Toll-free: 888-741-3475
Fax: 845-856-2110

Email: tharpa-us@tharpa.com
Website: www.tharpa.com

or

Tharpa Publications Canada
1155 Indian Road
Mississauga, ON
L5H 1RB, Canada

Phone: 905-274-1842
Toll-free: 866-454-5005
Fax: 905-274-1714

Email: info@tharpa.ca
Website: www.tharpa.ca

or

Tharpa Publications
Conishead Priory
Ulverston
Cumbria, LA12 9QQ
England

Phone: (0) 1229-588599
Fax: (0) 1229-483919

E-mail: tharpa@tharpa.com
Website: www.tharpa.com

Study Programs of Kadampa Buddhism

*K*adampa Buddhism is a Mahayana Buddhist school founded by the great Indian Buddhist Master Atisha (AD 982-1054). His followers are known as *Kadampas*. *Ka* means "word" and refers to Buddha's teachings, and *dam* refers to Atisha's special Lamrim instructions known as "the stages of the path to enlightenment." By integrating their knowledge of all Buddha's teachings into their practice of Lamrim, and by integrating this into their everyday lives, Kadampa Buddhists are encouraged to use Buddha's teachings as practical methods for transforming daily activities into the path to enlightenment. The great Kadampa Teachers are famous not only for being great scholars, but also for being spiritual practitioners of immense purity and sincerity.

The lineage of these teachings, both their oral transmission and blessings, was then passed from Teacher to disciple, spreading throughout much of Asia, and now to many countries throughout the Western world. Buddha's teachings, which are known as *Dharma*, are likened to a wheel that moves from country to country in accordance with changing conditions and people's karmic inclinations. The external form of presenting of Buddhism may change as it meets with different cultures and societies, but its essential authenticity is ensured through the continuation of an unbroken lineage of realized practitioners.

Kadampa Buddhism was first introduced into the West in 1977 by the renowned Buddhist Master, Venerable Geshe Kelsang Gyatso. Since that time he has worked tirelessly to spread Kadampa Buddhism throughout the world by giving extensive teachings, writing many profound texts on Kadampa Buddhism, and founding the New Kadampa Tradition–International Kadampa Buddhist Union (NKT-IKBU), which now has over one thousand Kadampa Buddhist Centers and groups worldwide. Each Center offers study programs on Buddhist psychology, philosophy, and meditation instruction, as well as retreats for all levels of practitioner. The emphasis is on integrating Buddha's teachings into daily life to solve our human problems and to spread lasting peace and happiness throughout the world.

The Kadampa Buddhism of the NKT-IKBU is an entirely independent Buddhist tradition and has no political affiliations. It is an association of Buddhist Centers and practitioners that derive their inspiration and guidance from the example of the ancient Kadampa Buddhist Masters and their teachings, as presented by Geshe Kelsang.

There are three reasons why we need to study and practice the teachings of Buddha: to develop our wisdom, to cultivate a good heart, and to maintain a peaceful state of mind. If we do not strive to develop our wisdom, we will always remain ignorant of ultimate truth—the true nature of reality. Although we wish for happiness, our ignorance leads us to engage in non-virtuous actions, which are the main cause of all our suffering. If we do not cultivate a good heart, our selfish motivation destroys harmony and good relationships with others. We have no peace, and no chance to gain pure happiness. Without inner peace, outer peace is impossible. If we do not maintain a peaceful state of mind, we are not happy even if we have ideal conditions. On the other hand, when our mind is peaceful, we are happy even if our external conditions are unpleasant. Therefore, the development of these qualities is of utmost importance for our daily happiness.

Geshe Kelsang Gyatso, or *Geshe-la* as he is affectionately called by his students, has designed three special spiritual programs for the systematic study and practice of Kadampa Buddhism that are especially suited to the modern world—the General Program (GP), the Foundation Program (FP), and the Teacher Training Program (TTP).

GENERAL PROGRAM

The General Program provides a basic introduction to Buddhist view, meditation, and practice that is suitable for beginners. It also includes advanced teachings and practice from both Sutra and Tantra.

FOUNDATION PROGRAM

The Foundation Program provides an opportunity to deepen our understanding and experience of Buddhism through a systematic study of six texts:

1. *Joyful Path of Good Fortune*—a commentary to Atisha's Lamrim instructions, the stages of the path to enlightenment.
2. *Universal Compassion*—a commentary to Bodhisattva Chekhawa's *Training the Mind in Seven Points.*
3. *Eight Steps to Happiness*—a commentary to Bodhisattva Langri Tangpa's *Eight Verses of Training the Mind.*
4. *Heart of Wisdom*—a commentary to the Heart Sutra.
5. *Meaningful to Behold*—a commentary to Venerable Shantideva's *Guide to the Bodhisattva's Way of Life.*
6. *Understanding the Mind*—a detailed explanation of the mind, based on the works of the Buddhist scholars Dharmakirti and Dignaga.

The benefits of studying and practicing these texts are as follows:

(1) *Joyful Path of Good Fortune*—we gain the ability to put all Buddha's teachings of both Sutra and Tantra into practice. We can easily make progress on, and complete, the stages of the path to the supreme happiness of enlightenment. From a practical point of view, Lamrim is the

main body of Buddha's teachings, and the other teachings are like its limbs.

(2) and (3) *Universal Compassion* and *Eight Steps to Happiness*—we gain the ability to integrate Buddha's teachings into our daily life and solve all our human problems.

(4) *Heart of Wisdom*—we gain a realization of the ultimate nature of reality. By gaining this realization, we can eliminate the ignorance of self-grasping, which is the root of all our suffering.

(5) *Meaningful to Behold*—we transform our daily activities into the Bodhisattva's way of life, making every moment of our human life meaningful.

(6) *Understanding the Mind*—we understand the relationship between our mind and its external objects. If we understand that objects depend on the subjective mind, we can change the way objects appear to us by changing our own mind. Gradually we will gain the ability to control our mind and in this way solve all our problems.

TEACHER TRAINING PROGRAM

The Teacher Training Program is designed for people who wish to train as authentic Dharma Teachers. In addition to completing the study of fourteen texts of Sutra and Tantra, which include the six texts mentioned above, students are required to observe certain commitments with regard to behavior and way of life, and to complete a number of meditation retreats.

All Kadampa Buddhist Centers are open to the public. Every year we celebrate Festivals in many countries throughout the world, including the USA and England, where people gather from around the world to receive special teachings and empowerments and to enjoy a spiritual vacation. Please feel free to visit us any time!

For further information, please contact:

US NKT-IKBU Office
Kadampa Meditation Center
47 Sweeney Road
Glen Spey, NY 12737
USA

Phone: 845-856-9000
Toll free: 877-523-2672
Fax: 845-856-2110

Email: info@kadampaUS.org
Website: www.kadampaUS.org

or

NKT-IKBU Central Office
Conishead Priory
Ulverston
Cumbria, LA12 9QQ
England

Phone: (0) 1229-588533
Fax: (0) 1229-587775

Email: info@kadampa.org
Website: www.kadampa.org

Index

The letter "g" indicates an entry in the glossary.

dependent relationship 271
desire realm 53, g
desires 72–74, 84, 144, 149, 177
Dharma (see also Dharma Jewel;
    teachings) 235, g
Dharma book 82–83, 199
Dharma Jewel 80, 174
Dharmakaya 244
Dharmarakshita 198, 204
direct perceiver 276, g
discrimination 143, 262, g
disintegration, extreme of 270
dissatisfaction 72, 73–74, 100
distractions 53
    dispelling 90, 149, 228,
    308–9
dog 85–86, 138, 173
    stories 139, 182–83, 214
door to liberation 34, 55
doubt 82
dream 24, 251–52, 287
    analogy (see analogies: dream)
    appearances 8, 251–52, 270,
    275, 286
    mind 8, 251–52, 286
    significance of 25–28

E

effort 44, 81, 89–91, 155, 200
    armor-like 162
eight extremes 269–74, 277
elements, four 41, g

emanations 138–39, 183, 185, g
empathy 169, 179
emptiness
    (see also emptiness of I;
    realization of emptiness)
    55, 243–88
    bases of 281–82
    conventionally existent 261
    lacks inherent existence 271,
    277
    of all phenomena 260–61,
    278
    of body 253–61, 277,
    280–82
    of eight extremes 278–79
    of mind 261–62
    same nature 281–82
    space-like 259, 266, 279–80
    studying 249, 280
    true 276–77
emptiness of I 262–67, 278–79
    identifying negated object
    249–50, 262–63
enemies 106, 117, 138, 194
    inner 130, 158
    kindness of 194–95
enlightened being
    (see also Buddhas) 98
enlightenment 98–100
    attaining 117, 126, 179, 221
    cause of 109
    happiness of 154, 244
    obstacle to 152

Further Reading

If you have enjoyed reading this book and would like to find out more about Buddhist thought and practice, here are some other books by Geshe Kelsang Gyatso that you might like to read. They are all available from Tharpa Publications.

How to Solve Our Human Problems

The Four Noble Truths

When things go wrong in our life and we encounter difficult situations, we tend to regard the situation itself as our problem, but in reality whatever problems we experience come from the side of the mind. If we responded to difficult situations with a positive or peaceful mind they would not be problems for us. Eventually, we might even regard them as challenges or opportunities for growth and development. Problems arise only if we respond to difficulties with a negative state of mind. Therefore if we want to be free from problems, we must transform our mind.

"Geshe Kelsang Gyatso has a unique gift for addressing everyday difficulties."
    —*American Library Association's Booklist*

The New Meditation Handbook

A Practical Guide to Buddhist Meditation

This well-loved and practical manual allows us to discover for ourselves the inner peace and lightness of mind that come from meditation. The author explains twenty-one step-by-step meditations that lead to increasingly beneficial states of mind, and that together form the entire Buddhist path to enlightenment.

"Geshe Kelsang Gyatso's expert instructions on meditation will help anyone learn the basics of this life-changing art."
—*BookLetters*

Joyful Path of Good Fortune

The Complete Buddhist Path to Enlightenment

We all have the potential for self-transformation, and a limitless capacity for the growth of good qualities, but to fulfill this potential we need to know what to do at every stage of our spiritual journey.

With this book, Geshe Kelsang Gyatso offers us step-by-step guidance on the meditation practices that will lead us to lasting inner peace and happiness. With extraordinary clarity, he presents all Buddha's teachings in the order in which they are to be practiced, enriching his explanation with stories and analogies. A perfect guidebook to the Buddhist path.

A full catalog of all our books, audio books, and artwork is available online at www.tharpa.com, or you can receive a mail order catalog by contacting us (please see page 343 for contact information).